THE WAY WE WERE

THE WAY WE WERE

Volume V
The Final Years
(1970-1979)

Russell Annabel

Illustrated by
Louise Lopina

SAFARI PRESS INC.

P. O. Box 3095, Long Beach, CA 90803
USA

The trademark Safari Press ® is registered with the U.S. Patent and Trademark Office and in other countries.

Annabel, Russell

Second edition

Safari Press Inc.

1997, Long Beach, California

ISBN 1-57157-102-7

Library of Congress Catalog Card Number: 95-69973

10 9 8 7 6 5 4 3 2

Readers wishing to receive the Safari Press catalog, featuring many fine books on big-game hunting, wingshooting, and firearms, should write to Safari Press Inc., P.O. Box 3095, Long Beach, CA 90803, USA. Tel: (714) 894-9080, or by visiting our Web site at http://www.safaripress.com.

TABLE OF CONTENTS

RUSTY ANNABEL

(Information from a clipping in an Anchorage newspaper Jan. 28, 1979)

Rusty Annabel, who lived in Montana Creek and Anchorage during territorial days, died Thursday in Los Tepames, Mexico. He had injured his leg while riding a mule on his ranch, and developed an infection that caused his death. He was buried Friday in Los Tepames.

Annabel worked in Alaska as a United Press International correspondent during the early days of World War II. He also wrote for such magazines as *Field & Stream* and *Sports Afield*, and was a writer until his death.

There are no known survivors.

[Editor's note: Actually, at the time of his death Russell Annabel was survived by his sons, David Russell Annabel and Michael Annabel, and his former wife, Dell Annabel Lamey.]

Blue Blizzard in Sonora

*Thick as mosquitoes at a lake resort, pigeons dive-bomb the
Mexican grain fields and bruise what they don't eat.
Justifiable shotgunicide!*

"**O**kay, knock off the daydreaming. Here come a couple thousand
blue pigeons. Right on schedule," I said to Pop Lovett just before sunrise this hurricane-hazed September morning at Guasaguari
hacienda, southwestern Sonora, Old Mexico. Pop was sprawled
comfortably with his back against a dooryard mango tree, lost
in some private fantasy. An interesting one, I gathered. "Up
and at them, mister."

"Damn it, I never daydream," Pop roared. "How many times
do I have to tell you that?" He sat up and laid hands on the
Browning Auto 12 across his knees. "Well, where are they?"

"Cast your gaze westward."

The pigeons were high enough to catch the sunlight. I
said two thousand—there could have been twice that many. They
bore in fast between blunt, monte-shaggy hills. The leading
flock was three-hundred yards wide decked ten or fifteen birds
deep. They were making for a milo maize field in front of
the hacienda buildings. Passing us out of gun range, they pitched
down into the twenty-acre field without the customary reconnaissance sweep. They didn't alight. Instead they hovered
above the almost ripe grain, greedily snatching kernels, win-
nowing the red-tufted seed heads with their wings. It was a
wildly dramatic spectacle. Within seconds the broad field had

1

become an undulating blue mass of pigeons. The sound of their wings was like wind rushing across a prairie.

Haysoos, the fifteen-year-old Mayo Indian kid who retrieved for us, touched my arm. "More pigeons arriving," he said.

Pop was on his feet, sore or pretending to be, when the second flock, perhaps five hundred birds, streamed through the pass. The sun was in their eyes, and we had the mango tree for cover. Wings set, coasting, the birds headed straight at us and the milo maize field beyond. Pop stepped into view. The Browning racketed. Four pigeons spun out of the loose formation. Very pretty shooting. Pop may take the cake for absentmindedness, but he is absolutely the fanciest scattergun genius I ever saw perform south of the border. He could charge admission. Haysoos went out and picked up the birds. As he handed them to Pop, desperate activity erupted from the hacienda.

I had heard our two rancher hosts, Moses and Oliver Castro, yelling commands.

Four mounted *vaqueros* now spurred to the maize field. They took cannon firecrackers from their saddle pockets, lit them with cigarettes, and threw them out toward the feeding pigeons. Another rider appeared dragging a cluster of five-gallon tin cans tied to the end of a riata. A pack of youngsters ran past us with bullslings, and heaved rocks amongst the birds. Somebody was blowing a police whistle. The great congress of birds lifted, to drop back down jam-packed at the far side of the field and resume feeding. But presently, as the *vaqueros* galloped around the perimeter of the field, coyote-squalling and still throwing firecrackers, the tin cans clattering, the whistle shrilling, a gun of some kind banging now, the birds thundered up and made a wide swing over the hacienda.

"I wouldn't have missed this for anything," Pop said.

He stuffed replacement shells into the Browning's magazine. The vast flock of pigeons banked into range. Pop deliberately picked high birds on the rim of the flight, and dropped three with three shots. The flock turned north over brushy hills, where it disappeared into the horizon haze. But I knew the birds would be back. So did our rancher hosts. The latter were coming to make a damage appraisal, looking plumb agitated. Milo maize currently had a market value of seven hundred *pesos* a ton. The field out front produced two tons per acre. And such a mob of blue pigeons could easily strip the entire

2

crop in a single day. That had happened here. It wasn't only the grain the birds ate, but the havoc they wreaked breaking stalks and battering seed heads to the ground with their wings.

Pop made a speech.

"When you accused me of idle daydreaming," he said, "I was thinking about country Mexicans and conservation. Practically anywhere else in the world, man, these blue pigeons would be classed as public enemies. Legislators would make emotional speeches demanding that farms be protected from the blue menace. Newspapers would run scarehead articles, emphasizing how many hungry children could be fed with the grain the birds pillage. TV cameramen would show blue pigeons descending on a maize field, then switch to a work-worn defeated farmer and his weeping wife. So right away, man, state and federal bounties would be placed on the birds. An army of heroes would arise to defend the nation's breadbasket. It would be a campaign of near extinction. Legalized wholesale killing by any means, including poison.

"But the country Mexican, give him credit, is a civilized gent in the best sense of the word. Also he is a philosopher. He knows you can't have wildlife and destroy it too. And he don't fall for propaganda. Despite the grain they steal, he likes to see blue pigeons around him. He sings sentimental songs about them. Have you heard that *Blue Paloma* ballad? He calls his wife and daughters *Palomas*. When blue pigeons raid his fields, he doesn't holler piteously for the government to reimburse him. Nor does he stand on his rights as a citizen and ask that a state of emergency be declared, and the national guard sent in. He just throws firecrackers, blows whistles and beats on tin cans, and hopes that his friends the pigeons have left him enough maize for tortillas.

"That's why I think I am gonna build me a '*dobe* house near some Sonora grain fields and live there until the character on the pale horse comes looking for me. Because, man, this is the sportsman pigeon hunter's last frontier, and I wanta enjoy it while I can."

I said I would visit him now and then. Pop is a goateed, white-headed, pint-size little Tennessean who wandered down into Mexico three years ago for a week of bird shooting, and

3

never did get around to going home. The previous day we had driven north from Guadalajara, glumly listening to hurricane warnings being broadcast over the radio. We had collected Haysoos at Huatabampo, and come on to Guasaguari ("Yellow Baskets" in the Mayo language) as thunder crashed and lightning forked down. For once Pop was grateful that we had Haysoos with us to do the retrieving. Until last autumn he had bitterly lamented the fact that nobody in Sonora uses bird dogs, that human retrievers are preferred. Because, Pop said, having shot over pointers and setters thirty years, he plain didn't feel right without a good dog working ahead. He didn't think he would ever become accustomed to a human retriever.

But he had. It had taken a nightmarish experience at a nearby place called *Bariste* ("Snorting Horse") to make him appreciate Haysoos' expert services. I had better tell you about that and a couple of other episodes before I finish relating what happened at Guasaguari hacienda. It'll give you the local slant on blue-pigeon shooting.

Bariste was a Spanish outpost before the Indian uprisings. Today nothing remains except some gnarled orchard trees, traces of adobe buildings, and a mysterious twenty-foot-deep dry shaft sunk into solid rock with the legend *SAN LORENZO 1775* chiseled below the shaft's heading. Blue pigeons haunt *Bariste* in early autumn. At daybreak this particular morning Haysoos and I went out to check on the horses. We found them in a meadow down the trail, and as we were hazing them closer to camp a flock of around fifty blue pigeons passed over us bound for the old orchard. We heard Pop's Browning stutter. We saw birds fall. The flock flared away, wings clapping together on the upstrokes, and vanished around the *sahuaro*-studded shoulder of a hill. Taking our time because one of the horses had hobble sores, we went on to the orchard.

Pop was nowhere in sight. But we heard muffled shouts and imprecations issuing from the aforementioned dry shaft. Fearing the worst, I plowed recklessly through stiletto-thorned *toro prieto* brush to the shaft and peered over its masonry heading. Well, Pop was down there all right. Flattened against the near shaft wall, he had a blue pigeon in one hand and his beat-up Jalisco sombrero in the other. He was holding the hat out in front of him, shield-wise. Except for this hat business, I comprehended the situation at a glance. The pigeon had fallen into

4

the shaft, and Pop had attempted to retrieve it instead of waiting for Haysoos. There had been a notched log ladder. But it was termite-riddled, and had collapsed under his weight.

However, he hadn't been hurt much. At least he was on his feet and plenty vocal. The blue pigeons had now come back and were circling us. Nine times out of ten small flocks arc spooky and suspicious, but this one wasn't. Probably, I thought, they were unsophisticated birds that had never been exposed to gunfire until this morning. At any rate, some good shooting was going to waste. I was about to tell Pop that we would hoist him out of the shaft any time he was ready, when I'll be doggoned if he didn't begin fervently addressing the Deity as follows:

"Lord, don't let that monster rattlesnake hit me. Save me from the ugly brute. You know I'm just a poor, humble shotgunner a long way from home, bent on salvaging my blue pigeon. If I have ever done anything to deserve being in this horrible predicament, Lord, believe me I am sorry. So please smite that son-of-a-bitching snake. Hurry, or I'm a goner sure enough, and I don't wanta die all alone down in this serpent pit that I have stupidly fallen into."

I couldn't see any rattlesnake. Or hear one either. But I advised Pop to freeze where he was and stop sounding off, and got out the .38 Colt I carried. Pop looked up at us, with the awed expression of a man reprieved by miraculous intervention. He pointed shakily at the tumbled remains of the log ladder. I moved around the shaft heading for a better angle of view. Behind broken sections of log I caught a glimpse of coils and movement. It was a snake, but not a rattler. In a moment it straightened out and I identified it as a fair-size valley boa. About seven feet long and as thick through as my arm. Now of course boas are harmless, and I figured this one was as panicky as Pop was. It opened its mouth and hissed like a busted steam pipe.

Don't ask me how come it happened to be in the shaft. Maybe it lived there. But there was no use trying to tell Pop that the big snake wasn't dangerous. He was too close to coming completely unstuck. So I put a slug through the hapless reptile's head. When it had ceased threshing about, I tied a bos'n chair bowline in my riata and we hauled Pop out. At this point the blue pigeons settled onto the orchard. They aimed to eat breakfast there, come whatever. Pop, forgetting his jangled nerves, at once started sneaking toward

5

a pomegranate tree where he had left the Browning. Then he halted, achieved a grin of sorts, and shoved a hand out at Haysoos.

"Son, I owe you an apology," he declared. "From now on the retrieving job is all yours. You won't hear me bragging anymore about the wonderful dogs I used to work. Because," he shuddered, "I don't suppose that even the greatest field trial grand champion dog that ever lived could reasonably be expected to climb down into a ghastly place like that Spanish shaft and take a blue pigeon away from such a monstrous deadly snake."

A week later, at San Antonio Spring, out of Huatabampo, Pop undertook to teach Haysoos how to score on blue pigeons with a shotgun. We had stationed ourselves so that the birds were crossing in front of us instead of barreling in head-on. There were a lot of small flocks, and no other water readily available. "Now don't shoot at a pigeon like it was hanging motionless in the air," Pop instructed the kid. "Swing your gun with the bird, see, and shoot where it's gonna be when the No. 6s get there." Well, this is what took place: *Blam*— "*Chihuahua*, I missed"—*blam*— "*Ay carajo*, missed again"—*blam*—"What went wrong that time?"—*Blam*— "I could do better throwing rocks"— *blam*. Haysoos had emptied the magazine without touching a feather. He handed the gun back to Pop.

"The trouble with this blue-pigeon shooting, patron," the kid commented resentfully, "is that the pigeons won't cooperate with me. I shoot where I think they are going to be, but they don't go there. They always turn off to somewhere else."

Exactly. That's been my headache these many years.

Mexico has twenty-four species of pigeons and doves, and most of them are admirable game birds. But the blue pigeons (*Columba flavirostris*) are tops, in an elite status by themselves. Not only are they big, beautiful and interestingly hard to hit, but they are a gourmet delight on the table. Non-migratory, they inhabit the settled lowlands and Sierra foothills of both coasts. Usually you find them hanging around farms. I have hunted blue pigeons pretty well throughout their range, and the largest populations I know about are here in Southwestern Sonora, in the grain-rich valleys of the Mayo and Yaqui Rivers.

Shooting blue pigeons gets much less tricky when the huge harvest-time flocks have assembled. As intimated, I have no idea what ordinary measures it would take to make an outsize flock permanently abandon a field of ripe grain. Pancho Sanchez, another farmer friend of ours in the Mayo valley, once came up with a scheme that deserved to work, but didn't. He had a phonograph record made from a World War II American movie soundtrack, and rented a public-address truck. One morning, when several hundred blue pigeons were feeding in his fifty-acre wheat field, Pancho drove as close to the birds as he could and broadcast the fire-fight record full volume. Pop, Haysoos and I were present as observers, and naturally for some shooting. But we had taken a stand at the far side of the field, where the action promised to be.

Well, it sounded like one of the busy mornings I had sweated through on Okinawa. Cannons, mortars and machine guns. Airplanes strafing. Bombs bursting. Men yelling. In the midst of the earsplitting pandemonium, an actor's amplified voice bellowed, "We're *pulverizing* them." The blue pigeons lifted, made a casual circuit of the field, and dropped back down on our side to finish their meal. Many were feeding within forty yards of the *guinolo* thicket in which we were concealed. Pop took his limit in five minutes. With all the high-decibel sounds of phony conflict hammering at us, the Browning's reports had been singularly flat and unimpressive. None of the pigeons apparently had even suspected they were being fired on with real lead. We returned to the public-address truck. Pancho, who had wads of cotton stuck in his ears, resignedly shut off the broadcast.

"*Caray,* I ought to hate those blue *cabrones,*" he growled. "They are putting a disastrous dent in my finances. But still I can't help admiring them. They have the true Mexican revolutionary spirit. Combat doesn't dismay them one damned bit."

Back to Guasaguari hacienda.

We had arisen shortly before sunup. Thunder was rumbling continuously. A radio newscaster stated that the hurricane would clobber the Sonora coast sometime today. That, Moses and his brother Oliver assured us, meant there would be an invasion of blue pigeons. Lowland flocks would band together and seek higher hill-sheltered feeding grounds such as Guasaguari offered. It turned out they were dead right. I have already told you about the epic flock that raided the milo maize field. I was positive the birds would come back any moment. Pigeons and doves invariably go to water immediately after feeding, and the only water nearer than six miles was in the cement stock-watering troughs alongside the main corral.

I looked around for a suitable blind. Parked behind the hacienda was a canvas-covered range chuck wagon. I requisitioned help, and we moved it to a spot two-hundred feet east of the troughs. So the rising sun would be at Pop's back. Then we climbed into the wagon and waited.

Assorted ranch animals came to drink. Several mules, a couple of steers, some burros, a horse, and a band of goats. Then I sighted a dark, wavering cloud low in the northern sky. Only it wasn't a cloud. It was an enormous flight of blue pigeons. I believe that other flocks had joined the one that had just looted the milo maize field. As to how many pigeons may have been in the flight, I won't even make a guess. They filled 45 degrees of the close, hill-humped horizon. Unafraid of the drinking stock animals, they swept directly in. There were four fifteen-foot troughs. The wheeling, hovering, crowding storm of pigeons blanked them from our view. Bizarre as I know it must sound, birds were alighting on the backs of the grouped animals.

I nudged Pop. He was sitting on a pile of grain sacks, wearing that expression again. Lost to the world. He grunted something, and stepped over the wagon's tailgate. At sight of him, the pigeons zoomed up in a crazy aerial traffic jam. Pop was three birds short of his limit. He cut loose with the Browning and killed them. The flock orbited the hacienda, unwilling to fly six miles for their morning water. I thought, *what the heck, let them drink in peace,* and herded Pop and Haysoos to the ranch house.

Moses and Oliver had broken out more firecrackers for *vaqueros* to explode in case the pigeons made another raid on the maize field. But there was little likelihood of that. Shucks, the birds had already eaten breakfast. As we watched through a front window, they swooped back down to the

8

watering troughs. Thunder cannonaded, and lightning hit a mesquite tree across the valley. Then a preliminary rain shower drummed the roof tiles, with a hard gust of wind behind it. The hurricane was showing its teeth, and soon water would be in every *arroyo*. But Pop stalled a while longer, giving the pigeons ample opportunity for a drink on the house. Then he handed the Browning to Haysoos.

"Go out there and knock down a few, son," he said. "This time take birds going away from you at 150 feet. I want you to build up some confidence."

Haysoos went across the veranda into the yard. He could have shot almost anywhere and hit pigeons. But he assumed Pop's easy stance, and waited until he had the gun on a pigeon going away at the right distance. The Browning boomed, and the bird fell. Then the kid downed another as the great flock rose to head westward over the valley against a slaty wall of oncoming cloudburst rain.

"What took you so long out there at the wagon?" I asked Pop. "Daydreaming again, huh?"

"Damn it, I never daydream," he replied indignantly. "I was just enjoying the show the pigeons were putting on. Then I got to thinking that that must have been the way passenger pigeons behaved in our country a century or so ago. Before we cut down the virgin timber and polluted the streams and lakes in the name of progress. Before we began commercially slaughtering the pigeons and shipping them packed in barrels to market, and feeding them by tons to hogs. Thinking about those barbarous matters made me sad, and that's why I didn't leap out of that wagon all eager and start blasting pigeons right and left.

"But young Haysoos' performance just now has made me feel better. He handled himself real good. Between us, man, we have helped a budding sportsman gunner get oriented with blue pigeons, and that's something we can be proud of."

Which, I guess, winds this up. See you someday on a blue-pigeon hunt in Sonora. Until then, *adios*.

Epitaph for Killer Grizzlies

The last of the murdering trio was true to form.
Ignoring an easy escape route, he charged.

"There he is, mister. The blond whopper on the right. That's the last of the Kutnoo-killer grizzlies," I informed young Pete Hadley, Jr., half shouting to make myself heard above the uproar of wind and water. "So watch yourself. I am going to put this craft ashore. I hope."

"Hooray," Pete said, and checked the chamber load of his .300 Weatherby Magnum.

Seconds ago I had warped our flat-bottomed, stampede-poling boat into Silver Salmon Alley, a narrow side channel of Alaska's Susitna River. Dead ahead of us, 150 yards distant, the two grizzlies stood belly-deep in a riffle. Presumably they were stalking salmon. But whatever they were doing, they sure gave rise to an urgent situation. The current here was running anyhow fifteen miles per hour. And we had a sand-laden September williwaw near-gale quartering against us. Our problem was, if Pete shot the Kutnoo outlaw on the riffle, recovering the carcass would be a chancy business. Equally frustrating, if we waited for the animal to beat it ashore, by the time he got there we probably would be past him barreling around another bend.

So the answer was to attempt a quick landing—which prospect didn't fill me with enthusiasm, much as I wanted to see the Kutnoo killer get his comeuppance. I would have to swing the heavy-loaded boat end for end, hold her in the stiff current, fighting the wind, hoping the pole wouldn't become wedged between rocks or stuck in soft bottom, and then, if lucky, angle her bow precisely so the current would nudge her safely ashore. And do it without help. Pete didn't know how to use a pole in fast water. There aren't many guys left around who do. It is practically a lost skill. I wished that we had a husky outboard motor.

"Hang on," I said.

The two bears stared at us through level-blowing sand and cottonwood leaves as I muscled the boat into a bucking turn. The Kutnoo outlaw, I told myself once again, was absolutely the handsomest grizzly S.O.B. ever seen in these parts. Pale cream yellow with cinnamon legs. High-humped and short-snouted. His undercoat, revealed by the wind, was blue-gray. By comparison, the mahogany-colored specimen alongside him looked third rate. That one, I figured, was a female who had lost her cub or cubs. Otherwise the two wouldn't be associating amicably at this time of year. As yet the animals hadn't spooked. They couldn't have heard us. The visibility, as stated, was lousy. Maybe they thought the boat was a drift tree.

I now had the craft turned and was braking her, with good bottom for the pole. I congratulated myself. The way things were working out, we had it made.

And then, holy suffering, we struck. Hard aground. With a heck of a jolt. On a gravel bar that I hadn't seen because wind-lashed water was washing over it. I grabbed at a thwart, but the pole got in my way and I fell skidding on my knees. Pete took a couple of off-balance running steps aft, encountered a seat, and went down in a flat dive. The Weatherby clattered onto the dunnage planks. I got to my feet and vaulted overboard, to lighten the craft and steady her before she swamped. Meanwhile the two grizzlies had concluded, I guess, that we weren't a drift tree or anything else innocent. With the mahogany-colored female leading, they were splashing ashore—but taking their time, looking back at us.

"Where'd the bears go?" Pete demanded, lurching erect and gazing upstream instead of downstream, on account of the boat had turned 90 degrees. "Where'd they disappear to?"

Pete was a lanky graduate biology student from the University of Washington. Ten days ago he had come north for his first grizzly hunt. But he couldn't afford packhorses. So I had borrowed the poling boat, and we had shipped it and an outfit by rail eighty miles up the Susitna, to float back down. It was as likely a way as any to hunt grizzlies, and it especially suited me. Because while I was at Anchorage waiting for Pete, a sourdough wolfer had brought me hot intelligence regarding the Kutnoo outlaw. Two days earlier he had sighted the bear in a black-currant patch partway down Silver Salmon Alley, but hadn't got a shot at him. That's how come we were here today being clobbered by the wind, instead of snugly camped under some sheltering headland.

"Damn it, behind you," I said.

The bears were ashore now. There was a strip of fireweed bar and then an alder-fringed cutbank. The mahogany-colored female went up the bank in a scrambling rush, and disappeared from our ken. But the Kutnoo outlaw of a sudden got tough. He whirled to face us at two-hundred feet, and let out a challenging roar. Then he swaggered back to the water's edge. If his mane hadn't been soaking wet, it would have bristled to make him look a third bigger than he actually was. And that was big enough. I gave him 750 pounds. Grizzlies didn't come much heavier on this watershed. *Wagh-h*, he roared again, swinging his head. With no way to prove it, I believe that he intended to charge the grounded boat.

Pete, I suppose, had been waiting for the exact target he wanted, and now had it. The Weatherby blasted. I saw the 180-grain softnose knock hair off the bear's neck close behind and above the mutton-chopped bulge on his jaw. *That's the button. Leave it to a biologist*, I thought. With his cervical vertebrae shattered, the bear crumpled in a heap, snorted blood, and died. Well, we horsed the boat into navigable water and I worked her ashore, the wind assisting me for a change. We parked ourselves on a drift log. I sweetened the edge of my knife while Pete admired his trophy.

"What did he do to get himself on the outlaw list?" Pete asked.

"He helped kill an Indian boy, five years ago. Name of Nikolai. The teenage son of old Mishkah Chickaloosun, a Denna Bear Clan second chief."

I was remembering the parka squirrel-trapping camp in frost-painted birches above Kutnoo Creek, thirty miles east of here. Mishkah and I sitting on a roan moose hide. And Mishkah's sad voice as he told me what had happened. That was the September of my twenty-third year, and I had just come afoot across the mountains from Cache Lake. Spotting the tent, I had angled down to pass the time of day. Then I saw the new grave. A mound of earth and a two-armed Russian cross. Above it a peeled pole spirit-offering platform. On the platform, lashed there with snare wire, was the raw skull of a grizzly. Mishkah's wife Christina, sat at the tent entrance, mourning.

"We journey up here seven days ago, with two pack dogs," Mishkah was saying in Denna. "Day before yesterday, early, I kill a moose. A fat mulligan bull. In a little caribou moss opening on the creek flat below here. I open the carcass up, but I ain't strong enough to turn it over so I can do a good job of dressing it. So I come back to camp for help. Nikolai and Christina aren't here. They have climbed the mountain to tend their squirrel snares. I holler and whistle. After a while they come down through the willows, and I tell them about the moose. That makes them happy. They are laughing, and planning a fine feast of marrow bones and blood soup, as they cinch the canvas-pack panniers onto the dogs.

"'Chain the dogs together,' I advise them. 'So they can't chase rabbits. And don't forget the camp ax, for chopping bones.'

"Happy, joking, grateful, we head down to the creek flat. Nikolai runs ahead with the dogs. Christina tries to keep up with him. Me, I plod behind. My stiff joints make me slower and clumsier every day. I notice that we now have a cross-wind, blowing straight down the creek. Nikolai and the dogs go out of sight around some frosted willows at the foot of a crooked spruce snag. The caribou moss opening and the moose carcass are a few yards beyond. Two ravens are perched on the snag, afraid to pitch down for a meal of guts. That should have warned me. I don't know why it didn't. Maybe I thought it was because they had spotted us. Anyway, suddenly I hear terrible sounds.

"Nikolai yells, a grizzly bawls, the dogs are screaming. So now I know why the ravens were afraid. I curse myself for a fool. The worst of it was that, except for the camp ax and his knife, the boy is unarmed.

"'Hurry, man, with your rifle,' Christina shouts. 'Grizzlies are killing our son.'

14

"Hell, I can't hurry. But ahead of me is a steep bunch-grass bank. As I head for it, I hear Nikolai call my name. That's the last time I ever hear his voice. Christina is running toward the trouble, stumbling and falling, getting up to run again, a knife flashing in her hand. I climb the bunchgrass bank as fast as I can. From its top I look down four-hundred yards over the willows to the caribou moss opening. I see three yellow grizzlies humping away from the place. A big female and two long yearlings. Nikolai is lying facedown beside the moose carcass. Not moving. Off to his right the two pack dogs are piled up in the broken top of a birch windfall, also motionless. The grizzlies have now crossed the creek. They are climbing the mountainside through clumps of wild celery. Above them is a round patch of very thick alder brush.

"I stretch out on the bank top, elbows propped, and try my damnedest to kill the big female. I have a good rifle, a .30-06 Winchester with Lyman iron sights. But I am panting, and the range is more than five-hundred yards. I shoot. The bullet busts a shale slab ten feet behind the bear's rump. I hold higher, and shoot again. This time I see rock dust fly close on the bear's left and even with her. She turns right toward the alders. The last shot scared her. She wants cover. A dozen more bounds and she will be in the brush. I take a couple of deep breaths. Then I lay the gold bead six feet ahead of her nose and two feet above it, and shoot. Her front legs buckle like she has tripped over something. I hear the solid *whoomp* a softnose makes when it hits meat.

"But she keeps going. Before I can chamber another shell, she reaches the alders. The two yearlings have abandoned her. They are now on the rim of a deep wash that cuts down the mountain, seven-hundred yards distant. I let go a shot at one of them. The bullet glances off a rock and howls out over the valley. The yearlings jump into the wash. I don't see them again.

"Well, I start down to where the trouble is. Pretty soon I hear Christina wailing. I ain't gonna tell you what the caribou moss opening looked like when I got there. It was a massacre scene. The boy is dead, all right. So are the two dogs. With their chain tangled in the windfall's limbs, the dogs didn't have a chance. But the boy died fighting. There is blood on the ax blade. I tell myself that it is all my fault because I didn't pay

16

attention to the ravens. You understand how it happened. The bears found the moose carcass while I was at camp. Then the boy and the dogs come sprinting crosswind into the opening. I figured the bears were taken completely by surprise. So naturally they attacked. But Christina, wagging a finger at me, argues that I am wrong.

"'The bears deliberately ambushed the boy,' she screeches. 'I saw everything through the brush. They heard the boy and the dogs coming. They had plenty of time to leave. But they wanted the moose carcass. They killed the tangled dogs first, then the boy. They were all on him. The big female had his whole head in her mouth. Shoot me those bears, man. At least the big female. Bring me her skull and her heart. Today. Before we bury our son.'

"'Maybe I can do that,' I say.

"I cut a birch staff because I need it, and climb the mountain to where the bear was when I put lead into her. I find blood. It looks like blood from her lungs. Well, the patch of alder is about two-hundred feet across. With redtop grass growing under the twelve-foot-high bushes. I decide to set the grass afire and burn the bear out. But the grass is too wet. It won't burn. So I sit down and wait. I know the bear can hear me and is getting my scent. She wants me to go into the brush after her. A half-hour passes. Two ravens, I guess the same ones, slide down the wind and circle me. Then they circle a spot out in the middle of the alder patch. A bush shakes there, and I hear the bear growl.

"An idea strikes me. It's something I remember my father told me.

"I take off my parka squirrel jacket and button it around a clump of wild celery. I put my hat on top of this dummy. Then I climb two-hundred feet above the alder patch. With my staff I pry up a wheel-shaped slab of shale, and send it rolling down the mountain. It smashes halfway through the alders, hits a boulder, and busts apart with a sound like an explosion. I roll another slab after it. I figure the bear can't stand much of that, and I am right. Alder tops shake. Then the bear roars and gallops out of the brush on three legs, upwind at the dummy that her nose tells her is me.

"I let her discover the mistake she has made. She takes one swipe at the parka squirrel jacket, and sees nothing is in-

17

side it but a clump of wild celery. I guess at that instant she realizes she is finished. Anyway, she faces up the mountain, and bellers at me. She don't try to escape. She only wants me to know that she hates me and wishes she could get hold of me just once before she dies. I line the Winchester's sights on her open mouth as she bellers again, and shoot. Blood, brains and broken teeth splatter. She tumbles 150 yards down the mountain, and ends up against the creekside willows.

"Christina wades across, knife in hand. 'Come back down here, man,' she calls. 'You have done well. Now we can bury our son.'"

Well, Mishkah was a popular sub-chief. And not only with his fellow Denna tribesmen. He had also made himself a lot of friends among the sourdoughs. As a result, for the next four years assorted hunting parties set out determined to destroy the surviving two killer bears. They failed. The bears (Indian trackers asserted they were males) apparently were not only unusually crafty, but also loaded with luck.

But their numbers were up. The following September a towheaded pilgrim from Denver, Bill Clements by name, got luckier than one of the outlaws. We had backpacked in from the railroad, for a grizzly and a goat. Forty miles over beautiful but mean country. We made a siwash camp under Cave Mountain near the headwaters of Montana Creek, one tall ridge south of Kutnoo Creek. It was a chill morning, with scattered clouds blowing along the range crests. Two thousand feet above us a mixed band of twelve goats was bedded down on a grassy terrace. A couple of the heads were promising. As soon as I finished washing the breakfast dishes, we were going to climb up there.

"I have located another goat," Bill said. "A monster. Big as a pony. But I can't see his head."

That was too much goat. I reached for my 16X glasses. The animal referred to was lying partly behind a lichen-encrusted red boulder. It wasn't a goat. The color was approximately right, but Bill had somehow overlooked the fact that goats have hoofs. This beast had paws. Platter-size hind paws anyway. I steadied the glasses against the lean-to ridge-pole and cut the focus finer. As I did so, the animal backed into full view and raised its head, checking the wind. Well, it was one of the Kutnoo outlaw grizzlies. No chance of a mistake. Their pale cream-colored coats were unique here-

18

abouts. The shaggy brute obviously had goat meat on his mind. In the band were several top-knotted kids. I mean, no grizzly with good sense will tackle an adult goat, but bears do occasionally kill youngsters.

We went up a steep glacier trough, ice on one side, blank rock on the other. The wind was cooperating nicely. During the climb I briefed Bill, gave him the Kutnoo outlaws' background. Another cloud had drifted across the mountain face. We fumbled our way out of the glacier trough, in a smother of wet mist. You couldn't see one-hundred feet. Directly below us now was a sheer cliff that dropped halfway to camp. We halted, waiting for the cloud to move on. It didn't. The favorable wind was pushing, but the cloud must have reached plumb to the horizon. I could hear the goats coming toward us. Shale tinkling. The bear surely would take advantage of the cloud cover, I thought.

"Get set," I whispered. "I am going to try something."

I cupped my hands at my mouth, and grunted like a frightened kid. I had once trapped goats alive for a government stocking project, and had practiced imitating the various sounds they uttered. Somewhere close ahead on the mist-shrouded terrace an adult goat snorted in reply. A warrior billy, probably. Then here came the grizzly. We heard him before we saw him. He was charging headlong down a scree stringer. Coasting on the loose stuff between bounds. Bill knelt, .375 Winchester Magnum at his shoulder. Cool and collected as though we were on a target range. The bear appeared sixty feet distant.

Bill fired. The sledgehammer wallop of the 300-grain slug racked the bear back on his haunches, but he stayed upright. He slammed past us, scrambling. He skidded off the scree onto grass, and swapped ends, his claws furrowing the turf. For perhaps two seconds the bear and I gazed at each other. The cliff brink was twenty feet behind him. Bill had hit him in the chest. I could see blood jetting. Most likely he was wondering how everything could have gone so horribly wrong in such a brief space of time. Then the heavy magnum boomed. The bear kicked himself backward over the cliff. A long moment later we heard him smash into an alder jungle one-thousand feet below.

Well, remember this account began down on the main river, in gale-swept Silver Salmon Alley. Young Pete Hadley, Jr. had just killed the last of the three Kutnoo outlaw grizzlies. I didn't

19

feel particularly triumphant. Instead there was an odd sense of loss. It could be, I thought, that a frontier needs a few outlaws around. Bears or whatever. As I got busy with my skinning knife, I told Pete that Bill Clements had let me have the skull of his bear. I had toted it over the ridge to Kutnoo Creek and placed it on the spirit-offering platform above Nikolai Chickaloosun's grave. Alongside the weather-whitened skull of the big she-grizzly.

"Do me a favor," Pete said. "Take the skull of this outlaw, and put it on the platform with the others. To complete the drama. I'll be proud knowing it's there."

Pronto Was a Lion Killer

*My old blaze-faced sorrel was a tough caballo,
a natural hunter with an ear for hound music,
a stubborn mind, and a hate for big cats.*

"**M**issed again. Man, it's like terrible. I can't hit that lion,"
big Tom Harkins said desperately, between shots, this cold
November afternoon atop a bleak cactus ridge above *Copeche*
(Firefly) *Barranca* in the Sierra Madre foothills of southern Sonora.
"I dunno what's wrong with me."

I had 8X glasses on the lion. The sandy-tan beast was now
five hundred yards distant on the *barranca* floor, loping up a
dry rain-season flood wash. My five hounds were bellering a
quarter-mile behind. The lion had set course for a rimrocked
point that jutted into the *barranca* at the next bend. If he reached
the point, he would lose the dogs. I could see that the jumbled
rimrocks were too formidable for anything but cats, goats and
reckless humans. We had found the animal's trail forty minutes ago. Paw prints and a urine signature told me it was a
fair-size male. I figured it would make for the *barranca* when
it heard the dogs. So we took a shortcut over two ridges, pushing
our horses, to this vantage position. Immediately after we arrived there, the lion showed up.

"Keep blasting away," I said. "You'll either kill the cat
or make it do something stupid. Your trouble is, you're cold
and shivering."

Tom had his scope-sighted .270 Winchester rested over a basalt boulder. He fired, and the bullet kicked up gravel eight feet ahead of the lion and an equal distance downwind. As I opened my mouth to call the shot, the lion bounded aside at the slug's impact spot. It whapped the gravel with both front paws, like a huge house cat catching a grasshopper. I had never before seen a lion do that. It curled its lips in a snarl and switched its long tail. It looked back at the oncoming dogs. Then it took off again. I told Tom where the shot had gone, and he let go another. This time the slug hit three feet downwind from the lion's right shoulder. The cat bucked as rock fragments stung him, and he veered sharply to the left, off his course to the rimrocked point.

Big cats are cut from a pattern. They are intelligent and crafty, but they can't stand pressure. Apply the squeeze, hooraw them into the open, crowd them, create unseemly racket, and they start making dumb moves.

Dead ahead of this one was an isolated flat-topped red boulder some ten feet high. He jumped onto it. He flattened himself there, watching the dogs. He was hiding. He had laid an ambush. Through the binoculars I could see the intent expression on his tawny triangular face. He didn't even glance up at the ridge crest. But of course he knew we were there. After such a spate of gunfire, every animal and bird in the countryside must have had us located. He wasn't using his brains. The dogs' bawling and the slugs smacking around him had plainly given him an attack of the stupids. If he had kept on, he probably would have gained safety in the rimrocks. Now his pelt was as good as nailed up to dry.

Tom lined the .270's glass sight, and fired.

The wicked 130-grain slug struck the boulder top two feet in front of the lion's head. There was no ricochet wail. The cat half reared, and either jumped or fell off the far side of the boulder. It didn't come back into view. So presumably it was hit. The dogs were closing in fast. If the lion was only wounded, there could be some casualties down there in the next several minutes. Loba, my black *xoloitzcuintli*-bluetick pack leader, wouldn't get hurt. She was a grimly cautious pro. But her four black-and-tan assistants, youngsters, had the notion that they were tough. They wouldn't settle for anything less than a brawl. You can't teach some young dogs to lay off wounded cats. They have to learn the hard way. That is, the lucky ones learn. The mortician buzzards and ants take care of the others.

I ran to my saddle mount, a lion-scarred sorrel named Pronto, and swarmed aboard him. I advised Tom to take it easy off the ridge. Then I touched Pronto with the spurs and gave him slack reins.

Pronto was getting old. A little sunk in at the temples, with that pinched look above his nostrils. A little stiff-jointed on cold mornings. I had ridden him six years. But he was still the best mountain horse I had ever put a saddle on south of the border. He took me down the broken ridge in his own special slam-bang manner. Jump, squat and slide. Dodge the boulders or sail over them. Zigzag in headlong plunges. Rocks rolling, hoofs clattering, grunt and snort, saddle working onto his withers, hurdle a wash, bust through a thicket, sideswipe a ledge but what of it? That's what bull hide chaps and *tapideros* are for. Down onto level ground, and out across the flat to where the black-and-tans were bellering frustration.

Their biggest problem was that they couldn't get at the lion. It had landed in dense bull thorn, and was now backed up against the boulder, protected on all sides. Tom joined me presently, and gave it a finishing shot through the head. I had a Sam Collins machete and used it to hack a passage to the lion. It was a fine trophy cat. Seven feet, one inch. Its pelt thick and prime. Tom's ricochet slug had smashed its left leg. I skinned the cat and gutted the carcass for dog food. Meanwhile Tom had put on his slicker. I didn't have one, so I donned the lion skin cape fashion. Front legs knotted together to hold it in place. Tail doubled under my belt. Then I loaded the carcass onto Pronto, lashing it behind the saddle.

"Man, what a terrific hunting horse that old-timer is," Tom said. "The way he rocketed off that ridge. I salute him. I wish I had a horse like him, man. What are those scars on his rump? Some kind of Mexican brand?"

I said I would tell him about the scars when we were back at camp, over a pot of coffee. I was remembering an episode of wild and savage action. . . .

"Que le pasa, señor?" white-haired Chapo Maldonado, the Mayo Indian contract freighter, had asked softly when I sat up in my blankets, a hand on the cold breech of the

Winchester Auto 12 that has been my reliable bedmate these
many years. "What goes on?"

"I don't know. Listen to that owl down at the pond."

This was around 2 o'clock of a moonlit September morning at *Borogui* (Toad) Spring in the high pine-oak Sierra. I had
met Chapo and his outfit here at dusk. He was en route to a
silver mine with freight and mail. I was bound for Huatabampo
to meet a sportsman from the States. I pulled on my pants and
boots. I checked the buckshot chamber load of the gun. The
place seemed peaceful. Chapo's teenage son Miguel was pounding
his ear on the other side of the fading pine-knot campfire coals.
Loba and her four Walker apprentices, chained yonder at the rim
of a pigeonberry thicket, had raised their heads when I spoke,
then had gone back to sleep. Everything was normal, they thought.

But the owl claimed otherwise. It was a pygmy laughing
owl. A *lechusa*. As we listened, it chuckled, tittered and giggled.
Sierra Madre folks believe that *lechusas* are witch sentries. When
one of the tiny birds sounds off near your camp, they tell you,
beware. Thieves and killers are prowling. Quaint superstition?
I won't argue. But—

I motioned Chapo to stay put, and eased over dew-wet grass
to the margin of the 150-foot-long spring pond. I hunkered with
my back against a scrub oak. The owl was in a chalate snag
across the pond. It ha-ha-ho-ho-tee-heed up and down the scale.
Then hoofs thudded. Chapo's packstring, seven mules and three
Indian ponies, rawhide hobbled, were coming in crosswind for
a drink. Leading them was this blaze-faced bright sorrel packhorse
named Pronto. He splashed knee-deep into the pond and began gulping water. He was a couple of lengths this side of the
fifteen-foot granite ledge from which the spring issued. *Huisache*
brush fringed the brink of the ledge. I now noticed, with a start,
two sizable dark humps in the thin screen of brush that I didn't
think had been there a moment ago.

I turned my head, watching the objects from the corners
of my eyes. Seconds passed. Then one of the things vanished.
The other shifted position, and moonlight reflected reddish-or-
ange from a pair of eyes. Mountain lions.

Or anyhow one mountain lion. I brought up the 12-gauge
a pulsebeat too late. Before I could point the barrel and shoot,
the lion launched itself off the ledge at Pronto. It was im-

24

possible to shoot. I would have put lead into the horse. Sure, I know, I know. What did he have to lose? But he wasn't my cayuse. As split-second events turned out, however, the sorrel didn't need help. Not with that lion. *Quien sabe* what had warned him. Unless it was a flicker of moon shadow on the water. At any rate, he whirled and kicked. His sharp-shod hoofs connected with a sound like a sledge hammering a ripe pumpkin. The lion moaned as momentum piled it onto Pronto's rump. It clung there an instant, then the sorrel sunfished from under it.

While the lion floundered in the water making drowning noises, Pronto spun and struck with his hobbled front hoofs. Some Injun cayuse. At this juncture the other lion reappeared. It likewise soared off the ledge at the horse, to take over the project its partner had bungled. For me the timing was perfect. Pronto's lightning pivot had given me a clear line of fire.

The cat was in midair. With the buck and boom of the full-choked gun, I saw pieces of skull splatter. The would-be assassin hit the pond with a splash, on its back, legs galloping, coughing blood and water. I clobbered it with two more buckshot loads that rolled it over and drove it under. Pronto started ashore, but bogged briefly in soft mud bottom. He was between me and the lion he had kicked and stomped. As I maneuvered for a shot, here came the rest of the packstring. They had stampeded around the pond and were heading for camp. Pronto now extricated himself, and surged up onto the bank. To avoid being trampled, I dodged behind a tree.

"Santa Guadalupe de Tayopa," I heard Chapo yell.

He was charging down to the pond, moonlight glinting on the long barrel of his .50-caliber Martin Campos muzzleloader. Young Miguel, a savvy mountain lad, had ignited an ocote pitch-pine torch and was sprinting after Chapo. Behind them at camp the hounds clamored hysterically. They were believers now. I wanted to know where the first lion was. The one Pronto had worked over. During my mix-up with the packstring, it had disappeared. The three of us circled the pond, throwing rocks into the bordering *cariso* sedge. No lion. It had made a getaway. So I went back to camp and fetched Loba. On leash. She soon informed us that the lion had gone ashore at the granite ledge, then had fled eastward toward a stand of oaks.

"Okay, chum, get going. It's all yours," I told her, and slipped the leash.

I could control Loba. I had a whistle she would obey. Whereas her Walker apprentices were bullheaded bravos. Give them a chance, they would chase a lion hellbent plumb to Durango. And I sure didn't crave to get involved in any marathon pursuit tonight. Loba streaked into the timber. She had been gone only a few minutes when she belled "treed." The lion had run less than four-hundred yards. We found it crouched twenty feet up in a wide netleaf oak. I grabbed Loba and hauled her to safety, and offered the 12-gauge to Miguel. With a bashful smile of thanks, he took the gun. He and Chapo fired together. The lion sagged forward, fell, and lodged in a fork. We waited to make certain it was dead. Then Miguel jumped and latched onto its tail, and pulled it to the ground.

Chapo caught Pronto and we looked him over.

The lion had raked multiple gashes from his kidney area down across both sides of his rump. We cleaned the wounds with some Bacanora tequila that Chapo had, and smeared them with pine pitch to baffle blowflies. The sorrel kept his gaze on the lion carcasses. Tense and glaring. As though ready for another go-round. Of a sudden I coveted the character. I liked his courage and the way he was put together. He was short-coupled and blocky-hipped. Maybe 1,050 pounds. Four years old, according to his teeth. Wide-set eyes in an Arabian-type head. Hard dark hoofs. Long black mane and tail, and a smooth coat of the copper-bright sorrel shade that the Mexicans, who boast one thousand color names for horses, refer to as *alazan saino*.

"Sure, he's handsome and valiant," Chapo was saying. "He might make somebody a good saddle mount, once he's healed up. But what's that to me? Here I am, *caray* with sixteen-hundred pounds of freight and mail to deliver fifty miles from here day after tomorrow, or lose my contract. What am I gonna do?" Chapo watched me with anxious Indian eyes, to judge how his hard-luck recital was going over.

"Don't be downhearted, *compañero,*" I said. "I have a first-class packhorse. The bay pinto. It's possible I could be persuaded to trade him for this lion-clawed sorrel."

"My benefactor," Chapo cried, and quickly handed me Pronto's tie-rope.

In December I checked Pronto out as a lion-hunting horse.

It was a mean morning. Thunder cannonading. A half-gale of wind howling down the Dolores Fork of the Mayo River. The dogs were trailing somewhere ahead. But I hadn't had a position fix from them for ten minutes. The wind was making too much racket. Their voices wouldn't carry through it. So I was just heading Pronto, by guess and by gosh, up the willow-jungled valley bottom.

Bucking the brute wind, we came abreast of narrow *Tetajioso* (Picture Rocks) Canyon mouth. Here Pronto and I had our first serious argument. Of his own volition, he turned toward the canyon. I reined him back on our original course. To my astonishment, he balked. Flat-out defied me.

"Listen, hotshot," I said. "I don't know what you have in mind. But forget that canyon. That's not where we're going. Your job is to supply the transportation. Period. So, damn it, leave the strategy to me."

I still hadn't heard from the dogs. But I was positive the lion had continued on up the timbered main valley, where it could climb a tree anytime it needed to. Its belly was full of deer meat. It was hard pressed, and the canyon was a mere barren rift. I had never explored the place, but the visible three-hundred yards of it was sheer-walled. No convenient ledges. No talus slopes. No boulder heaps. I couldn't believe the lion would risk being overtaken in such a trap. Anyway, why was I arguing with a come-lately cayuse? I pulled the sorrel's head around, and hit him a lick with the sunflower spurs. He grunted, humping his back. I thought he was going to pitch. Instead he lit out at a dead run into the canyon.

Nothing like this had happened to me for quite a spell. Usually I have a pretty fair rapport with horses.

I came back hard on the spade bit. He couldn't take that. No horse could have. So then he did pitch. He went up high and whomped down stiff-legged, swapping ends with every jump. I lost track of him twice. I was all over the J.R. Thompson saddle. He might have tossed me, except that the brush handicapped him and he had bad footing. After twenty seconds or so he was ready to quit. But I thought I had better make him get it all out of his system. While I had the advantage. I whacked him across the ears with my hat. I told him I knew plowhorses who could out-pitch him any old day. With both hind feet in a bucket. May I be forgiven.

Because just then there was a lull in the wind's blaring. I heard, echoing down the canyon, faint but unmistakable, Loba's beautiful voice. The four Walkers chiming in.

They weren't trailing. They were telling me they had the lion bayed, and asking me to hasten with a gun. Well, I now understood. Partly, anyhow. The way it had to be, Pronto's ears were a whole lot keener than mine, and he had been homing in on the dogs all the while. Like a veteran of a hundred cat hunts. I don't suppose it is necessary to explain how I felt. I got down and petted the horse. I assured him that from today on he was an executive vice president of the outfit.

I stepped aboard, and let Pronto have his head.

We highballed up the canyon, into level-blowing sand. We rounded a bend, and the canyon widened. Ahead was a wedge-shaped flat, spiky with tall dead sotol bloom stalks. God's candles, the Mayos call them. At the west limit of the flat stood two scraggly crowned cottonwoods. I could now hear the dogs again. We slammed clackety-crash through brittle sotol palisades, and then I saw the lion. It was in the nearest cottonwood, stretched out on a crooked hangman's limb. With the wind blowing its fur the wrong way, it looked burly and disheveled. Loba and the Walkers were ranged in a circle at the tree, competing to see who could bawl the loudest. I reined Pronto to a skidding halt, slid the .30-30 out of its boot, and hit the ground.

The lion had known where it was going. Beyond the flat an ancient waterfall had spilled a steep alluvial fan into the canyon. On each side of it were ledges and terraces. Complete safety, if the cat had reached there.

I carefully shot the lion behind an ear, and it tumbled stone dead out of the tree. It was a large male. I gave it 130 pounds. Pronto snorted. I turned and saw him standing in the posture of a fighting range stud. Head craned out and his teeth showing. I knew then that he was a great lion-hunting horse. He had everything. . . .

Big Tom Harkins and I were riding into the outskirts of town. It was still cold, so I was still wearing Tom's lion skin as a windbreaker cape. We came to Chapo Maldonado's adobe house. Chapo and Miguel were sitting on the doorstep repairing a sawbuck saddle. Whenever we met, the venerable freighter and I put on a little act. He now came out into the road, and with a look of hammered-up surprise, said, "Are you still riding that crowbait sorrel, *compañero*? Are times so hard with you? *Pues,* maybe I can help. I have a first-class packhorse. And I might be persuaded to trade him for your sorry *alazan saino.* As a favor, you understand."

"My benefactor," I cried, and quickly handed him Pronto's reins.

Tom said, "Are you crazy?" And then, "Oh, I get it, man. A joke, huh? It's gotta be a joke because, man, we all know that Pronto is the most, bless him."

Wolf Trouble

As cubs, their lives were spared.
Four years later they had grown into killers.

"**D**amned wolf is fixing to massacre a few caribou. But he don't know we're here," my sourdough partner Tanana Stewart advised our current hunter, husky young Wes Thompson, of Santa Fe. Tanana had his 12X glasses trained on a whopper white wolf crouched in some gaudy willows four hundred yards distant. "Shoot your fancy bull caribou, mister. Then, by gosh, shoot the lousy no-good so-and-so of a wolf."

"Yessir," Wes said, grinning. "You're acquainted with the beast, huh?"

This was happening on a pretty, windless September morning above the west portal of Denna Lake Pass, deep in Alaska's northern Talkeetnas. We had taken a stand at the edge of the bordering spruce timber. The barren grounds caribou herd, around two-thousand head, was drifting down through a frosted pea vine meadow out front. Wes rested his .270 Winchester over a boulder. But before he could fire, the wolf broke cover and charged at the herd. He was larger than some of the caribou. I gave him 140 pounds, and ten feet tip to tip. The lead cow made a fast turn toward us when she saw him. The herd pounded after her. It was a curious sight, the multitude of caribou fleeing from a single wolf, hoofs thundering, antlers clattering, scared silly. But I guess each caribou thought it was the white killer's prime target.

31

Wes still hadn't shot. His trophy bull was five lengths behind the lead cow, partly hidden by other bulls. He looked great with his branchy, basket-type head, twin brow shovels, and elegant snowy cape. He was now about three hundred yards distant. I figured that in the confusion Wes had lost track of him. Which, if so, was tough, because we didn't have a prayer of pointing the animal out to him again.

The wolf swooped in and chopped at the hamstrings of an ancient, skinny bull, one side, then the other. You could see that he'd had plenty of practice working on caribou. The bull squatted and clubbed desperately with his antlers, but he was too slow. The wolf set teeth in his flank and tore out a mouthful. Intestines spilled.

But the wolf didn't bother to finish the bull. He raced on, covering ground at twice the speed of the caribou. He crowded a cow against the herd and slashed at her hocks. She stood on her hind legs, pivoted, and came down onto a bull's antlers, impaling herself. The two fell in a kicking tangle. The wolf swerved past them, yelping and baying. He was wrecking caribou for the fun of it—a sure-enough haywire wolf. But he had committed a tactical boner. He was no longer on the rim of the herd, but out in front of it.

"There he is. There's my trophy bull," Wes said, and fired.

A handsome bull one hundred yards from us stumbled and went down. Perhaps it really was the bull we had selected, I couldn't tell. At any rate, he hit the ground apparently dead, and the herd poured over him. The lead cow tried to swing the herd away from us, but didn't have enough room. Here she came, so spooked that her tongue was hanging out. As for the wolf, I guess he now understood what a blunder he had made. He looked over his shoulder at the herd. No opening in that direction, nor was an end run feasible. No time—the herd front was two hundred yards wide. So he attempted a bluff. He turned and threatened the herd, teeth bared, to make it split around him. In other circumstances he might have gotten away with that. Caribou aren't noted for brains. But Wes decided for them.

His .270 crashed. The wolf fell, scrambling. He was on his side, head lifted as though yowling a protest, when the hoofs of the herd blanked him from our view. Everything had occurred in high-speed sequences. The herd was now on top of us, but we had a chest-high granite boulder for shelter. As we bellied against it, caribou hurtled past so close that I could have poked them in the ribs with my rifle barrel. They jumped windfalls, busted the limbs off trees, flattened thickets. Then the last of them, a crippled bull, snorted slobber at us and disappeared down the pass. The stand of timber looked like a cyclone had visited it. We went out and examined Wes's two trophies. The damage they had taken could be repaired, we agreed, by a competent taxidermist.

"Yeah, we knew this white thug," Tanana said, answering Wes's question. "S.O.B helped kill a pet colt of ours. Also, he was a would-be man-killer. The only reason he didn't get out of the would-be class was, he and his pals lost their nerve."

I was remembering how it had begun on a cottonwood-perfumed May morning four years ago. We had just decided to build a commercial hunting lodge at the lake. The area was completely wild then with hardly an ax scar in it. This particular morning, we were over at the lake's outlet catching a mess of grayling for breakfast. A wolf pup yodeled on the hillside above us. We went up and found the den, a short tunnel dug under the roots of a spruce snag. The place stank of meat the bitch wolf had toted home in her stomach and vomited for the pups. Swarms of blowflies. Bones. Scraps of rabbit skin. Grouse and ptarmigan feathers. Getting down on our knees, we saw the litter of pups crawling over one another at the end of the tunnel. Six of them, fat and woolly: a black pup, a white one, two grays and two browns.

Well, there was a $50 federal bounty on wolves, including pups.

"Oh, boy," Tanana said, "the jackpot."

He cut a ten-foot willow pole, produced a length of fishline, and bent a slip-noose on the end of the pole. With this instrument he snared the black pup and dragged it, struggling, into the open. I grabbed the youngster. I was now supposed to kill it and stand by for the next victim. But nope. Tanana and I could qualify as pro wolfers. We had snared, trapped and shot our share of the animals, sold the pelts, and collected the bounty checks. But they were adult wolves. Knocking helpless pups on the head wasn't, I told myself, our style. Not mine, anyhow. I handed the pup to Tanana. He held it up for a look. It was a male. As it bit and clawed, trying to wriggle free, it wet copiously on Tanana's shirt front.

"Okay, I had that coming," Tanana said. "And I now vote that we let these junior wolves live. Shucks, we're too chicken to kill them anyway."

Well, with the help of Indian friends we constructed our lodge. The wolves grew up. We laid off them for three-and-a-half years because, in the first place, they were a business asset. When a visiting sportsman heard wolf song in the night he went home knowing he had hunted unspoiled country. In the second place, we thought these Susitna-Talkeetna wolves deserved some protection. They were magnificent animals, super wolves, the largest on the planet, *Canis lupus pambisileus.* Since they weighed up to 175 pounds, they made timber wolves and prairie wolves seem mere overgrown coyotes. They were dramatic. They contributed color and a sense of the wilderness. We thought they deserved a haven where everybody wouldn't be trying to knock them off for the money it would bring.

But it turned out to be a bad experiment. Coexisting with wolves had too many drawbacks. They kept the game nervous and on the move. They pulled down an almighty lot of meat— more than they needed. They killed off most of the grizzly cubs. We had spoiled them, and as a result they were bold and arrogant. They thought they owned the countryside. Then, one windy, aurora-lit December night when Tanana and I were alone at the lodge, they made the mistake that doomed them.

We had eaten supper and washed the dishes. I was fleshing a lynx skin. Tanana, costumed in red underwear and beat-up cabin moccasins, was mixing the next day's sourdough—a peaceful backwoods fireside scene. All of a sudden, we were electrified by wolf yammer at the outlet creek, just across the flat. As we listened to the hysterical kill chorus, our string of pack cayuses stampeded into the snowy clearing, en route to the log barn we had built for them. I took the .375 magnum down from its moose-antler rack, chambered a shell, and stepped outside. The horses were huddled at the barn door. I walked toward them in flickering wild-rose aurora light, making a head count. Two horses were missing: the pinto bell mare and her eight-month-old buckskin stud colt. The latter, name of Happy, was Tanana's cherished pet and mascot.

I headed for the outlet at a run. There was only six inches of wind-crusted snow, so I didn't need webs. As I passed the front door I alerted Tanana. "Get the lead out," I hollered. "I think the wolves are killing Happy and the mare."

The wolves were ominously quiet now. I plowed hellbent down off the homestead bench through second-growth spruce jungles onto the creek flat. One-hundred-and-fifty feet upwind in blowing snow I beheld a savage spectacle. The bell mare had backed up against a cutbank. She was rearing, with a monster black wolf hanging onto her right ear. Seven other wolves were ranged in a semicircle between me and her. I knew most of them. Only two were strangers. Happy lay stretched out on the snow, motionless. The mare came down striking, but her knees buckled and she pitched forward with a scream across the colt. The wolves swarmed onto her.

Her life expectancy right then was maybe three seconds, but I didn't try for a wolf. I probably would have hit the mare as well. I fired into the snow. The wolves whirled, staring.

"Here's luck, neighbors," I said.

I cut down on a pale-gray local bitch whose head, chest and forelegs were splashed with blood—Happy's, I gathered. I had good light. A tilted column of orange aurora radiance hung directly overhead. Its light made the flat almost as bright as day. I hit the wolf in the chest. The 300-grain softnose lifted her off her feet and spun her end for end. Scratch one shaggy raider. (That's what I like about the big magnum. It has the efficiency of a pile driver.) The other wolves streaked toward the willow-margined outlet creek. I worked the magnum's action with cold-numbed fingers. I fired, and missed. I blasted again as the wolves were entering the brush, and scored on the black wolf. He somersaulted and rolled, wailing, and dragged himself into the windy thicket. I sprinted past him to the creek bank.

Four wolves were loping straight away from me on the frost-flowered dark ice. They were dopes. They'd had no experience being outlaws. They should have stayed in the willows. But I was delighted they hadn't. I let go a shot at the nearest wolf, a brown specimen. It was a lucky shot. The slug went low, but glanced off the ice and hit him somewhere. He fell popping his jaws, then whacked his head on the ice and lay still. His three packmates bounded up the opposite bank. That was the last I saw of them.

I scouted back into the brush. The aurora pattern had changed. A vast comber of green fire was now rushing across the sky. By its light I spotted the black wolf, twenty feet distant, propped up on his front legs, snarling. Old ear-mangler himself; the character I had held in my arms when he was a pup. Well, the magnum was empty, but its barrel would serve as a weapon of sorts. I went up to the wolf. I thrust overhand for his face, and saw teeth fly. He lunged at me, raging. He moved pretty good. (He wasn't grievously wounded, I discovered later. The bullet had creased his backbone.) I belted him over the head with everything I had and felt his skull cave in. Momentum piled him against me. I hit him again, and jumped clear. He perished with his teeth clenched in a willow sapling instead of my leg. But I guess he never knew the difference.

"Happy's dead," Tanana said behind me, his voice grim, "and the mare needs considerable doctoring. Well, we asked for it. But from now on, partner, things are gonna be different. The only good wolf is a dead wolf. That's my motto."

Tanana was a lonesome guy, like most sourdoughs. He had adopted the buckskin colt as his special pal. He carried sugar around for the little cuss, combed and brushed him every day, tried to teach him tricks. Worried about him. For instance, take something he did one cold November night before we got the barn finished. I was awakened by a terrific racket at the door. A horse was pawing the planks, whickering and bellering. I got up to find out what it was all about. Partway across the room, I fell over an animal, which naturally startled the heck out of me. By then Tanana was on his feet, explaining. The animal, it seemed, was our Happy. Tanana had brought him inside because it was cold out there. But the bell mare didn't approve.

"Why didn't you bring her in too?" I asked, laying on the sarcasm.

"Don't be funny," he said. "The thing is, I like that colt. He's my friend. I mean, I aim to take care of him. Any trouble he has is likewise my trouble."

I shared his sentiments regarding the wolves. The sooner we cleaned out the rest of them the better. We made our opening move against them next morning.

It was the old big-bait dodge. Saddling a couple of horses, we dragged Happy's frozen carcass into the middle of a half-acre alder patch several hundred yards east of the lodge. We

hung fifty wolf snares in the brush. For come-on scent we used beaver castors crushed with the genitals of the gray bitch I had shot. The colt's carcass was, by design, visible from the east bunk-room window. We got our break a week later, on a forty-below morning. Three wolves paid us a sunrise visit. Any other wolves with good sense would have stayed clear of the lodge, but these bravos still had the delusion that they enjoyed privileges. I had just put the soapstone hot cake griddle on the stove, and was greasing it with a piece of bacon rind. Tanana was in the bunk-room shaving. I heard him cross to the window.

"Wolves at the bait," he bawled.

I hastily joined him. He had the window open. The sun was coming up through a notch in the hills. Its dazzle of light reaching across the snow revealed the three wolves: a white, a brown, and a silver-gray. They were snooping along the rim of the alder patch, visibly suspicious. I understood why. It was because we had moved the colt's carcass. They wanted to know how come. They figured they had exclusive rights to it. Tanana knelt at the window, and rested his .30-06 Remington on the ledge. He fired. The brown wolf seemed to chase its tail, then went down and stayed there. The other two wolves fled into the eye of the sun. Tanana fired steadily. I had picked up my glasses to call the shots, but there was too much glare. I thought he hit the gray wolf, but the animal kept going.

"That's four for Happy," Tanana said.

We pulled on our parkas, stepped into the hitches of the Denna webs, and headed down onto the flat. The brown wolf was stone cold dead, shot through both lungs. He was a lean, battle-scarred pirate. I estimated he would go 110 pounds. We cast beyond him and cut interesting sign—blood and a tuft of bullet-torn gray mane hair. So we took the trail. Ten minutes later, in a point of spruce timber, we found the gray wolf lying dead on trampled, bloodstained snow. His demise hadn't been due entirely to Tanana's bullet. The slug had only ripped a gash in his left shoulder. He had been killed by his white littermate. I suppose the smell of blood had been just too much for the white wolf. Probably, if he'd had time, I thought, he'd have treated himself to a cannibal breakfast.

"That's five," Tanana said.

Well, we didn't sight any wolves for a spell. Perhaps they were hunting down along the big river. Our next contact with them came on a gale-swept afternoon in March. It was a dandy. It revived all the old campfire tales of alleged man-killing wolves.

The hard wind had bellowed since morning off the glaciered slopes of Mt. McKinley. Toward dusk we snowshoed out to bring the horses in. They were on a hillside just west of the clearing, pawing for bunchgrass. In the clearing itself, feeding from our slash piles, were a half-dozen resident moose. The moose were almost as tame as the horses. They had a good thing here, and knew it—protection and ready-cut browse. Tanana was ahead of me. He halted in the lee of a brushpile to tighten the lamp-wick hitches of his webs. Forty yards downwind from us stood a huge roan cow moose whom we had named Kate (don't ask me why). She snorted. Her mane lifted. She laid her blanket ears back.

I threw a chunk of snow crust at her. I told her she was an ungrateful old bat. She snorted again, and pawed the snow. At which point, holy suffering, I realized that she wasn't looking at us. Her hostile gaze was directed past us and to our left. I swiveled, shedding my mittens.

Three wolves had appeared from behind a brushpile two-hundred feet upwind. They were walking toward us, spread out abreast. Two of them were local wolves—the white raider and a dun bitch that we believed was the dowager pack mother hereabouts. The third wolf was a blue-gray stranger. We had our rifles slung across our backs. As we reached for them the wolves broke into a run. They were headed at us, but we were between them and the cow moose, so maybe the cow was their target. They were upwind and so hadn't identified us by scent. Moreover, the visibility was poor at the moment, with a lot of snow dust blowing. (I'm doing my doggonedest to present a fair case.)

Tanana and I fired at the same instant. The dun bitch wheeled over and came down skidding in the snow. Unfortunately, we had both held on her; she had been in the lead. The white wolf and the blue-gray stranger veered off, and went out of sight among the brushpiles.

"That's six," Tanana said. "Those heroes aimed to pull us down, but lost their nerve. Gunfire panicked them. Except for that, boy, we would have had a battle on our hands."

Maybe, but so far as I knew, there was no record of Alaska wolves having attacked a human in modern times. A zoologist friend of ours had remarked that this was a mystery. European and Near Eastern wolves, he said, still occasionally ganged up on a wayfarer and killed and ate him. Whereas our giant wolves, the most formidable on earth, were plumb peaceful. The answer to that, in my opinion, was that there were no unarmed peasant types on this frontier. We roughneck woodsmen carried guns and knives, and had learned to use them in a most demanding school. The wolves had found out that it was practically suicidal to let themselves be sighted at less than a half-mile. Everybody was bounty hungry. But maybe our local wolves, because we had spoiled them, thought they could beat the odds and were out to eliminate us. I hate to say so, but it sure had looked that way.

Weeks went by and none of them showed up. Then, in May, just after the breakup, a brown wolf got into one of the snares we had set at Happy's carcass. We heard him at daybreak fighting the steel noose. Before we arrived on the scene, he jumped over a windfall and broke his neck.

"That's seven," Tanana said.

Well, I have told you how young Wes Thompson, in September, shot the white wolf at the forefront of a caribou stampede. I sat down and rested the wolf's battered head on my knee. He had been something. One of evolution's more spectacular jobs. Smart, powerful and swift, with endless stamina. But of a race headed for oblivion. His trouble was that he was too specialized, and was in competition with men. He hadn't had a chance to win. And it was too bad. His long blue howl in the night had been the voice of wilderness. We were going to miss it. Tanana stood up. He had been sweetening the edge of his skinning knife.

"That makes eight," he said, "and now Happy's ghost can rest in peace."

Fifteen Years
in a Grizzly Pasture

*Our sojurn at Toonakloot Creek with
a passel of brawling bruins provided one
wilderness adventure after another.*

"That grizzly has a hunch we're somewhere close-by," Baldy
Thomas said to eager young Matt Lawson, our current hunter.
"But it don't seem to worry him none. He must have some-
thing mighty important on his mind."

We were crouched behind a screen of pussy willow brush
at the edge of a redtop meadow above the forks of Toonakloot
Creek. The grizzly, eighty yards distant across the meadow,
had paused to stare in our direction and growl. Then he had
swaggered on toward the creek bank. He was a good-size coffee-
colored bear. Around seven hundred pounds. A fine poten-
tial trophy. But we needed to see both sides of him with our
glasses, to make sure he hadn't ruined his winter pelt rubbing
it against trees and boulders. He was pigeon-toeing along an
ancient trail that generations of Toonakloot bears had worn a
foot deep into gravelly hardpan soil. When he reached the
bank, he halted at a wonderfully scarred spruce "message"
tree. He cast another look toward us, then reared up, sank
his teeth into the tree as high as he could reach, and bit out a
mouthful of wood and bark.

"Take him," I said. I had seen both of his hips and shoulders. The pelt was unblemished.

41

Matt lined the sights of his .30-06 Winchester, and fired. The grizzly fell backward, bawling, then surged up facing us and started the all-out slam-bang charge of his species. He was valiant. But the 220-grain softnose had exploded one of his lungs, and before he had covered fifty feet, Matt fired again and blew the top of the bruin's skull off. We went over, with respect, and examined the trophy. Then Baldy explained about "message" trees. There were seven of them spaced along the forty-mile length of the creek. The bears periodically rubbed themselves against the trees, probably leaving scent information as to their sex, health, rutting status, and what they had been eating. The males, it appeared, competed seriously all their lives to see which of them could make the highest bite mark. Matt's bear had come within three inches of the record for this tree. Which is something considering that he was only five years old. Sure, I had known him. That is, I had seen him around since he was a cub.

"For the love of Mike, how long have you lived in this grizzly pasture?" Matt asked me.

"Fifteen years come the dog salmon run," I told him. "If I decide I like the place, I may stay."

Up to now it had suited me just fine. To the east were the ragged Talkeetna Mountains and five hundred square miles of first-rate grizzly range. It was total wilderness there. Not a human habitation or a road or man-made trail. The area would never be hunted out, I believed, because there was no lake or hospitable sandbar on which a plane could be landed, and a twenty-mile belt of lowland tundra swamp made it inaccessible to horses. The Alaska Railroad ran along the western margin of the region, but the swamp paralleled it. Thus, anybody who wanted to hunt this reach of gameland had to backpack in, or line a boat up one of the streams. My patented 160-acre homestead was on a beach at the confluence of Toonakloot Creek and the Susitna River, athwart the main game trail to the mountains.

I'd had various sourdough hunting-and-trapping partners here, but Baldy Thomas was in a colorful class by himself. The guy had recently, for example, won himself frontier folklore stature as the only man anybody knew who had taken a club to a full-grown Alaska grizzly and made the animal back down.

Baldy had accomplished that remarkable feat in August while we were lining a heavily loaded eighteen-foot stampede boat

42

up Kashwitna River, just south of Toonakloot. We had booked two Boston sportsmen for a fifteen-day bear and goat hunt at the headwaters, and aimed to establish a base camp there in advance of their arrival. But our medicine had the feebles. One of the notorious sand-laden Kashwitna gales had come bellowing down the valley. The wind-whacked boat refused to obey her bridle, no matter how we rigged it.

Towline over our shoulders, we were toiling along a brushy cutbank under those tall cottonwoods that mark the mouth of Slide Creek. Sheets of yellow sand were hitting the cottonwood tops and pouring down onto us. Baldy had taken the lead. The boat was out in the middle of a steep riffle.

We pushed through a clump of alder brush, and there stood the grizzly. Sixty feet distant.

He was a sizable taffy-colored beast, long-legged and high-humped. We had interrupted his lunch. Between his jaws he held the desiccated remains of a dark valley coyote that had perished in some careless bounty-trapper's hardtwist wire snare. The other end of the snare was looped around a birch toggle-pole behind the grizzly. Well, you could see that the bear didn't want trouble, but that it didn't want to abandon the tied-down coyote carcass either.

Our rifles were in the boat.

You can't battle brush and soft-bottomed sloughs, straining against the drag of a towline, and tote a rifle too. Baldy hollered at the bear. He waved his hat and whistled. The bear didn't budge. Instead it dropped the coyote carcass, planted a front paw on it, and let out a defiant roar. Then, proving that trouble comes in bunches, I guess, a further complication developed. We had been so concerned with what the bear might do that we had momentarily forgotten the boat. I now felt a change in the vibrations coming through the towline, and turned for a look. The boat, holy cow, was careening inshore. Wind and current had caught her just right. Before we could make a move to prevent it, she crashed into a sawyer snag on the bank and heeled over, water spilling across her upstream strake.

"Now look what you've done," Baldy yelled at the bear. "Beat it, damn you. Haul your fanny outta here."

The bear still didn't depart. So Baldy snatched up a driftwood club and ran at the animal, shouting lurid threats. I wouldn't have given two cents, right then, for his future. I had a split-second vision of myself gathering up his mangled remains and boating them back downriver. The bear had reared up in the blowing sand, massive paws weaving, like a vast, shaggy karate fighter. There was nothing I could do. If I let go of the towline and tried sprinting to the boat for my rifle, the boat would surely float away on the current before I got there. So I stood watching, horrified, certain that the worst was about to happen. But Baldy was, after all, a sourdough woodsman. He had the bear figured right. Its nerve broke. It whirled and took off. Baldy threw his club after it. Boosted by the wind, the club hit a rock, bounced, and whapped the bear across the rump.

Baldy walked back past me to the half-swamped boat, and abruptly sat down. "You know something?" he muttered. "A man could get kilt pulling a damn fool stunt like that."

I don't want to give the impression that grizzlies were abundant in the Toonakloot area, because they weren't. I doubt that grizzlies ever were abundant anywhere. But it's a fact that the animals did outnumber folks at least five to one hereabouts, and that the lower creek was their favorite rendezvous spot. Food was the attraction. Starting in June, four heavy runs of salmon came up the creek to spawn. There was a considerable acreage of blueberries, black currants, and highbush cranberries. Indian potatoes grew everywhere on the sandy stream bars. As a result of this bounty, bears always were here. There were four or five resident grizzlies, and perhaps a dozen that made pilgrimages to the creek. But even so, hunting them was a gamble. I have seen as many as six grizzlies fishing salmon within a mile of the cabin, and also have hunted hard for a week without sighting hide or hair of a grizzly.

Like all grizzlies, these bears were dramatic bravos, and full of surprises. Early one May morning, for instance, three of them fought a bloody battle royal practically in the cabin dooryard.

Baldy and I were sitting at the kitchen table in our red underwear drinking coffee when the sounds of strife arose. We hastened to the rear window. One-hundred-and-fifty yards distant in the snow-patched clearing, two medium-size brown grizzlies that I recognized as locals were challenging a huge blond stranger grizzly. We put our glasses on the trio. The two resident bears were closing in, shoulder-to-shoulder, uttering loud, menacing noises. I knew what the trouble was all about.

Twenty feet beyond the bears, the carcass of a winterkilled bull moose lay partly exposed in a snowdrift. We hadn't been able to bury the carcass—the ground was still frozen. Lately it had begun to stink. Blowflies had found it. But I guess the bears thought it was sure-enough gourmet banquet material, and worth fighting for.

The blond stranger interested me professionally.

He was the largest grizzly I had seen on the creek in several years. One of the rare eight-hundred-pounders. His thick silky-looking coat was honey colored, shading to dark mahogany on his shoulders and legs—probably the most popular trophy color combination. Of a sudden he took the offensive. The would-be hard-boiled locals had made the tactical mistake of staying close together. He gave a rasping war bellow and with one bound was upon them. The slugging, biting, claw-raking conflict that ensued lasted maybe thirty seconds. Then the outclassed local bears concluded that they'd had aplenty. Struggling clear, they lit out for other parts. Both were limping. They left bloodstains on the snow-stringers they crossed. The blond giant shook himself. He clawed chunks of turf onto the moose carcass. Then, after a suspicious glance at the cabin, he shambled into the timber.

"Some fighting trophy bear," Baldy said. "Man, I hope he's around when our new cheechako hunter gets here."

The hunter, a husky 65-year-old gent named Dave Merrill, arrived from Los Angeles two weeks later. This was during the likeliest part of the spring season. The king salmon run had commenced. The grizzlies were rutting. After the long winter the countryside had again come vividly alive. We got Dave out of the sack at daybreak the first morning, and took him upstream to a king salmon spawning riffle below a beaver dam on the North Fork. A pearly drift of ground fog hung over the stream. Climbing an aspen hillside, we sat down to wait. Two hundred feet below us we could hear salmon splashing on the riffle. After a while the sun burned through the fog. Baldy nudged me. Two grizzlies were standing in fast, shallow water at the head of the riffle. One was the battling blond nonpareil. The other was a chunky brown specimen, obviously a female.

I mean, she was making a big play for her formidable fishing companion. As we watched, she poked him with her nose. She nipped his ear. She sashayed around in front of him and coquettishly swapped ends. Our Dave sat motionless with his .300 Weatherby Magnum across his knees. We had cautioned him to hold fire until we gave him the word. He was cooperating, however impatiently.

The blond grizzly ignored the importunate female. He kept his attention fixed downstream, watching for salmon. All business. I had 8X glasses on him. I was trying my doggonedest to will him to turn around and give me a look at his off side. But he didn't, and then a third grizzly, a gaunt tobacco-colored animal, shouldered out of some willows at the foot of the riffle. The brown female winded him. She swiveled around, head up, nose working. Then she waded out of the riffle and went galloping down the bars. The tobacco-colored bear came to meet her. He didn't fool around. He wrestled her to the gravel, bit a divot out of her neck, and then hazed her headlong into a thicket. I thought, *the blond warrior won't hold still for that. He'll pulverize the dumb, too-aggressive Romeo.* But nothing occurred. Registering unconcern, the outsize slugger continued to watch for salmon.

Presently he was rewarded, in that respect anyway.

A king came rocketing up the riffle. A yard-long, ocean-bright, fifty-pound superlunker. Half its back out of water. The blond bear intercepted it easily, set his teeth in its hump, and paced ashore, the great fish belting him over the head with its spotted fluke of a tail. He dropped the salmon on the gravel and held it down with both front paws while he bit chunks out of it. Eating it alive. I could now see his off side. The pelt was good. I gave Dave the go-ahead sign. He brought up the Weatherby, and blasted. The bear, heart shot, made one bound toward the brush, and died. We zigzagged down to the kill. Examination revealed that the bear had been an authentic old, old-timer. His teeth were worn to yellow snags. His claws were splintered and scurfy. His big head was covered with combat scars. Bemused, I told Dave about the animal's prowess in the clearing last month, and remarked that it was mysterious why such a terrific fighter had let another bear walk off with his girlfriend.

"Not so mysterious," Dave said with a rueful grin, as he lowered his 65-year-old frame down on a boulder. "Hell, in the bear's place, I guess I would have played the situation about the same way he did."

Folks often ask me what the grizzly's chances for survival are. My answer is, he'll be around for a long while yet. But it'll be mainly in places like the Toonakloot region at this period. Because the grizzly isn't temperamentally suited to share his range with people. He's too tough. He makes too many enemies. There was actually at one time, I recall, strong agitation to outlaw grizzlies in Alaska; put a bounty on them. I knew sourdoughs, wilderness-traveling men, who had admitted that they shot every grizzly they could lay their sights on. The species really has taken a horrible beating from a variety of sources. When I was a kid, so help me, agents of a Chinese apothecary hunted grizzlies in the Chugach Range for their gall bladders. But all that is ancient history. It could never happen again. People nowadays realize that the grizzly is an asset. Especially dude-wranglers do.

One August a unique white female grizzly showed up on the creek. Baldy referred to her for a couple of weeks as "That beautiful $1,000 bear." Later he invented other names for her, none of them complimentary.

She first attracted attention to herself by making a nocturnal raid on our hillside strawberry patch and vegetable garden. Her technique, we discovered next morning, was novel. She was a sampler. After harvesting a twenty-foot row of ripe strawberries, she had bitten a large mouthful out of each of five fine cabbages. I took her trail. I wanted to learn everything I could about her. Because if she stayed around, I aimed to arrange her death. The vegetable garden was a pet project of mine. Two of those cabbages, I'll bet, would have won prizes at any county fair. Well, I found a tuft of her hair caught on wild-rose thorns. Then I found a urine signature, and a line of clear paw prints. I kept on until I came to a place where she had walked under a horizontal alder branch, scraping her back on it. That gave me her height.

I now had all the sign data I needed. The picture was complete. I would know her trail if I found it on Park Avenue, New York, ten years from this date. That night I took my rifle and sleeping bag out to the top of the garden plot, and waited for the bear to return.

She came in through the creek-flat birch timber shortly after midnight. Her arrival was heralded. I heard a snowshoe rabbit take off ahead of her. Then a couple of jacksnipe spiraled up, protesting. But she was cautious and crafty. Five minutes passed. Then she materialized one hundred feet below me at the foot of the garden, and stood there looking and listening, trying the wind. The midnight sun had gone below an Alaskan Range crest, but was still putting out reflected light. The bear's ivory coat in the red shadows appeared luminous. She would weigh around five hundred pounds. Her head was wide, with a short muzzle. If a grizzly can be beautiful, she was. I believe that she sensed she was being watched. At any rate, she spun around and faded into the gloom under the birches. I didn't move. I figured she would come back, and after several minutes she did—from the opposite direction.

It was spooky. It taught me a lesson.

I heard a snort behind me, and turned my head to see the bear standing sixty feet distant, crosswind, in a pool of tree shadow. She had circled and was hunting me. Maybe she was just curious, but I felt the hair on the back of my neck lift. She hadn't spotted me yet. I had spread my sleeping bag amongst knee-high Hudson Bay tea bushes. I slowly raised the .375 magnum and laid its sights between the white sow-bear's front paws. Then I said, "See you when your pelt is prime, smart stuff," and fired. She bucked and wailed as upflung gravel stung her belly. Still wailing, she took out in wild flight across the homestead bench. I rolled my sleeping bag and returned to the cabin. Baldy had gotten up. I told him what had taken place, and described the grizzly.

"Wonderful. Why, that bear is like money in the bank," he declared. "The country is full of sportsmen that would squabble for a chance to spend $1,000 collecting her pelt and skull."

That was a cheering thought. But it turned out fate was against us. September came, and the first hard frosts. The grizzlies' pelts were now prime again. We had two hunters scheduled to arrive the following week. Then one morning our friend Nikolai Stepan, headman of a tiny Denna Indian village over on lower Montana Creek, paid us a visit. We shouldn't, Nick told us, waste time hunting the white female grizzly. "She's dead," he explained. "The way it happened, yesterday morning I kill a bull moose on the creek bank two miles above the village. I gut and quarter it, stack the meat on the hide, and pack a ham home. After resting a half-hour, I go back for another load. I'm a couple of hundred feet from the meat pile, when I sight the white grizzly. She's at the rim of some blowdown, fifty yards downwind, watching me.

"I bring up my rifle in a hurry, but she jumps into cover before I can shoot. I know then I am in trouble. I go on to the meat. Of course she has been there.

"She has taken bites out of every chunk of meat, and then has clawed moss and dirt over the pile. I clean the quarters as well as I can. Then I try to figure some way to make a bear-proof cache. But that's hopeless. I ain't got the materials. So the only way I can protect the meat is to relay it home, staying in sight of both piles all the time. Unless I'm lucky enough to kill the bear. That settled, I start to lash the other ham onto my packboard. I'm bending over, the packboard in my hands, when I hear a growl close behind me. Well, I never move faster in my life. I don't know what the bear has in mind. It don't make no difference. I throw the packboard at her without looking, and dive for my rifle. She roars and I hear her fighting the packboard, and then I have the rifle in my hands, and I turn and shoot her between the eyes." Nick got out his pipe and tobacco pouch. "I thought I'd better tell you," he added.

"Thanks. We mighta known that she-grizzly was a no-good tramp," Baldy said bitterly. "Sneaking around like she did. The bum moved in on us and ate our cabbages when she wasn't worth two bits. Then just as soon as her $1,000 pelt got prime, what happens? She goes gallivanting off somewhere else to get kilt. Bah."

I remember one autumn morning when Baldy and I hiked up the forks to shoot some grouse and catch a mess of Arctic grayling. This was the marvelous time of year. The creek full of fish, the berries ripe, and all the animals fat and lively. When we came to the aforementioned spruce message tree, I shed my packboard and began ceremoniously rubbing myself, hips and shoulders, against the tree's wonderfully scarred trunk. Baldy, astonished, asked me what the hell the idea was. I told him I was making an autumn report to the bears. I was informing them that I was still on the creek, still salubrious and still eating well, praise be. The important point is, I wasn't kidding.

"Well, that's life in a grizzly pasture," Baldy said. "Move over, huh? Let's make it a joint report."

Berserk Brownies
I'll Never Forget

Sometimes, these great brutes will not retreat.
Instead, they will kill you . . . or die trying.

I grew up in an Alaska brown bear pasture, so it was no great surprise to me when this Cook Inlet specimen, an outsize straw-colored brute, suddenly got sore and opted to fight.

We had worked through a belt of spruce timber to the open bars of Cottonwood Creek, several miles west of Redoubt Bay. I spotted the bear as we ducked under the last screen of rain-wet boughs. He was 250 feet distant, on the opposite rim of a dark salmon pool, swaggering along the pool's narrow strip of gravel shoreline with an eight-foot cutbank behind him.

Ordinarily I would have insisted on seeing both sides of the animal to make sure he hadn't rubbed his handsome June pelt. But, this time I waived the precaution, because said pelt would square close to ten feet and, given that dimension, a hunter can afford to overlook a rubbed spot or two. My customer, young Bart Wagner of St. Paul, bought that. He had stepped ahead of me, and was bringing up his .300 Weatherby Magnum.

Presumably the bear saw the movement. Anyway, he swung his massive head around, stared at us, then whirled to climb the bank. Bart fired and missed. The 180-grain softnose chugged into the bank where the bear's left ear had been a split second ago.

With that, everything happened. Of course the bear was plenty startled. The .300 sounded like a cannon at close range. Gravel fragments had sprayed his face. We were trying to kill him. So he let out a roar, and here he came. It was the classic brown-bear attack, motivated by pure resentment. He wasn't wounded, and he could easily have beat it up the bank before Bart got another shell chambered. But instead, the big so-and-so's intention was to swarm onto us and demonstrate exactly who owned this piece of salmon creek. He had just reached swimming water when Bart raised the magnum again. I asked the kid to hold it. Downstream fifty yards, a logjam stuck out into the stream. If the bear's carcass was carried under it, we'd have a mean salvage job on our hands. The kid nodded that he understood. This attacking brown bear didn't have a prayer, but you had to applaud his courage and spirit. He was Big Ivan, the glamour bear, America's No. 1 trophy animal, dream target of sportsmen all over the world, with twenty seconds to live because he couldn't forget that his tribe had once been dominant hereabouts. He came across swimming low, only his head above water. Then he got his paws on bottom and charged, splashing through the shallows at us, bawling, mouth wide open, an apparition to make anybody's neck hair lift.

I laid my .375 magnum on him, and waited. The kid held fire until the bear was on the gravel. Then he let go a shot that wrecked the animal's muzzle and smashed into his chest on the left side. The bear went down, skidding on one shoulder. He rolled over, and pushed himself to a sitting position. He was looking me squarely in the eye, twenty feet distant, when the kid fired again, a head shot. The bear fell over, finished.

"You just met a natural brown bear," I said.

That's a label I invented. Perhaps it isn't generally realized, but the brown bears bossed this coast for millennia. They were the biggest and the toughest. Nothing could stand against them. According to legends, the Stone-Age Indians tried, but apparently for every brown bear they killed, some several Indians were rubbed out. The brown bears didn't become hunted animals until recently, when white men arrived with high-powered rifles.

They still haven't learned to be really afraid. Sure, they get out of your way, but they don't panic. Most of their attacks on humans have been made when they were guarding meat, when they were wounded, and when females believed they were protecting their young. I'm speaking of normal, average brown bears. But every now and then one shows up who would rather fight than run—a natural brown bear.

There are two open seasons on brown bears: one in the spring, the other in autumn. The latter season is popular because it gives the sportsman opportunity for a combination hunt. When he has taken his brown bear, he can try for other species. But nevertheless, I have always recommended spring hunts. The bears' pelts are better then. So is the weather. There are no leaves on the ever-present and accursed alders to hinder spotting the animals. The mountainside redtop grass, waist-high in summer and autumn, has been flattened by winter snows. Further, the bears are livelier during the spring season, and a heap more interesting. Probably because their rutting period begins at this time. Actually, the spring season is for dyed-in-the-wool brown-bear fans.

Whenever I hear the cost of brown-bear hunting discussed, it reminds me of the extraordinary circumstances under which Hank Burgess, of Tucson, took his spring bear trophy.

I had just returned to Anchorage from a late-May hunt at Iniskin Bay with a Los Angeles real estate agent. For me, the hunting season was ended. It was now time to resume work as chief smokechaser for the Forest Service. I found Hank waiting for me. A red-headed, twenty-two-year-old zoology student, he had signed on to be my assistant. The next day we went down to Kenai Lake, to open up the Forest Service station there for spring inspection. As usual, a herd of moose had wintered out behind the buildings. Some of the animals were still hanging around, and a brown bear had been scouting them. We found his platter-size tracks in a melting snowdrift while backpacking through the timber to the station. Hank was fascinated. He asked for time off to make a hunt for the bear.

"You want to get me fired?" I said. "The Forest Service Supervisor himself is going to inspect this station next week. It'll be ready, or else."

Ten minutes later, we sighted the brown bear. I was whittling white-spruce shavings for a fire, when I glanced out the front window and saw the bear herding a gaunt bull moose toward us along the lakefront. The animals were a quarter-mile distant. We hastily put our glasses on them. The bear was long-legged, with a grizzly-type hump. I gave him nine hundred pounds. His shaggy coat was the color of a burlap sack. As for the bull, he had problems. He had been hurt. I could see raw, bleeding gashes in his left shoulder and foreleg. He kept stumbling. His tongue was hanging out. The way it looked to me, the bear had attacked and wounded him, and was waiting for him to collapse, or else was working up nerve to tackle him again. A bull moose is no patsy even for a brown bear. He's fast, and has a trip-hammer wallop in his front hoofs.

"This is my chance," Hank said. "Here's where I collect myself a brown-bear trophy." He hurried into the bunk-room to fetch his rifle.

The bull had been traveling at a trot. Now, as he approached the station, he broke into a gallop. Maybe he thought the bear would be afraid to follow him into the clearing. If so, it was a fatally bad guess. The bear sprinted to catch up. Watching him cover ground was most educational. I doubt that a good quarter horse could have stayed ahead of him for fifty yards. The bull turned up off the beach, passed the flagpole, and was in front of the toolshed when the bear raced alongside him. I have heard various theories as to how a brown bear pulls a moose down. This bear didn't conform to any of them. He used a variation of the bulldogging technique. Heaving himself upright with a roar, he hooked his left front leg over the bull's neck. Then he slugged the moose on the head with his right paw, and set teeth behind his ears.

The bull's knees buckled. He came down on the side of his head and somersaulted. The bear hung on. Sprawled across the bull, holding him down, he began biting chunks out of his throat. Jugular blood drenched the whole front third of him. Hank had appeared beside me at the open window, with his .30-06 Winchester in hand. I was about to make room for him when a thought struck me. The ground was still frozen, and, as I said, we had an inspection coming up next week. We would have to bury the moose carcass, and I didn't think we could do it with pick and shovel. We'd probably have to use rock drills and dynamite charges. But if Hank killed the brown bear in the clearing, and we had to bury it, too, it was a cinch we wouldn't get the place cleaned up in time for inspection.

"Look, don't hate me," I said. "But you can't shoot that bear on the premises. Haze him somewhere else."

Hank didn't savvy. He gave me a betrayed look, and stalked out the rear door. I picked up the .375 and followed, to back him up if he needed it. The bear was eighty yards distant. He whirled to face us, one paw on the dead bull's head. He uttered a warning growl. I had hoped he would retreat into the

timber. But nope. I could see he was going to fight. He was a hard-boiled brown bear with a fresh moose carcass to guard. We could kill him, but we couldn't make him abandon it. He bobbed his head, and took a step toward us. Hank shouted at him, then threw a rock. That was all it took. The bear charged. Well, it developed that Hank was a deadeye rifleman and a mighty cool hand. He put a 220-grain slug into the bear's right shoulder. But the animal kept coming on three legs. So Hank shot him in the other shoulder, and then through the head.

"What else could I do?" he asked, while his delighted expression said that despite me and the upcoming top brass inspection, he figured he had just made the quickest, most economical and exciting brown-bear hunt in the local history of the sport.

Conservationists are proposing that a hunter should be allowed to kill only one brown bear—just one in his entire life. Well, it sounds like a good idea. I don't know why any sportsman, everything considered, would want to take more than one brown-bear trophy. But I will add this: In my opinion, the brown bear's chance for survival doesn't depend as much on new legislation as it does on the goodwill of Alaska's wild-country residents. They are the people who meet the brown bear and share land and stream use with him. They know, to a degree, how much trouble he is in. If they want him to survive, he will.

I have worked and sojourned with several Cook Inlet old-timers who told me they had always shot every brown bear they could lay their sights on. I know others who admire the animals, and would kill one only if forced to. Somewhere in between these extremes my friend Beluga Jack takes his stand. Jack is a white-haired, pint-size sourdough coaster who used to make headquarters in a sod-roofed cabin at the mouth of Big River. He trapped beaver and mink, gill-netted salmon for a cannery outfit, and did some guiding. Big River, it happens, is prime brown bear country. The huge animals outnumber humans thereabouts by ten to one, and appear to know it. Listening to Jack talk, you might have thought he was running a brown bear ranch. A good trophy bear, he would declare, was an asset that could be cashed in for at least $1,500. Therefore, the animal rated the consideration given blue-ribbon livestock.

"Lookit what a deluded damn sow bear did to me," he said by way of greeting one autumn evening when I beached my dory in front of his cabin. He pointed at his footgear. He was wearing a rubber boot on one foot, and a moose-hide moccasin on the other.

"The way it happened," he went on, "I had hiked a mile upriver to those cottonwood-bordered pools with my black eighteen-month-old Injun dog, Tuktoo, to catch me some fat Dolly Varden trout for mild-curing in the smokehouse. I land a nice one, better than six pounds, and stake it out alive in an eddy. All at once Tuktoo bristles and growls. I can tell that he has winded a bear. So I make a fast pass at his collar. But he dodges, and I get a handful of air. At this point there's a commotion in the willow brush close downstream. I swivel around and see a mustard-colored yearling brown bear lope out of the thicket. He's got my big Dolly Varden in his mouth. I know it's mine because he's dragging the stake I tied it to. Seeing Tuktoo and me, the yearling puts on speed, but the stake catches on a bush and throws him.

"Well, I holler at Tuktoo to stay put, but he pretends he's stone deaf. All summer he's been looking for a bear he might have a chance to whip, and this is the first one he's seen. So he gives a war-beller and streaks at the yearling. It could have been an interesting set-to. The two are the same age, and although Tuktoo is outweighed some, he's faster. But the yearling takes another look at me, and decides to play it safe. Backing up against a boulder, he squalls for Mamma.

"Mamma answers from fifty yards back in the timber. A hoarse *wahg-h*. That's the cue for me to depart. Of course, I have my .30-06 Winchester ready for business, but you know how I feel about these bears. They are my stock-in-trade. They are valuable. I need them. So I look around for a hospitable tree. Two-hundred feet up the bank there's a bright-yellow frosted cottonwood with a convenient low limb. Standing my rod against a bush, I head for the tree. Usually I get over the ground pretty good when I'm in a hurry, but today I am handicapped. It's my boots. I sent to Kenai last week for a pair of No. 9s, but Squarehead George, the storekeeper I deal with, didn't have any No. 9s, and sent No. 10s. Even with two pairs of socks, the things are loose and clumsy. I am tripping over my own feet, which is discouraging because I can hear Mamma behind me. Too close behind me.

"She hasn't bothered with Tuktoo. It's me she's after. But I still think I can beat her to the tree. I hang the rifle over my left shoulder, so I'll have both hands free, and really stretch out. I stumble again, but I'm practically under the tree now. So I make an all-out running jump at the low limb, and latch onto it.

"Then Mamma arrives. Before I can muscle myself completely up onto the limb, she grabs hold of my left boot. She's got it by the heel. She braces her paws and yanks, trying to pull me to the ground. But I manage to hang on, both arms wrapped around the limb, and I kick at her with my other foot. I give her a couple of good ones on the snout that make her roar, but she don't ease off any. She pulls harder. There's no way I can use the rifle. I'd have to let go with one hand, and if I do that I won't have time to shoot. She'll drag me off the limb in half a second. I figure I'm a gone sourdough. Sooner or later my arms will give out. But then it turns out that old Squarehead George did me a favor after all. Because the doggoned boot comes off. I guess the bear thinks it's my leg. Anyway, she starts tearing it apart, and don't even look at me as I climb up into the tree.

"I suppose you're about to ask me if I shot the bear. The answer is, hell, no, I didn't. She's a fine, husky brood sow. Mahogany-colored, with black legs. About eight hundred pounds. She looks young. She ought to produce three or four more cubs. Think what that means. I'd be nuts to shoot such a valuable bear. So I just sit there till she and her yearling take off. Then I collect Tuktoo and resume fishing for Dolly Vardens. You know, it's remarkable how a man can get along with one boot."

Or, consider the climax of an autumn hunt I made at Chinitna Bay with Bill Jarvis, of Albuquerque. It was a half-hour after daybreak. We were crouched at the downwind edge of a wide beach-grass flat. Out in the middle of the flat, four brown bears were busily breakfasting on eulachon fish. Last night the season's highest tide, with a stiff southeast wind behind it, had stranded tons of the silvery, smelt-like fish. I looked the bears over with my 12X glasses. The nearest one was our likeliest bet. He sported a thick, taffy-colored coat set off by fancy reddish-brown points. I estimated the pelt would square around nine feet. The range was 120 yards. Bill took a look, and approved my choice. He then got down for a prone shot with his .300 magnum. It should have been a quick, clean kill. But something went wrong. The slug kicked up mud under the bear's belly. The four animals at once stampeded diagonally across the flat, downwind, toward the nearest alders.

Bill let go another shot, and missed. The bears had galloped into grass so tall that only their heads and humps were visible. Fifty yards more, and they would be safe in the alders. Bill tried again, shooting through grass. I heard the solid *whoomp* of the softnose striking home. The taffy-colored bear faltered, but kept going. I couldn't tell where he was hit. A six-foot cutbank marked the dividing line between the grass flat and the alders. Lunging up the bank, the bears paused to look back. They'll do it every time. I saw blood on the taffy-colored bear's ribs. He had been hit too far back and too low. As the bears started into the alders, Bill fired a third shot. I saw the slug clip hair off the taffy-colored bear's shoulder. It wasn't a center shot, though, it looked quartering. The bear staggered, bit at his shoulder, and fled into the alders.

We went over to the alders. It was a circular thicket, some eighty feet across. The crooked, interfretted bushes stood twice my height. Their foliage was so dense that you couldn't see into the thicket at all. I could smell the bear. Also I could hear his breathing—a bubbling, wheezing sound. He seemed to be at the center of the thicket, either unable to move, or waiting to find out what our plans were. It would, of course, be suicidal to go into the alders after him. Even if you were lucky enough to get a shot at him, it would be at such close range that he'd almost certainly lay hold of you before he died. So our best hope was that he had drive enough left to come out and fight. There is no formula for this situation, no backlog of tradition. What I did was my own idea. I began talking to the bear, to hold his attention.

"He's coming out," Bill said.

An alder top had weaved against the wind. In a moment other tops moved on a line toward us. I kept talking. The bear took his time. He spent nearly a minute covering forty feet. He was coughing now. Bill's last shot, I gathered, had nicked a lung. Then he was at the rim of the thicket. I had a glimpse of him, a shadowy shape behind wind-brushed leaves. The next instant he gave a roar and charged. We had allowed ourselves fifty feet of operating space. He was halfway across it when Bill fired and hit him in the chest. It was a heart shot, but the bear came on another dozen feet before he fell. He was valiant. At the moment he was the greatest. He was Big Ivan, the brown bear, at his best.

The Demon Bull
of Denna Lake

*This even-tempered giant was an
antlered engine of destruction.*

"**I** got a strong hunch that crazy snag-fighting bull is our best
bet," my sourdough partner Tanana Stewart whispered to the newest
cheechako hunter at Denna Lake Lodge, young Dave Peters. "But
there ain't no way to prove he is until he turns around."

We were hunkered behind a boulder on the floor of the
lake's outlet canyon. Three hundred yards above us, in an
autumn-painted willow thicket, six trophy bull moose were assembled. We had appraised five of the heads. None was under
sixty inches, and two were well over that. But it was the head
we hadn't gotten a good look at that intrigued us. It was carried
by a huge roan bull, a twelve-hundred-pounder. Facing away
from us, he was waging a busy sham battle against a tall, fire-
killed jack-spruce snag. He lunged, raking with his antlers.
He feinted and sidestepped. He backed off, grunting—*aghrr-
uh aghrr-uh*—to charge with abandon. The snag's top gyrated
wildly. With my 12X glasses I saw that it was deeply fire-
scarred. It wouldn't stand much more punishment.

"Uh-oh, there she goes," Tanana said.

The exhibitionist bull dug his hoofs in and really leaned
on the snag. There was the sound of splintering wood and the
upper part of the snag broke off in two sections. They seemed
to fall slowly. The bull was still shoving at the snag for all he

was worth when the two heavy chunks crashed down on him. One hit him across the neck; the other landed on his antlers. He slumped to his knees. Through the glasses I saw that his eyes were shut and his tongue was hanging out; I thought he had been killed. But he was tough. He bounded up and glared about belligerently. Clearly he believed he had been clobbered by a sneak assailant. The other bulls didn't seem to comprehend what had happened. They milled, then came stampeding hellbent down the canyon. The snag-fighter joined them. Then I got my first good look at his head.

"Take him," I said.

The kid's .300 Weatherby crashed. Dust jumped from the running bull's shoulder. He went down hard on his brisket and rolled half over, an antler blade gouging the gravel. The other five bulls plain hated the idea of passing us, but they were committed, so they poured on coal and slammed headlong through the brush and boulders, shaking their antlers and walling their eyes. They were magnificent. I saluted them as they passed within forty feet of us to go out of sight in a stand of cottonwoods. We went over to the carcass, and I got out my steel tape. The head measured seventy inches. It was massive and beautifully symmetrical. It had a brave array of points. I knelt for a look at the bull's left front leg. As expected, there was a white scar around it above the knee. Tanana solemnly inspected the scar. Then I took a seat on the bull's rump, fumbled out cigarettes, and passed them around. The kid was perceptive, for a pilgrim.

"I guess you knew this bull, huh?" he said.

My thoughts went back over events of the past five years, back to when Tanana and I first opened the lodge. There weren't any moose there then. The animals had been burned out. Eight years before our time, a forest fire had raged over ten square miles of watershed south of the lake. The moose that weren't barbecued in the big blaze moved elsewhere. Naturally the lack of moose was a severe business handicap, but we made out. There were plenty of sheep, caribou, grizzly, and black bears. When a customer insisted on shooting a moose, we took him to the Susitna Valley or down on the Kenai Peninsula. But then, one July morning, a kind of backwoods miracle occurred.

I had hiked over to Granite Creek, two miles east of the lodge, for some grayling fishing. Champ, our husky pet Labrador, was with me. At the moment we were bemused by the curious behavior of two black bears.

The bears, summer-fat and glossy-coated, were loping across a fireweed bar 150 yards upstream in a terrific hurry. Champ yearned to pursue them, and I told him to lay off or I would braid his ears. Without slackening pace, the bears disappeared into a point of spruce timber. I resumed fishing. A sixteen-inch, lavender-spotted, sail-finned, jumping wonder of an Arctic grayling arced out and came down headfirst on my Silver Doctor, and I missed the strike.

Before I could cast again, bedlam busted loose in the timber. Bears roared. Something floundered heavily. I heard an odd mournful bellow. Swiveling around, I made a fast grab at Champ's collar, but not fast enough. He whipped past me, stretched out like a coursing greyhound.

I had hung my .375 magnum on a drift log limb. I retrieved it, left the fly rod in its place, and sprinted after the dog. After battling through raspberry and wild-rose thickets, I arrived, panting, on a scene of violent action.

Fifty feet ahead of me in a caribou-moss opening, a tremendous roan bull moose was down, struggling desperately, with the larger of the two black bears sitting cowboy fashion astride his hump. The bear had his teeth set in one of the bull's soft, velvet-stage antlers, and was slugging the hapless moose on the head and neck with both front paws. As I stepped into the opening he saw me, turned, and let out a threatening bawl. Maybe he intended to get tough with me, too. But I didn't wait to find out. I shot him in the face. The thunderbolt wallop of the 300-grain softnose knocked him backward off the bull, finished. Champ had the other bear bayed against a windfall. It was smarter and didn't waste time demonstrating. It belted Champ sprawling and galloped over him, making for cover. I shot it through the shoulders and it fell, wailing its last. Champ hobbled in vengefully and latched hold of its throat.

The bull had surged to his feet, but he just stood there, groaning and breathing heavily. In a moment I saw what his trouble was. He had gotten into a wolf snare, one end of which was spiked to a spruce toggle pole.

The rusted wire noose was embedded deeply in the bull's leg, and the leg had swollen plenty, but I saw no indication of gangrene. I suppose the bull had thrown himself fighting the snare, and the bears had heard the racket and believed they were a cinch to harvest a lot of easy meat.

"I can't imagine what you were doing up here, bull," I said. "I guess you must have been lost. Anyway, I am now going to shoot that snare off you, and I hope you don't get any wrong ideas. Believe me, I am your friend."

I laid the .375 muzzle on the bent-washer lock, and fired. Metal fragments flew and the snare dropped to the ground. The bull glared boggle-eyed at me, and reared straight up. He came down gritting his teeth, blanket ears laid back. He didn't know yet that he was free. He wanted to attack, but didn't dare. He was afraid he'd end up in a heap again. I backed away from him. When I had fifty feet between us, I fired a shot past his head. He was in such a desperate state that for an instant I thought he was going to charge the gun. He whirled instead and took off for the timber. It must have surprised the heck out of him when he got there right side up. He swung his head around and gave me another dirty look, then went out of view. His gimpy leg was functioning.

Bands of immigrant moose began drifting up from the lowlands. By the first of September there were an estimated eighty of the animals on this short reach of lakefront. The attraction, of course, was available food. After nine years the aspen, willow, and birch browse was again plentiful enough on the burn to support a moose population. We got up one snowy November morning to see fourteen moose—bulls, cows, and young stuff—gathered in our new ten-acre clearing, feeding from the slash piles. Alaska moose have an affinity for backwoods human habitations. Give them a chance and they become almost as friendly as horses and cattle. These moose were declaring themselves a part of our winter domestic setup, which was wonderful.

It developed, however, that I had an enemy among them. I didn't recognize him at first, but he sure jogged my memory.

Champ and I were coming in late from marking beaver houses over on the south shore. It was a pretty night. A foot of snow lay on the ground and gaudy aurora combers blanked the stars. As we entered the clearing, a moose snorted. I ordered Champ to get behind and stay there, and pivoted on my webs to see a

couple of cows waggling their ears at me. Then I saw movement in the shadow of a brushpile this side of them. It was an
enormous bull. He came swaggering at me, his mane rucked
up. He was uttering hoarse, chesty grunts, telling me what a
dangerous so-and-so he was. His eyes reflected the aurora's
changing colors. The white vapor of his breath swirled around
his narrow but wickedly point-studded antlers. I mean, he was
something. And I now remembered him. He was the roan bull
I had rescued from the black bears on Granite Creek.

"Don't try it, stupid," I said. "Why be dead?"

He shook his antlers, and kept coming. Experience told
me to blast one through his ugly head—he was asking for it.
But instead I took a chance. I put the .375 on his right antler blade where the palmation began, and fired. To my vast
surprise, the heavy slug ripped the antler clean of the bull's
skull. Visibly stunned, with his head suddenly lopsided, the
outsize animal fell to one shoulder. When he did that, the
other antler dug into the snow with his weight on it, and it
also came off. Of course the antlers were loose; it was that
time of year. He probably would have shed them naturally
in a day or two. But the way it had happened, I guess he
thought he was being systematically taken apart. He scrambled
up with a hollow, defeated groan, and fled out across the aurora-
lit clearing.

I went on to the lodge. Tanana stood on the doorstep, rifle
in hand. I told him the knotheaded bull had a vendetta going
against me because he figured I was responsible for his experience with the wolf snare and the black bears. "Aw, it musta
been just a mistake," Tanana said. "You gotta remember these
moose are still strangers here. They are bound to be a mite hair-
triggered. But he didn't mean anything by it."

Nuts. If the moose felt like strangers, it was their fault.
We were being as hospitable as we knew how. Tanana was
going so far as to present a special radio music program for
the animals every evening. No fooling. Silly as it sounds,
we had discovered that they enjoyed music. When we turned
the radio on after supper, they would gather in front of the
bunk-room window, big ears at attention, eyes gleaming in
the lamplight. They seemed to prefer vocal pieces. So Tanana
would shop around the dial for them. One evening he ab-
sentmindedly made a bad selection. He tuned in a certain

mauve-voiced crooner who had always given us the creeps. The roan bull happened to be standing squarely in front of the window. When the swishy singer came on, he spread his legs and abundantly relieved himself on the snow. It had to have been coincidence, but Tanana claimed otherwise.

"That bull is a fine critic as well as a fan," he declared. "I allus told you these moose are extra smart."

But they weren't smart enough to deal with a combination of wolves and drastic weather. In January, a three-day blizzard bellowed out of the southern peaks. You couldn't see fifty feet. Inside two hours the south side of the lodge was drifted under to the eaves. The moose deserted us when the first wild gusts hit. They went down over the homestead bluff into a narrow cove fronting the lake, and yarded there. All moose appear to hate wind, maybe because the noise worries and confuses them. At any rate, although the cove gave our moose guests shelter, it nevertheless was a trap. The great wind scooped up several hundred tons of snow off the homestead bench and dumped it, as from a score of conveyor belts, into the bowl-shaped sink. By dawn of the third day, when the wind had begun to slack off some, the moose were buried to their withers.

Then the wolves found them. The shaggy killers came in off the lake ice, upwind. If they had kept quiet they might have accomplished a massacre, but wolves are loudmouths. They are fascinated by the sound of their own voices. Tanana and I had built a fire and put the coffeepot on, and were breaking trail to the woodpile and the cache, when we heard wolf yammer out front. It was a sizable pack; at least ten or fifteen of the slant-eyed pirates. They passed the lodge in blowing snow and turned into the willow cove, still sounding off. We had already snowshoed over to the rim of the cove and sighted the gang of snowbound moose. So there was no doubt as to the wolves' target. We got our rifles and hurried to the lee of a sandstone buttress overlooking the cove's entrance.

The moose, alerted by the shrill tallyho chorus, were starting back to the clearing. They were practically swimming in the feathery drifts, not making much headway.

We waited in ambush until the wolves were fifty yards inside the cove. A handsome blue-gray king wolf, a 120-pounder, led the pack. He apparently was a newcomer on this watershed. Neither of us had ever seen him before. He came plunging through the tops of a submerged willow thicket, his face plastered with snow, yowling ecstatically. He was closing in on a brown heifer. A couple more bounds and he would be chopping at her hamstrings. I whistled. He halted two hundred feet below us, and stepped behind a snow hummock. Only his tail was visible. I lined the .375 on the hummock, and pulled. Maybe the slug hit a branch, or maybe the snow mushroomed it—it would be interesting to know which. The wolf sprang into view, lunged fifteen feet down the hillside, and died. Later we found that, except for a few scraps of hide and bone, his whole head had been shot off.

Tanana dropped a brown wolf. Then another series of blizzard gusts whirled more tons of snow off the bench and unloaded it into the cove. When we could see again, the rest of the wolves were gone. Presumably they had made a getaway east along the wind-cleaned shore ice. The moose were coming up over the rim into the clearing. I made out the roan bull on the far side of the band. He saw me presently, and snorted. I was remembering how dumb he had looked the night he lost his antlers. It made me laugh. I hollered crosswind asking him why he didn't fatten up and grow trophy-size antlers for a change.

Well, the moose prospered. There was a good calf crop. During the summer other groups of immigrants joined them. When September frosts turned the birches and cottonwoods yellow again, we estimated there were 150 moose in the watershed. We booked two moose-hunting parties. The hunters took first-rate trophies less than a mile from the lodge. A week later we set out to kill a fat bull for our winter's meat. Finding moose for the pilgrims had been easy. Finding one for ourselves proved a tough problem. Everything went wrong. The moose were rutting, and had no routines. There was an inch of noisy crusted snow on top of crisp leaves. We hunted two long days without sighting a single bull.

So we switched tactics. "We'll show 'em a thing or two," Tanana said.

Next morning, an hour after daybreak, we found where a bull had spent the night stretched out on the crest of blueberry brush knoll. We took his trail. Perhaps it isn't generally known in civilized parts, but a man can walk a moose down. In fact, when I was a kid hunting with the Indians, that was a standard way of killing moose. We made no attempt to be quiet.

The crust was so noisy the bull would have heard us anyway. Besides, it didn't matter. With some jerky and smoked
salmon on our packboards, we aimed to walk the bull plumb
into the ground if we had to follow him to the Yukon. But
it turned out easier than we expected. The bull made a mistake. He tried to mix romance with the unforgiving business of survival.

We had been on his trail fifteen minutes when we spotted him in a tundra swale eight hundred yards distant. He saw
us at the same time. I put my glasses on him. He was a dark,
blocky beast, in good flesh, carrying trophy-size antlers. He
ran a mile, then climbed a ridge to watch his backtrail. Sighting
us again, he circled and got our scent. He acted as if he couldn't
believe humans were following him as persistently as hungry
wolves. Next he headed into the hills north of the lake. At
the timberline he maneuvered for another look at us. Then
he turned down the brush-jungled floor of Ptarmigan Creek
Valley. Toward midafternoon, in a rocky flood channel at the
forks of the creek, he met a cow and collected her. The sign
showed that the cow wasn't willing, but he hazed her along
anyway, at antler points. We had now covered twenty-odd miles,
and were about four miles from the lodge.

The bull was losing time on account of the cow. She balked
and dodged and fought him. She was plumb notional. He should
have abandoned her. But he didn't, and then of a sudden he
encountered more trouble—competition.

We were crossing a cottonwood bottom when, close ahead,
we heard sounds of moose conflict—clash and clatter of antlers, war grunts, drumbeat of hoofs on the frozen ground. To
our right a steep bank rose. We climbed it. One hundred yards
across the creek, our dark Romeo bull and a gaunt, skimpy-antlered
roan bull—the hard case I kept running afoul of—were doing
their doggonedest to destroy each other. They weren't fancy
Dans. They stood head to head swinging their antler blades
like scythes. Both were bleeding. The cow they were fighting
over, a trim brown specimen, was poised nervously at the edge
of a thicket. We had the wind and good cover, but she knew
we were present. Maybe she couldn't prove it, but she knew,
all right. She was trying to watch the fight while keeping a
lookout for us in every direction.

Our dark bull was the likeliest candidate for the meat house. He had some padding on his ribs. Tanana shot him through the neck, high enough to smash the vertebrae, and he was dead when he hit the ground.

The roan bull and the cow wheeled, stared at us, then lit out down the valley. This time the cow didn't require any encouragement. She trotted right behind the big roan, matching her gait to his. She had it made. She had found a rutting-season partner as ornery as she was. We forded the icy, crotch-deep creek and dressed and quartered the carcass. We lashed the two hams on our packboards, and hung the rest of the meat from a cottonwood limb. We waded the creek again, changed into dry footgear, and headed for the lodge. As the hams weighed better than one hundred pounds each, we took our time toiling homeward. The sun was down and the moon had risen when we reached the clearing. Tanana halted with a strange exclamation, pointing. A fine upstanding bull had walked out from behind a brushpile. Then we saw other moose across the clearing; three or four bulls and a couple of yearlings.

"It ain't fair," Tanana said brokenly. "It just ain't fair."

Well, I began this account by telling you how young Dave Peters shot the roan bull during a moose stampede in the outlet canyon. I parked myself on the bull's rump and broke out cigarettes. The Denna Lake watershed was becoming an important moose range, and we had witnessed its resurrection. Up to now the road builders hadn't gotten authority to move in with bulldozers and dynamite and spoil it. I patted the bull's hip. Not only had he grown a grand set of antlers, but he had put on some fat.

"Sure, we knew him," I said. "He was a pioneer in these wilds. A character, like most pioneers. I'll tell you about him at the lodge tonight."

Die-Hard
Dueler of the Crags

*Those needle-sharp spikes on a billy's
head aren't there for decoration.*

"**G**o ahead and shoot, Paleface," my Susitna-Denna Indian partner, Billy No-Dogs, said when the four mountain goats appeared unexpectedly on a snow-plastered cliff fifty yards above us. "Hell, I can stand a little muzzle blast."

"Sure. That's because you've got an audience down on the river bars," I said.

This was late of a gray October afternoon near the top of Wolf Point, in Alaska's Knik Valley. Billy No-Dogs and I were bound upriver to make our cabins and caches ready for the trapping season. A half-hour ago we had sighted the goats loafing in a snow-weighted serviceberry thicket on the point's summit. We urgently needed meat, so we climbed for the animals. But while we were toiling up the lee face of the point, our goats came down onto the higher cliffside. Billy No-Dogs was ten feet ahead of me on the steep, drifted slope, clinging to an alder bush with both hands. I had halted to take a look with my glasses at a band of Indian wayfarers who had been behind us all day on the trail.

At this point the four goats walked into view. As Billy No-Dogs ducked his head to the snow, covering his ear with his forearm, I laid the sights of my .270 Winchester on the lead goat.

He was a fine, upstanding billy, a 150-pounder, prime-coated and still summer-fat. The others were large females—his current harem, no doubt.

After an appraising look at us, he made a desperate bound forward. I followed him with the sights and pulled as he landed running. I saw the 130-grain slug slam him against the rock wall, but he was tough. With his heart exploded he ran forty feet before his front legs buckled. He fell sideways and hit the snow on his back. He didn't roll, he slid. I floundered out through a knee-deep drift to intercept him. If the carcass tumbled on down the point it would probably lodge in some goshawful place and we'd have to spend the rest of the day salvaging it. So the thing to do, I thought, was to latch onto it here if I could.

It was one of those swell ideas that can get a man killed.

The carcass tobogganed at me, picking up speed. I made a fast pass and got hold of a hind leg, but I was off balance. The momentum of the carcass yanked me backward, and by luck I managed to grab an alder limb. That left me spread-eagled on the snow, clutching the limb with one hand and the carcass with the other. The Winchester was speared into a drift. Thirty feet below me there was a vertical drop-off, and I mean my situation was thought-provoking.

But then Billy No-Dogs came plunging down the slope. He held the carcass while I got my feet back under our backtrail and hauled it on down to me. We then took the carcass over to the river bars. The Indians were waiting for us. It was a band of wild-looking Goat-Eater Denna, twelve of them, under a sometime guide named Esai Raven. You could tell they were plenty meat-hungry and expected to share our goat.

"We watched you two perform up there," Esai Raven said in Denna, a big, friendly smile on his face. He took me by the elbow. "Come sit at a fire. The women will skin and dress your goat." I knew the guy by sight and reputation. He was a tall, hard-jawed gent, mission-educated, with a truly remarkable gift of gab. "We decided a moment ago," he went on, addressing me, "to invite you to tell the story of that goat kill at our next spring gathering of the Goat-Eater people at Eklutna Village. Or the story of some other goat hunt if you wish." He glanced over his shoulder. "I know you won't mind if the women borrow a few pounds of meat. We are short today."

Parking myself on a pile of spruce boughs by one of the fires, I began reviewing some goat-hunting episodes. Presently I came up with one that I thought might be dramatic enough for a talk. It was the climax of a hunt I had made near the headwaters of Carbon Creek, with a twenty-four-year-old sportswriter named Tom Logan.

We sighted Tom's goat at daybreak, while eating breakfast. It was a fair-size billy with a beautiful snowy pelt. He was on a seven-thousand-foot summit behind camp, lying down, maybe asleep. We looked him over carefully with 16X glasses. Since his horns were only a little shorter than his skull, I gave them nine inches, which is good.

But otherwise, the prognosis was lousy. For one thing, the western half of the summit was socked in, hidden under a mass of lead-colored cloud. The cloud was stationary now, but it could bulge out in five minutes and blank the whole mountaintop. For another thing, three veteran Dall rams were assembled on a terrace below the summit, watching us. Spook them and they'd go tearing boggle-eyed up onto the skyline and spook the goat. Tom didn't covet their heads, as he had taken his white ram.

Hoping to fool the sentinel sheep, we hiked a half-mile down-valley, then made our climb with a buttress ridge for concealment. Luck was against us. Three hundred feet below the summit, everything went haywire. Shale tinkled close ahead. The instant I heard it I motioned Tom to freeze. I knew what was about to happen. Sure enough, out of a quartz-banded V-notch filed the three Dall rams. I suppose they had moved over to this slope hunting some morning sunshine.

We tried to resemble pieces of the scenery. No success. One of the rams snorted. Another struck the shale with a front hoof. Then the trio wheeled and lit out in panicky flight for the summit, crowding, knocking their horns together and rolling rocks. A couple of keg-size boulders thundered down, hit an outcropping above us, and burst like bombs. The rams humped themselves up a rimrock onto the summit. Without a backward glance they fled westward.

"Damned meddlesome fancy-horned aristocrats are about to spoil our stalk," Tom cried, and made for the summit in a scrambling run.

He was right. If we didn't get up where the action was in an almighty hurry, I figured we could say good-bye to the goat. Thus instead of advising Tom to slow down so he'd be in condition to shoot, I matched pace with him. Naturally we reached the summit panting like wind-broken draft horses. The goat stood 150 yards distant on the acute crestline, facing us. Eighty yards beyond him the rams were posed picturesquely atop a broken six-foot-high reef that slanted wall-like across the summit. Towering behind them was the cloud mass. At sight of us the rams jumped off the far side of the reef, but the goat didn't move. He seemed more curious than worried. Tom knelt and leveled his .30-06 Remington.

At this point the goat took off. Tom let go a shot. The bullet wailed off a boulder three feet to the running animal's right. Tom worked the bolt and fired again. Another miss, at eight o'clock this time. Muttering savagely, he chambered another shell, fired, and busted fragments off a tilted shale slab ahead of the goat. That really hoorawed the animal. It swerved around the impact spot and laid on speed. Goats aren't noted for fleetness, but if there was any way to prove it, I'd bet this one was doing thirty-five miles an hour. Tom drew in a deep breath and held it. Using the slingstrap for support, he fired again. For a split second I thought the shot was good. A tuft of hair had dropped from the animal's hump. But he went on without faltering, so he had only been grazed. A moment later he made a soaring bound over the reef and out of sight amongst the rams.

"Terrible. Give me a minute to get my wind back, huh?" Tom wheezed.

On our right rose a splintered rooster-comb formation, fifteen feet high. We climbed it. We could now see the four animals. They were crowded together and resented it—no integration for them. As we watched with our glasses, one of them attacked. The billy faded aside, and the ram crashed head-on into the reef. It sounded like a sledgehammer walloping cement. Before the ram could reorganize himself, the billy stabbed him in the flank with both horns. Blood gushed, and a loop of intestine spilled out. The other two rams now attacked. One caught the billy on the rump, belting him half around. The other missed. As the latter blundered past, the billy hooked him between the hind legs. He hoisted the ram, then wrenched free. Impaled on his left horn were the ram's testicles and torn scrotum.

That ended the battle. The two wounded rams headed westward along the crest, their backs humped, walking carefully. The third ram milled, afraid to venture into the open, but then got reckless and left at a gallop.

The goat was fidgeting. He didn't know where we were. The fact that we hadn't in any way followed up the spate of shooting must have baffled him plenty. I guess he figured it was dangerous to stay where he was, but would also be dangerous to depart. Then a hard gust of wind clobbered the summit. We saw that the cloud mass was moving toward us. Its front was laced with white streaks like tracer bullets—hail. You could now hear the barrage of ice pellets, a sullen roar.

The goat contemplated the oncoming squall. I could almost read his mind. The squall would provide perfect cover. All he had to do was wait for it. But of course while he was waiting he might well get shot. Abruptly he opted to run. Tom, in better shape now, rested the Remington over a shale cornice and fired. The goat dropped and lay motionless. We hastened over to the carcass. Hailstones whizzed down, bouncing higher than our heads.

"He was a killer," Tom said as he knelt beside his trophy goat in the battering storm, admiring the silky pelt and the bloody, dagger-pointed horns.

Back to the Goat-Eater Denna camp. The sun had gone down. The air was filled with the smell of roasting meat. In the hope it would help me remember an equally interesting goat-hunting episode, I mentally played back a talk I had heard Esai Raven put on a couple of years ago during a spring gathering at Chickaloon Village.

"This concerns goats and golden eagles," Esai Raven had begun in the eloquent old-time Denna manner of speaking. "It happened at the headwaters of Friday Creek in September. I am guiding a professor from Matanuska, named Walter Richards. At the moment, we are lying behind a screen of waist-high wild celery, glasses glued to our eyes. Three hundred yards above us, crosswind, a mixed band of eleven goats is strung out along the rim of a one-thousand-foot cliff. When we commenced our stalk twenty minutes ago, there were twelve goats. The missing animal is a husky trophy billy with horns that will measure anyway 8 ½ inches. I figure he has somehow spotted us and taken cover. As I am trying to locate him, two golden eagles join us. They zoom over the snout of a hanging glacier to the north, and come coasting down toward the goats. Since

it is a cinch they see us, I suppose they will go on around the mountain, but the dark birds have other ideas.

"They scream. I realize that they will attack, and that they have picked their target—a top knotted three-month-old kid standing with its mother on the cliff edge. The female turns to face the eagles. She is a trim, slick-coated matron, under average size, with mean-looking skinny horns. The eagles check her out. They bank around and reverse their heading. They let the wind drift them over the two animals. They hang there a moment, black cross-shapes against the sky. Then one of them half closes its wings and pitches down at the kid. The female rears to fight the bird, challenging it with her horns and front hoofs. Opening its wings, the eagle skids aside. It has trouble regaining altitude. The female bounds after it, covering two feet to the eagle's one. But the bird catches an updraft and is lofted before she can get close enough to knock it out of the air.

"'She can't stand them both off,' the professor says. 'Shall I break it up?'

"I tell him no, he'd ruin our chances for a shot at the trophy billy. But it's true that the female and her youngster are in bad trouble. The first eagle now swoops at the kid, feathered legs stuck out, talons reaching. It talon-slashes the kid's face and chops at an eye with its beak. The kid dodges behind a boulder. The eagle hops over to finish it, and then the female goat is there. She jumps onto the eagle, hoofs bunched. She hooks left, right, left with her horns. But the other eagle now comes in slow and fast, and strikes at her head. She rears. She is on the very brink of the cliff. The kid comes running and crowds against her, and the airborne eagle strikes again at her head. She trips over the kid, and falls. She falls five hundred feet, bounces off a ledge, falls another three hundred feet, smashes the top of a spruce snag, and ends up smeared over a moraine dump.

"But at least she has partly crippled one of the eagles, and the other goats are now closing in on it. The bird heads down the mountain, toward us. It is able to stay in the air only a few yards at a time. The goats charge in pursuit.

"At first the eagle manages to keep ahead of the goats. But then it attempts a steep downwind turn, maybe because it knows we are hidden in the clump of wild celery. It don't complete the turn. Its wings give out. It goes into a spin and piles up a hundred feet from us. The goats swarm onto it. They are stomping it into the ground when, ninety yards above us, we see another goat step around the point of a ledge. It is the trophy billy. He comes sprinting down a scab-rock stringer. No matter what the risk, he wants to help destroy the eagle. The professor stands up. He puts the sights of his .300 Weatherby on the goat, and fires. The goat, shot through the chest, makes one jump off the scab-rock, and drops. The professor shakes hands with me.

"'Well, Esai, I will declare as follows,' he says. 'If that was a fair sample of the way mountain goats deal with predators, nobody needs to worry about their ability to survive. They will probably be around, fat and handsome, until the final whistle blows.'"

We had eaten and turned in. That is, Billy No-Dogs and I had. The Goat-Eater Denna people were still stuffing themselves. Before I went to sleep I remembered another promising goat-hunting episode. It had occurred on a hunt I made on the South Fork of Carpenter Creek with young Pat Jarvis of Seattle. Pat was the cheechako grandson of an early day sourdough.

Pat's billy was eight hundred yards distant when we sighted him. We had just come to the mouth of a tributary creek, a quarter-mile below South Fork glacier, and were scanning the area with our glasses. One moment the scarlet cloudberry slope above us was empty. The next, over at its east limit, the goat appeared. I suppose he had climbed out of a wash we couldn't see from there. I put the 16X glasses on him. He was a sizable specimen with horns that would go close to nine inches. He hadn't seen us. He was facing the opposite direction. But with his telescopic eyes, all he had to do was turn his head. We scrooched down behind a cutbank whose rim was fringed with gaudy frosted wolf willows. I found a spy-hole through them, and we began planning a stalk. Something moved on my left, and I craned my head to see what it was.

What I beheld was a plump, terrier-size silver marmot sitting upright at the entrance to his burrow, twenty feet distant. We looked each other in the eye for maybe two seconds. Then he opened his mouth, let out a piercing alarm whistle, and dived underground.

Instantly the goat spun around, gazing straight at us. Other marmots began sounding off. From timberline to the glacier, both sides of the valley, clear up to the last grass, colonies of lookout rodents were whistling a red alert. Since the goat had a mighty good idea where we were, a stalk was going to be difficult—if not impossible. First we would have to get across the creek. Then take cover under a continuation of the cutbank we were now using. After that, it would depend on what moves the goat made. I got down on my belly and eased toward the water. Some willows upstream just barely gave me concealment. I could see only one way to ford the creek undetected—crawl across on our hands and knees. I went back and acquainted Pat with the situation. He said to lead on.

The creek was glacier-fed and milky, some ten feet wide and, I hoped, less than a foot deep. We slid down its low bank otter-fashion and headed across. At the deepest part the icy current sluiced against my ribs. We crawled up the east bank and, keeping low, worked fifty yards along a reach of barren gravel bar to where the cutbank resumed. The marmots had shut up, but you could be sure they were vigilant. One glimpse of us and they would notify the countryside. Choosing a scalp-lock of willows for cover, we cautiously poked our heads above the cutbank. The goat had moved out of range. Most likely trying to get our scent, he had beat it over to the west side of the cloudberry slope. I realized that he still didn't know what we were. Perhaps he suspected the first marmot had gotten excited over nothing more formidable than a fox or coyote, and wanted scent confirmation.

"I hate to tell you this, boy," I said, "but we've got to ford the creek again. It's your only chance for a reasonable shot."

Pat was shivering miserably, but didn't protest. We retraced our route down the open bar and across the creek. When we emerged into the glacial wind I felt the cold plumb to the marrow of my bones. The goat was now seven hundred yards distant, and was intently watching the creek mouth. He knew dog-goned well we were in the vicinity. Raising his head, nose pointed at the sky, he sampled the wind eddies being bounced off the mountainside. I guess they didn't tell him anything. He took a long look around, then started back toward the east limit of the slope. Pat stiffened. "No, you don't, friend," he grated. "You don't sucker me across that creek again." He racked up the iron receiver sight of his .30-06 Springfield sporter, took a rest on the cutbank rim, apparently willed himself to stop shivering, and fired. The goat turned toward us, and fell dead. It was the most astounding feat of marksmanship I have ever seen in my life.

I woke up around two o'clock. The Indians were still eating. Before I went back to sleep I remembered another goat-hunting episode that I thought might do. It had taken place on a hunt I made above iceberg-dotted Lake George with Dave Watson, a middle-aged banker from the Wheat Belt.

Dave and I were washing the breakfast dishes. I looked up and spotted a goat running across a wire-grass meadow at alder-line. Reaching for my glasses, I saw that it was a medium-size critter, a female, judging from its slender horns. Obviously she had recently bedded down in a blueberry patch. Her thick, cream-colored coat was mottled with large blue stains. She was heading for a boulder-field on the brink of a waterfall canyon, where several non-trophy billies were visible. One hundred yards behind her I caught a flicker of pale yellow in the alders. Into view trotted a giant, square-built billy with a phenomenal set of horns. I couldn't use his skull for comparison because he never stopped moving. It didn't matter. I knew the horns would go ten inches or better.

The billy hastened after the female, nose to the ground like a trailing hound. I estimated he would weigh 220 pounds. In these parts the rutting season had just begun. I guess the female hadn't yet succumbed. But clearly the billy had the urge bad.

As the female approached the boulder field, a chunky young billy moved out to meet her. He herded her against the side of a ledge, and tried to drape a foreleg companionably over her neck. She broke past him, galloping. But he caught up with her, and this time got a kind of half-nelson on her. He was so preoccupied that he didn't even turn when the big boss billy raced up to them. The female inadvertently alerted him. She wrestled clear, and as he whirled in pursuit he found himself face-to-face with his outsize rival. The two reared and came together, striking and stabbing. It was a brief contest. The big billy hooked the other in the mouth and threw him sprawling. Meanwhile the female had made a getaway. We saw her disappear over the edge of the waterfall canyon. The huge boss billy took her trail.

We made a quick climb up through a quarter-mile of alders. The billy was nowhere in sight. But the blueberry-stained female had gone out onto the dizzy waterfall cliff at the canyon's head. I couldn't see what she was using for footholds. Mist swirled about her. A rainbow spanned the two-hundred-foot falls, one end of it touching her shoulders. I suppose she figured she had a reliable refuge from romance. But then we sighted the big billy. He was on the canyon side between us and the falls. And he had located the female. He made for her across the sheer expanse of wet rock. The female saw him coming, but had no avenue of escape. Dave, with his .270 Winchester poised, waited. If a goat falls onto rock, his horns will shatter. The billy came up behind the female, dancing eagerly over invisible footholds. He was now above the waterfall pool. Dave fired. The billy stepped into space, fell through the rainbow, turned over twice, and hit the churning water.

"I'll wonder about that billy the rest of my life," Dave said when we had climbed down and retrieved the carcass. "Do you think he really was serious? In a perilous place like that?"

When Billy No-Dogs and I arose at first light, the Goat-Eater Denna people were breaking camp. They had feasted all night. There was no meat left. They had even cracked the marrow bones. Esai Raven didn't look our way. Of a sudden I made up my mind. At last I had a goat-hunting adventure to relate at the spring gathering. I would let Esai Raven introduce me. Then I would describe how we had risked our necks to kill a fine, fat goat, and how a fast-talking Injun operator had conned us out of the carcass. But I really couldn't blame him too much, at that, I would add, goats being as wonderful to eat as they were to hunt.

Beach Bears Can Be Fatal

*Along Alaska's seacoast, brownies can be counted
on to do only one thing—the unexpected.*

"**M**an, that ain't no ordinary fracas. Those bears are murdering each other. I figure they met a friendly sow and they're battling to see who gets her." Aleut Bowen was speaking to our current hunter, young Bart Wilson of Los Angeles, as we hearkened to sounds of savage bruin strife coming from the far side of some spruces two hundred yards inland from the beach and upwind. "Come on, gents, let's get over there afore they claw their expensive spring pelts to scrap rags." Aleut took off at a trot, and we followed.

This was early of a crystal June morning at Chinitna Bay, on the west coast of Cook Inlet. We had left camp at daybreak, scouting for beachcomber brown bears, and had just found a tangle of platter-size tracks when we heard the fight begin. A salmon stream came in here. We hastened up its alder-shaggy bank to a redtop opening beyond the spruces. Dead ahead of us, 150 feet distant, two huge coffee-colored brown bears were locked in dire conflict. They rolled and tumbled on the new green grass, slugging, biting, raking with their hind claws.

Aleut had been right. It was a mating-season hassle. The cause of it, a handsome taffy-blond female, stood off to one side watching. She was small and trim by comparison with the burly combatants. Probably she was a four-year-old making her debut into the roughhouse springtime mating rituals.

"Now hold everything till I get a good look at their pelts," Aleut muttered. "I wanta see 'em fore and aft, on both sides, 'cause they may be rubbed as well as fight-tore."

What with all the activity, it would be easy to make a mistake, but the pelts looked all right to me. The two fighting males were apparently fine trophy-grade specimens in the nine-hundred-pound range, and could be identical twins except that one had a bald-face. (That is, he had a pale-cream forehead patch, a blaze.) The pair lurched up and clinched, to lumber around on their hind legs in a kind of grotesque waltz, busily chopping at each other's throats. All of a sudden the bald-faced bear grabbed the brown-faced bear's nose with his teeth and started chewing it off. At that the brown-faced bear flipped backward, kicking his opponent in the crotch with both feet. The bald-faced bear gave a bellow of anguish. He came down hard on the back of his neck, letting go of the other's nose.

From the corner of my eye I now caught a glimpse of surreptitious movement to the left of the embattled suitors. It was the blond female departing. I don't think she could have seen or heard us. We had good cover, and the creek was making a lot of noise. Besides, she didn't act spooked—she was just sort of sneaking away. I suppose she had concluded that she didn't especially like either of these mayhem-dealing would-be boyfriends, and thought she could do better elsewhere.

"The bald-face," Aleut said. "Take him."

Bart brought up his .300 Weatherby Magnum and fired. With the *whoomp* of the 180-grain softnose, tissue jetted from the bear's neck. He made one bound toward the alders, and crumpled in a heap. As for the brown-faced warrior, the rifle's report hadn't panicked him. He stared at us, then cast a wild look around, presumably trying to locate the blond female. But she was long gone. For an instant I thought the battered Romeo was going to attack. He bristled and sank his head. A snarl rumbled in his throat. You couldn't blame him if he hated the world right now. He had survived a hard fight, and for what? All he had to show for a heap of valor was a shredded snout. I felt sorry for him as I watched him over the sights of the .30-06 Winchester. He snorted blood at us, wheeled, and loped into the brush.

When he turned I had seen a rubbed spot the size of my hand, completely bare, on his right hip. That was a solid lesson to me, one I wouldn't forget. We went over to the trophy carcass. The pelt was thick and silky, no blemishes. I got out my skinning knife. My chores with Aleut were diversified. I was, as the situation required, packer, deck hand, skinner, cook, weapons cleaner, and clam digger—also student.

A year previously, when I turned nineteen, I had apprenticed myself to Aleut. I aimed to make a career of dude-wrangling and realized that I needed to know more about brown-bear hunting. Aleut was tops in the field, a craggy, humorous roughneck with a weather-seamed face and the bull shoulders that come from paddling kayaks. He was maybe fifty-five, half-Bering Sea Aleut, and he had been born alongside a brown-bear trail over near Unangashik Village. His whole life had been spent observing and hunting brown bears. I think he knew more about the brutes than any other man living. If he had a major fault as a guide, it was that he got so interested in outsmarting bears that he neglected the ordinary comforts of his customers. I had found that out on the first hunt I made with him, the year before.

It was a real lulu. Aleut had booked an elderly Chicago grain buyer, name of Frank Mallory. We loaded grub and camp gear into Aleut's twenty-foot, outboard-powered Kodiak dory, and headed down the Inlet for brown-bear country. This was the last week of May. Chunks of breakup ice still rode the Inlet's notorious river-swift tides. I knew the bears would be fresh from hibernation.

Late the second day, below Anchorage, as we were cruising some four hundred yards off the west coast, a mean southeaster blared out of the Kenai snowpeaks. The dory bucked and wallowed miserably. Our Mr. Mallory became seasick. The wet motor started missing. But if Aleut was concerned, he didn't show it. His gaze was fastened on a great assemblage of seabirds circling under the lee of a snow-patched cliff close ahead. In a moment we saw what had attracted them. The carcass of a finback whale—a forty-footer. I put my glasses on it. The painted shaft of an Umnak lance jutted from its shoulder, broken rawhide float-line trailing. Aleut stood up and scanned the beach, looking for a good landing spot. There wasn't any. Hooligan Creek came in between us and the whale, but its mouth was narrow and rocky. The beach was strewn with ice.

"You ever been ashore there?" Aleut asked me.

I said I hadn't. I added that the place didn't look exactly hospitable.

85

"Well, maybe it ain't," he said. "But you can't beat a ripe whale for bear bait. So hang on, we're going in." He turned the dory on the slope of a wave, and aimed her at the creek mouth.

It was some landing, and some campsite. We sideswiped a rock. A following wave broke across the stern. The motor quit. Aleut and I jumped overboard and muscled the dory into calm water. We unloaded the outfit and pitched the tent. Then we discovered that the creek drained a tidal marsh and was salty. It had been raining here, and there was no dry wood. We were soaking wet, shivering in the wind.

Well, we ate sandwiches for supper, washing them down with canned milk, and turned in. Toward morning the wind hauled around, blowing from the whale to us. The goshawful stink awoke me. Aleut and the pilgrim, though mercifully asleep, were making gagging sounds.

I lit my pipe and was stoical. At last sunlight touched the tent roof. Seabirds screamed overhead. Aleut and the pilgrim woke up. I guess the pilgrim must have been still queasy from seasickness, because when he got his first waking noseful of whale stink, he tuned green. His eyes glazed. "Mister, I give you credit," he said brokenly to Aleut. "There are good camps and bad camps, and then there are impossible camps. But you have come up with something new. You have introduced me to a camp so horrible that it defies classification."

Well, hardly had he finished speaking when we heard a brown bear roar. The animal was upwind on the beach at the whale carcass. Then two, maybe three bears roared in basso chorus. It was a most impressive sunrise serenade. It abruptly ended the pilgrim's interesting and absolutely justified remarks about our camp.

"Of course you're plumb correct, and I got no excuses," Aleut said stiffly. "But as soon as you're ready, I'll also introduce you to some brown bears."

Dressing hastily, we plowed through salmonberry brush and devil's club to a vantage point two hundred feet back from the grounded whale. An extraordinary bruin drama was developing out front. The pilgrim and I watched it as Aleut appraised the cast of characters. The whale carcass lay broadside to us, wet and gleaming, surf battering against its ribs, a noisy mob of gulls and other seabirds orbiting above it. Six brown bears had arrived for a blubber feast, but they were having trouble.

Two of them, a tobacco-colored sow and a blond yearling, must have gotten there ahead of the others. At any rate, they had taken possession. They had climbed onto the whale and were militantly patrolling its length.

The other four—obviously males, since there was no young stuff with them—stood below on the sand gazing up at the sow in dumb frustration.

"I like that yellow-maned bear. The one on the right," Aleut muttered above the pounding surf. "But wait'll I get a better look at his off shoulder."

That's when I saw the king wave rolling in. At the same moment the yellow-maned bear edged toward the whale's fluke, obviously with the idea of snatching himself a mouthful. But the sow was alert. She uttered an outraged *wagh-h,* and crouched to spring. He whirled back to safety. It was a thoroughly ridiculous spectacle. He was a massive 1,100-pounder, whereas she wouldn't go better than 700. Yet she had him and the other males buffaloed. She was making them respect her incredibly greedy claim to the whale. I hoped they were hungry and got hungrier. They deserved it. The king wave was now fifty yards out. Gray and foam-mottled, the wind tearing spray off its crest, it lifted ponderously above the horizon. I knew what was going to happen, and I stood there fascinated.

"Go ahead and take him," Aleut was saying. "His pelt's okay."

The pilgrim slipped the safety latch of his .375 magnum, but before he could line up his sights and shoot, the king wave struck.

It hit the whale with a howitzer crack. It climbed straight up, a sunlit wall of water, towering high above the sow and her yearling. It toppled and broke, and the formidable weight of green water sluiced them off the whale. I had a split-second view of the sow upside down in the air. Then she crashed on the beach amongst the male bears. The falling wave bludgeoned them all to the sand.

As they were scrambling up, the wave's backwash caught them and piled them in a heap. I can't report further on the yearling, I lost track of him, but the sow emerged from the confusion fighting. She clobbered one male and bit another. She was roaring like a crazy bear, but she had crowded her luck too far. The males retaliated. It looked to me as though they all took wallops at her.

Another big wave smashed in. The six bears came galloping up off the beach ahead of it. The pilgrim had knelt. The bears were in an open group with the wave now creaming around their legs. The yellow-maned bear was leading. He bounded up a low cutbank as the wave smacked into it. The pilgrim fired. Hair flew from the bear's chest. He bawled, went down, and stayed down. The other bears veered off into salmonberry brush. Well, the pilgrim had taken a swell trophy. The two-toned pelt was winter prime, it had a nice sheen, and the hair was three to four inches long on the hump and back. Aleut said the hide would square ten feet.

"Forget my comments at camp, please," the pilgrim said. "I'm so happy, men, that it's a fact that whale stink is beginning to smell sweet as roses."

Like many old-timers on this wild coast, Aleut was superstitious. He had been mission-educated, but he believed in medicine—medicine animals and animist magic. For instance, the guy had the notion that in 1912 he and a certain brown bear had somehow triggered the volcanic explosion that blew the top off Mt. Katmai and created the Famed Valley of 10,000 Smokes. Yeah, I know. But the way Aleut told it, you could see why he honestly thought so. Here's the story, in his words.

"I'm over on the Shelikof Coast north of Kanatak, in June," he said, "shooting hair seals for the $2.50 government bounty. This particular day I've got me a promising project. I'm bellied down on an alder-brushed point overlooking a narrow cove. It's dead low tide. About ninety seals are loafing on the exposed mudflat. I place my cartridges handy and plant my elbows for some fast shooting. I figure that with luck I may score ten kills before the herd reaches water. But everything goes wrong. I'm lining the sights of my .30-06 Springfield on a dozing bull, when I hear something in the alders off to my right. I raise up for a look. It's a brown bear, a sizable dark character. He don't see me. He eases down the side of the point and, damn him, makes a rush at my seals.

"At first it's a comedy routine. The mud is blue clay, slippery as grease. A man can't run on it. I've tried. The bear skids and falls, snorting, gets up and falls again, mud all over him, sore as hell. But then he gets the hang of it, and starts making time. The seals are desperately humping themselves for the water.

The bear charges among them, and it isn't funny anymore. He clobbers seals right and left. He grabs seals between his jaws and shakes them. He bounces around faster than you'd think a bear could. I have my glasses on him now. He's slobbering and letting out hysterical moans. But seals are hard to stop unless you hit them square on top of their thin skulls. A thick layer of blubber protects their bodies. So the bear ain't scoring many clean kills. He's got cripples flopping all over the haulout.

"'Okay, Ferocious. I'll take a hand now,' I say. 'It happens I have use for a bearskin bunk cover.'

"I snuggle my cheek against the Springfield's stock. The bear has paused to pull the guts out of a big cow seal. I put the gold bead on his shoulder and start the trigger squeeze. There's almost no wind. The range is only two hundred yards. Shucks, I've got the bear. He's mine. You know how you can tell when a shot is going to be good. But just as I'm applying the final squeeze, the ground shakes. The sights joggle off the bear. It's an earthquake, I think. Nothing unusual in these parts. But the bear's reaction is unusual. He whirls around, picks up one of the crippled seals, and comes floundering across the mud toward the point. He's abandoning all that seal meat. It don't make sense. Well, I put the sights on him again. And as before, the ground shakes. The sights wobble off. Coincidence, I tell myself. Life is full of coincidences.

"The bear is halfway to the point, slipping and scrambling, mud flying, in a heck of a hurry for some reason. I grit my teeth and cut down on him again. This time the ground don't shake. Instead the light fails. All at once it's deep twilight. I look over my shoulder to where the sun ought to be, and it ain't there. An inky black cloud has covered half the sky. Well, this is when I realize that I'm up against a medicine bear. But, doggone it, I am supposed to be carrying pretty strong medicine myself. I've got an *oodoochilah* charm around my neck that my grandfather, an Atka chief, wore. It's guaranteed by the shamans to give protection in cases like this. I reach up and touch it. The bear is now climbing the point. Well, the light ain't good, but it's good enough for short-range shooting.

"'You're no high-powered medicine bear,' I say. 'If you were, you'd have done a better job of seal killing. Anyway, it's you and me. I am gonna try to bust your skull with a slug.

So let's see you stop me. Fly at it, sucker,' I say. 'Shake the ground, darken the sun, bring the world to an end. . .'

"Me and my big mouth. There's a rumbling and booming. A gust of hurricane wind whacks the point. It gets darker. Stuff like ashes falls out of the sky. Well, the bear is coming over the top of the point. He's still got the seal in his mouth. I shoot, and hear the slug hit. He gives a strangled roar, drops the seal, and falls over. I keep shooting. I empty the magazine. Then I reload, and go over to him. He's dead. But the sun don't come back, and ashes are still falling. I take off the bear's pelt. I tote it to the sod *bara-bara* I'm camped in. The ashes are ankle deep now. To the northward there's a red glow like a fire in the sky. I figure it's the end of the world, and all my fault.

"But a week later I find out I'm wrong. Partly, anyhow. I hike over to Kanatak, and the people there tell me what's happened. It ain't the end of the world. Mt. Katmai, sixty miles north of here, has blown up, that's all. Naturally I am relieved. But even today a thought keeps bothering me. Just suppose I hadn't been wearing my *oodoochilah* charm. Maybe the whole works would have blown up, huh?"

Aleut had a gift we all coveted. He was at home in the ubiquitous mountain alders—the only man I ever knew who was. We would spot a bear bedded down on a mountainside and decide to climb for it. Then Aleut would make his special reconnaissance. He would park himself on the beach a few minutes and contemplate the intervening maze of alders. I guess he photographed them mentally—he'd seem to go into a trance. When we started climbing, he'd know exactly how to proceed from one opening to another, always on course to the bear. No sweat. It was as if he had electronic aids and a map in his head. I used to kid him that someday this ability to ghost through alders right up onto bears that no doubt thought they were safe would get him into trouble. And it did.

We were at Iniskin Bay in early June, shepherding a pleasant, middle-aged California real-estate dealer named Herman Bosworth.

The bear was eight hundred yards up from the beach, lying asleep on sunlit winterkilled grass between a granite outcropping and a snow stringer. It was a chocolate-colored bear with a tan patch across its hump. A male, it turned out. Thanks to Aleut's genius, we made a quick, easy climb to a ridge from which the bear should be visible. No bear. So we angled over to the animal's bed. The grass was still warm. There was a pile of dung, steaming. Aleut must have had a primitive hunch. He looked and listened. He sniffed the wind. I saw him reach up and touch his medicine charm. He started to say something to the hunter, but just then, directly above us and too close, the bear snorted. I jerked around and saw the animal rear up on the lip of a terrace thirty feet distant.

I understood in a flash what had happened. While we were climbing, a peak shadow had fallen across the bear's bed. So he had moved a bit higher, back into the sunshine. Until this moment he hadn't been aware of our presence on the mountain. Well, the bear made a perfect target, and our Herman had climbed up here to shoot him, so that's what he did, without a go-ahead from Aleut, probably without thinking. He was carrying a .400 Whelen Mauser. Fortunately a mighty weapon. He whipped the gun up and pulled, and it looked like the 520-grain softnose blasted anyway a quart of meat and blood out through the bear's back. The animal weaved under the tremendous impact, uttered a coughing wail, and pitched forward like a tree falling. I was already leaping into the clear.

The bear pinwheeled and slid. Herman tried to move aside, but didn't get started soon enough. I believe his first idea had been to chamber another shell. Aleut had stepped up beside him. He was hogtied by ethics. But gravity solved that. The bear's rump slammed into Herman. Then he and Aleut were down and the bear was rolling over their legs. The bear wheezed and flailed the air with his paws. I couldn't shoot. There was too much chance of hitting one of the men. The bear heaved himself partly up, then collapsed with a windy grunt and slid against a boulder. He lay there blinking his eyes, ribs heaving. I laid the Winchester on his head, but didn't shoot. He wasn't going anywhere, and let Herman finish what he had started.

Herman and Aleut untangled themselves. Herman sat up and gave the bear a finishing shot through the neck. Later, when we were taking off the pelt, I told Aleut the whole scary episode was because he was such a spook in the alders. He grinned. He liked compliments—even kidding, left-handed ones.

The last time I saw Aleut he was at Seldovia, getting ready to take a congressman bear hunting. The congressman was a robust type, he said, who wanted to rough it, siwash-style, on the beaches. So he wasn't taking much of an outfit. I thought, my gosh, somebody ought to warn the congressman. Rough it with Aleut? He'd probably never be the same again. But then I wished I were going with them. They might come back lean-bellied and ragged, but they'd have a fabulous hunt. Because, as I've been saying, Aleut was the best.

Champ Dalls Come Tough

*The men who hunt these snow-white sheep are a
special breed, letting nothing, not even the risk of death
come between them and a tape-breaking trophy head.*

"**M**ister, I admit it. That place scares me spitless," young
Pete Donnelly said as, with williwaw wind gusts clawing
at us, we sized up the forty-foot-wide empty snowslide chute
that lay between us and the next good cover. The chute was
steep. There were no visible footholds. A short way below us it ended abruptly—in dizzy space. "And what's with
those rams?" Pete continued. "Why are they prancing around
like that?"

"Seems they've decided to fight," I said.

That was an easy conclusion. The two chunky white Dall
rams we had stalked for the past hour were five hundred yards
crosswind, at the brink of a boulder-strewn terrace, demonstrating. I put my 12X glasses on them. They stood twenty-
five feet apart, heads lowered in combat readiness. They pawed
the scree and made stiff-legged crow-hop jumps. They faked
and feinted. They were advertising that they were the veri-
table terrors of the peaks.

Then of a sudden, as though there had been a signal, they
slammed full-tilt together. The impact sounded like whacking
a plank with the flat of an ax. Manifestly dazed, they stood
spraddle-legged a moment, sides heaving. Then they backed off
several yards to glare at each other.

"You'll have to figure out another approach," Pete was saying. "That chute is too much for me. And I sure couldn't score a killing shot from here. Not in this crazy wind."

Our sheep-hunting drama was taking place partway up a seven-thousand-foot peak above Tonzona River, on the wild north slope of the Alaska Range, in early September. We had spotted the rams from camp. Companionable then, they had been posed side-by-side, gazing down into the frost-painted valley. One was big-bodied but no great shakes as a trophy specimen—too young. The other, a patriarchal type, carried marvelous horns. As nearly as I could estimate, they would go 15x41 inches. I heard Pete suck in his breath. The guy was a complete mountain sheep fan. He had taken Stone and Fannin trophies, and now was hellbent to collect a fine Dall head. As he studied the elderly ram with 16X glasses, he muttered delightedly. His hands were shaking. He'd had to rest the glasses against a tent pole.

Well, the only way to avoid the snowslide chute was to climb above it. I was looking for a route that offered cover, when Pete touched my arm. Turning, I saw that the rams were about to resume fighting.

This time the wonder-horned veteran was slow getting started. Before beginning his rush, he made a fancy buck-jump ahead and to one side. That bit of show-off won the fight for him, because as a result of it he went in at an angle, and the young ram didn't alter course to meet him squarely. It could be the young bravo had his eyes shut. I've heard it claimed that most rams fight that way. At any rate, the young slugger was barreling straight ahead when the two crashed together, and thus took the collision on his left horn. His nose dug into the loose shale. His rump came up and over. He finished the somersault on his back and then rolled, kicking, down against the face of a deeply undercut boulder. As for the patriarch, he slumped to his knees, but got up at once, still full of fight.

Attacking, he smashed the downed ram a piledriver wallop in the ribs. But the boulder's overhang cramped his style. He couldn't make efficient use of his weapons. As he drove in again, his right horn hit the rock so forcefully that I saw a sizable chip break off its ridged striking surface. Beside me Pete uttered a moan. I thought he was sympathizing with the young ram, and advised him to forget it. After all, I said, the young hard case had asked for trouble. Pete made agitated sounds. Shoving his glasses back into their case, he stepped past me. The old ram was boring in vindictively, and his young opponent was stretched out absorbing the punishment, blood dripping from his open mouth, a pathetic warrior indeed.

"Man, I've gotta get over there," Pete said.

With that, taking me by surprise, he headed at a run, quartering across the snowslide chute. It was a hair-raising performance, a combination of balance and speed. Maybe for him nothing else would have succeeded. Anyway, he got across, and seconds later I joined him. We now saw what had made the rams so belligerent. Six ewes were bunched on a cliff above them. Crawling, we cut the range to four hundred yards. The trophy ram had sighted us. Pete opened up with his .270 Winchester. It took him two shots to drop the old-timer. At this point the young ram recovered his senses. Battered and bloody, limping, he lit out up the mountain. We went over to the kill. As Pete got busy with a steel tape, I remarked that he certainly had conquered his fear of the snowslide chute in a hurry.

"Hell, I had to. It was a desperate emergency," he said. "This idiot sheep was damaging his trophy head."

Sheep hunters are special. They tend to be colorful, adventurous gents probably because it's that kind of sport. Some of them, in fact a lot of them, get plumb single-minded in their pursuit of trophy horns.

For example, take an episode that occurred during a Dall sheep hunt I made with a dedicated stalwart named Pat Jarvis. We were at brushline on a ragged peak near the headwaters of Wood River, deep in the Alaska Range. Forty minutes earlier a golden eagle had inadvertently done us a favor. The great bird, circling, had pointed out a notable trophy ram and his harem of four ewes, plus a supernumerary lamb, and then had cruised on around the mountain when we began our stalk.

We were now in good cover two hundred yards below the sheep. I had my glasses on the ram. I was concentrating, willing him to make a half-turn toward us. Sometimes the thought-projection business works for me. But not with this ram. He wasn't cooperating worth a doggone. And then the eagle came back.

The ram had herded his ewes and the lamb out onto a dead-end shelf that weather had gouged into the face of a five-hundred-foot cliff. He was now loafing, leaning against the cliffside, no doubt enjoying the afternoon sun on his ribs. I wanted him to turn so I could get a look at the tip of his left horn. I suspected it was broomed. I had got a quick glance at the horn from farther down the mountain, and it had looked short. Otherwise he toted a first-rate head. In contrast to the massive but narrow coastal heads, the amber horns rose above his skull to sweep outward, then down and around in wide twin curls, flaring handsomely at the line of his jaws. Beautiful, but I needed a look at that left horn tip. I gave the right horn 15x38 inches. Growth rings indicated the animal was nine years old.

A shadow passed over us just as I decided I would have to try something more direct, like hollering at the ram. Looking up, I saw the eagle bank around and make a shallow dive at the sheep.

I assumed that the bird had spotted us, and that we didn't worry it much. Its attention plainly was centered on the lamb. And you could see that the ewes knew that. They had at once gathered around the lamb and were starting off the shelf with it. The eagle pitched down at them, screaming. It battered the air with its wings. Its strategy was evident. It wanted to stampede the sheep. In the confusion it would scoop the lamb off the shelf into a 150-foot fall. And if the ram hadn't been an ornery character, the scheme probably would have worked. The ewes were eager to stampede. But the ram, head down, hoofs planted stubbornly, refused to let them pass. The eagle swooped again. Then one of the ewes, a skinny old bat, reared and struck at the ram's face. He reacted violently. Bounding at the aggressive female, he belted her six feet backward and upside down on top of two other ewes.

"Now there's a ram I admire," Pat said. "In fact, I am gonna take him without seeing his other horn."

When Pat fired, I saw the ram flinch. Then it stepped off the shelf. It turned over once in the air, and thudded into the alders. We went up to the carcass. Pat knelt to examine the head.

"Aw, don't worry about it," Pat said. "There's only about two inches of horn broomed off. I think it gives the head character, sort of."

Then there was a chancy Dall sheep hunt I made with Bill Wilkins back in the cloud-busting Knik River peaks. A lean Westerner, geared for climbing, Bill got a kick out of estimating horn dimensions. He had become expert at it. We made camp at Wolf Point, and next morning sighted a lone ram high on the mountain above us. I checked him with my glasses. He stood on a ledge between two shale turrets, gazing directly at me. I doubted that my 12X magnification gave me much advantage over him, if any. He carried a good Chugach-type head. The horns were heavy and close-set, with clean tips that reached well above his eyes. I gave them 15½ by 37 inches. Bill had set up a tripod-mounted 24X scope. He fiddled with its focus. He got out a camel's hair brush and delicately removed a speck of dust or something from its front lens. He then took a long look at the ram.

"Well, I have just made a reckless bet with myself," he said presently. "If those horns measure 15x37 inches or better, I will treat myself to another Alaska sheep hunt next year. If they go less, I'll stay home and work."

It figured to be a tough stalk. Since the ram had seen us, we would have to put terrain between him and us. Trying to Injun undetected from one bit of cover to another on the slope facing us would be wasted effort. The ram had spent his life watching the mountain's pitches. He knew every boulder and patch of vegetation. He knew where the shadows belonged. He would quickly spot us and beat it. So we went upriver a quarter-mile, turned into a side canyon, and began climbing the mountain's formidable east face. We came to a chockstone chimney, a four-foot-wide vertical cleft with boulders wedged in it. There was no alternate route. We worked around three boulders, and squeezed behind another. Then trouble clobbered us. Reaching up for a handhold, Bill dislodged a shale slab. It struck his head, knocking his hat off and cutting a gash in his cheek.

With sixty feet of space under him, Bill sagged against the chimney wall. His eyes were shut. Blood trickled down his face. And at the moment I couldn't help the guy. I was ten feet above him, hanging on with both hands. Then he looked up at me. "It's okay," he mumbled. "I've got a mighty hard skull. Let's get on up there and measure those sheep horns."

We topped the broken summit a half-hour later. There was an inch of snow here, with fresh sheep tracks in it. Shivering in an icy wind, we hastily took a look down the riverfront face. The turret-flanked ledge was empty. But off to its right, peering down toward our camp, stood a ram. We put our glasses on him. Bill groaned. From this distance, 150 yards, and from this angle, the head was small. I gave it 14x34 inches. Bill muttered sadly that there went next year's sheep hunt. He said he didn't get it, he had never made such a mistake. I understood his dismay. I knew he had spent a heap of time in museums guessing the dimensions of sheep horns. To keep his eye sharp he went around estimating the circumference of saplings. Once I had found him, tape in hand, squinting at the tent's stovepipe.

"Listen, that can't be the same ram," I said. "I think I know what happened. Come on, and be ready to shoot."

We went back to the tracks in the snow. They had been made by a large ram. He had come up from the riverfront side, and had gone west along the summit. Fifty yards in that direction, upwind, stood a huge red boulder. It hung on the brink of the Friday Creek drop-off. The ram's tracks appeared to end there. I glanced at Bill. He was ready.

So I threw a chunk of rock at the boulder. Our ram walked into view. Silhouetted against snow-topped peaks, he was magnificent. Bill's .270 banged. The ram took two steps, fell, and kicked himself over the rim. I ran after the animal. If he tumbled down that face, it might take us days to recover the trophy. Friday Creek Canyon lay down there, a ghastly piece of country. Well, I made a fast grab and got hold of the carcass as it was sliding off a rock flange into emptiness. Thankfully, I dragged it back to the summit.

Bill whipped out his steel tape. The horns averaged 15x38 inches. I was remembering Friday Creek Canyon's windy cliffs and hair-triggered rockslides when Bill slapped me on the back, his bloody face creased in a wide grin. "My friend, I just can't tell you how relieved I am," he said. I assured him that made two of us.

And then there was the dramatic climax of a Dall sheep stalk I put on with Walt Beecham above a nameless creek flowing northward off Mt. Deborah. It was a sullen, snow-threatening morning. We were four long days east of Healy railroad station, and during the night our ten horses had deserted us. We tracked the string up through timberline thickets to where the valley narrowed between saw-toothed ridges. Not a horse in sight. But across the creek, just below the last willows, a band of twenty-odd sheep was gathered on a blue-gray mudslide. They were eating the sunbaked mud. Several were crouched in tunnels that sheep had pawed or gnawed into the slide, mining the stuff. At least four of the rams had trophy heads. Obviously the place was a so-called mineral lick. I noted that deep-worn trails led to it.

"That's a trophy bonanza," Walt declared excitedly after surveying the scene with his glasses. "But I wouldn't want to shoot my ram right there on the lick. So make a suggestion."

Commendable of him. And I decided our best bet was the ridge top six hundred yards above the sheep. It was a cinch, I thought, the animals would climb when they got their fill of the presumably tasty mud. If they didn't, I could easily fetch them by rolling a few rocks. Scattered dry snowflakes were ghost-dancing on the wind when we began our climb. By the time we reached the crest, it was snowing good. We could no longer see the sheep. I told Walt I had better send some rocks down. But hardly had I got the words out when we heard shale clatter below us, then a fast drumming of hoofs. The sheep were arriving. Something, I gathered, had spooked them. Three ewes came plunging up the slope, shadow-shapes in the blowing snow. Then two rams appeared. Their horns looked heavy, that was all I could make out.

Walt laid his .250-3000 Savage on the leading ram, but didn't shoot. I guess he wasn't sure of his judgment, or else had concluded he could do better. The two rams fled past us and went out of sight. I could hear the rest of the sheep coming.

Then the wind blew a hole in the storm and we saw what had frightened the band. Our horses. Led by my black pinto saddle mount, the runaways were hobble-hopping down through the willows en route to camp. I suppose the snowfall had given them second thoughts. Then here came the sheep. Rams, ewes, and young stuff, making a panicky rush for the summit. But it was a miserable setup for judging heads. One ram went past us fifteen feet distant. I saw that his horns were full-curled and reasonably massive, and then he was gone. A ewe nearly ran over us. Then two rams came into view, and one had a terrific head. You can always tell the really heavy-horned rams by their gait. Even in reckless flight they travel tippytoe, balancing themselves. I nudged Walt, and pointed. He fired, thoughtfully holding behind the shoulder

101

so as not to bloody the cape. The ram fell twenty feet from us, stone dead.

Walt knelt at the carcass in the level-blowing snow. He produced a steel tape. The horns averaged 15¼x39 inches, a grand trophy. Up to a couple of minutes ago I had been plenty worried. Losing track of your horses at this time of year in these parts, with wolves and grizzlies around, was a disturbing matter. It would have been a long walk back to the railroad. So we were loaded with luck, and I said as much. Walt chuckled. "Yeah. You noticed it, huh?" He patted a slight bulge, a malformation, at the base of the ram's right horn. "This lucky nubbin, by gosh, gave us a good inch and a half on the tape." Clearly he had forgotten all about the horses.

Pete Donnelly, the sheep fan I told you about at the beginning of this account, made a comment about sheep. We had fired up cigarettes. We were sitting on a lichen-shaggy ledge alongside Pete's trophy kill. I was sweetening the edge of my knife. We watched the beat-up young ex-combatant ram and the six ewes make for the summit at their best speed. "They crave altitude," Pete said fondly. "One instinct dominates the whole aristocratic species. I mean no other creatures in the wilds are so doggoned single-minded."

Except sheep hunters.

Deadly Hunter
of the High Country

*Does the mountain grizzly
rate as the greatest trophy of all?*

"Comes competition, mister. It's a mountain grizzly," I said to young Paul Dalton, my current pilgrim, without lowering the 12X glasses. "He's in ambush. Sixty feet above the point caribou."

"Well, hooray," Paul said.

This was on a frosty September morning at the head of Cabin Creek, in Alaska's Tonzona Basin. Led by a ribby cow, the herd of around two thousand barren ground caribou was funneling down through timberline thickets onto the narrow creek flat. The point animals were 150 yards distant. I had already begun appraising heads. Then suddenly the lead cow spooked. She tried to turn the herd, but there wasn't room enough. So she put on speed. She was rolling her eyes at the brushy hillside.

I checked with the glasses, and in a moment spotted the grizzly. Crouched under some gaudy willows, he was staring down at the jam-packed caribou. Clearly he had meat in mind. He would weigh maybe 550 pounds. His pelt was dark brown except on the forehead and snout, which were blond-baldface. Paul took one look and brought up his .300 Weatherby Magnum. He was a couple of seconds too late. The grizzly had started his rush.

Plenty fast, he came off the slope in ten-foot bounds. His target was a chunky, white-maned bull. The bull saw him, but was so hemmed in he couldn't turn back. Desperate, he elected to fight. With his array of ivory-tipped war tines he looked fairly formidable at that. But the bear went straight in.

The shaggy assassin struck with a sledgehammer front paw, slamming the rack of antlers aside. His next wallop smashed down on the bull's neck. That one did it. Masses of caribou were streaming past. The bear roared continuously at them. Probably he had never before been so close to so much meat. Paul and I moved toward him. We had cut the distance to thirty yards when he saw us. He reared, chomping his jaws. Paul carefully shot him through the neck. Our baldface toppled across the bull's antlers and died—his shattered skull would not make a trophy, but we were alive and safe.

"Spectacular," Paul said when we had gone over to the kill, with caribou still trotting past. "Man, I claim the mountain grizzly is our No. 1 trophy animal. You agree?"

I said I would answer that later, over a pot of coffee, and got out my skinning knife. I was remembering a gallery of six sourdough grizzly hunters. They were guides, grizzly specialists. When I was a kid I had apprenticed myself to them. I wrangled horses. I backpacked. I lined river boats. In one long season I saw five mountain grizzlies taken by visiting sportsmen. I mean, I learned the business. By the time I was twenty-two, I knew one thousand miles of grizzly country. I had also learned to admire the mountain grizzlies. I admired them because they were colorful, dangerous, and dramatic. I was their fan.

Take the climax of a spring hunt I made in the Wood River country with iron-maned, green-eyed old Tex Cobb. I was the party's horse wrangler. Tex was guiding a lad named Jim Blake. . . .

It was a fancy bear, taffy-colored with cinnamon legs. Tex gave him four hundred pounds. When we sighted him with our glasses he was 650 yards distant, at the forks of Kansas Creek. He had found the carcass of a winterkilled moose buried in a snowdrift, and was feasting. It should have been an easy stalk. We had the wind, and the brush wasn't noisy. But weather fouled us up. Slate-gray clouds were drifting along the range shed, and the edge of one blanked the forks. We eased within sixty yards, then sat down to wait. We could hear the bear feeding. He crunched bones, he snuffled, he belched and broke wind.

At last the cloud thinned. You could make out the shine of snow-banks bordering the creek. Tex decided to move closer. A moment later we got a vague glimpse of the bear. But just then everything went haywire.

A pair of willow ptarmigan burst up ahead of us, squawking. The bear let out a startled *whowf-whowf*. We heard him run, then saw him. A mere shadow-shape, he was passing in front of us on the creek bank about one hundred feet distant. "Shoot," Tex said. "If you don't kill him, maybe you'll make him do something dumb."

Jim fired, and missed. I heard the slug glance off a boulder and hit a tree across the creek. Jim fired again and missed. Then the half-visible bear made a mistake. There was only scanty brush cover on our side of the stream, but on the opposite side alders came down to the water. The bear opted for them. To his right, in the murk, an ice bridge spanned the stream. He started across it. Of course the ice was sun-rotted. With a boom and splash it collapsed under his weight. We headed for the scene at a run. I figured the bear would climb the other bank, but Tex was pointing at some misty pussy willows on our side. They moved. The grizzly shouldered into view. He had changed his mind. He was going to battle us. Bawling, he charged. Jim brought up his .30-06 Winchester. (Almost every grizzly hunter I knew carried a .30-06.) He dropped the bear with a heart shot at twenty-five feet.

"They'll run and they'll fight. It keeps a man in suspense," Tex said. "And that, gents, is what makes grizzly hunting such a fabulous sport."

The mountain grizzly's exuberant sex habits often make stalking him a cinch. Take an episode that occurred during a spring hunt I made with tough, moon-faced Baldy Thomas at the headwaters of Montana Creek, in the Talkeetnas. Baldy was guiding a broker named Walt Ballard. I was backpacking for them. We hunted four days without seeing a bear. Then, early the fifth day, we sighted two sizable dark grizzlies high on the mountain above camp. They were engaged in a rut-period necking session.

The female, a hulking brute, was being coy. As we watched, she yielded to the boyfriend, then thought better of it and struggled free. He hauled off and belted her. She fled. He pursued and overtook her. They sat down on a patch of blueberry turf, gaz-

ing at each other. Walt was so eager he had a case of the shakes.
He had turned pale.

We made our climb. (Mountain grizzly hunters can expect
to do a heap of climbing. You sometimes see the bears higher
than sheep.) We came out on the brink of an alder-fringed shale
cliff. Our bears were now seven-hundred yards above us. As
we got out glasses, the female put on her act again.

She became affectionate, then broke free to swap ends
coquettishly. The male slugged her. She took off slantwise down
the mountain, with the male following. Their course, if they
held it, would bring them past us at close range. We knelt in
the alders. The bears came on, and went by seventy feet distant. Baldy said, "Take him." The pilgrim let go with his
Remington. Hair jumped from the bear's shoulder. He fell and
rolled. I believe Baldy had figured the alders would stop him.
They didn't. Still alive, bawling, he crashed through them. At
the cliff's edge he lodged against a boulder. With his rump hanging
in emptiness, he looked up at us and snarled. He tried to muscle
himself back onto safe ground. Walt shot him between the eyes
as he grabbed an alder with his teeth. The animal fell sixty feet
into a snowbank.

"Well, he was terrible as a Romeo," Baldy said. "But as a
trophy grizzly he has everything."

The mountain grizzly possesses a strong sense of curios-
ity, and many a trophy hunter is indebted to it. Consider the
happy conclusion of a hunt I made with the Watana Kid in the
Yanert country. The kid was guiding a gent named Tom Howard.
My job was to wrangle the party's ten horses. We went up Nenana
River and headed over Louis Creek Pass.

At the summit of the pass we encountered a handsome
yellowtip grizzly, but circumstances were against us. In the first
place, it was raining, a cold downpour with williwaw wind. In
the second place, right at the top of the pass there's a mean tundra
bog. I succeeded in putting our horses across without mishap.
But just as we reached solid ground, the yellowtip grizzly walked
into view, thirty yards dead ahead. Rearing up, he let out a snort
that panicked the horses. They stampeded back the way we had
come. Within seconds they were bogged to their briskets.

Worse, Tom didn't get a shot. The bear galloped to the
right, and Tom made a discovery. He found out that one o'clock
is about as far as a mounted right-handed rifleman can swing

louise
epina

Dudley Kquinten of the hights.

his gun clockwise. If he'd been a horseman, he would simply have kneed his mount around. As it was, the bear made a clean getaway.

The Kid was disgusted. With wind-driven rain whanging against our slickers, we unpacked the horses. We toted the freight and gear out of the bog. Then we helped the horses extricate themselves. By this time it was too late to move on so we pitched camp in the willows. I found a set of the bear's tracks. The front paw prints measured six inches across, thus, he was in the five-hundred-pound range. We followed his trail fifty yards over mushy caribou moss to a low bald knoll. He had climbed the knoll and lain there a while, presumably watching us. I remarked that he seemed to be a snoopy sonofagun.

"That's good," the Kid said. "If he's curious about us, he'll come back here for another look."

Next morning it was still raining. We climbed to a terrace on the downwind face of the pass, 250 yards from the tents. An hour dragged by, then we saw the grizzly. He was humping himself up the side of his lookout knoll. So the Kid had been right.

Tom rested his Winchester over a boulder. The bear had topped the knoll and was peering at the tents. Tom fired. I heard the softnose hit. The bear coughed, and tumbled off the knoll. He got up and lurched into a thicket. He stood there biting at his chest. Since we were above him, he had no cover. Tom fired again. The bear dropped. We went down to him. He was stone dead, shot twice through the lungs.

"A grand yellowtip with a bump of curiosity," Tom said. "Outsmarted by a perceptive guide."

There are no blasé grizzly hunters. The wonderful animals are too dynamic. They produce too many surprises. For instance, there was the eerie ending of an autumn hunt Tanana Stewart and I made with young Ross Bailey. This was on Knik River. Tanana had hired me as his assistant. We loaded our outfit into a sixteen-foot stampede boat and headed for the glacier, lining the craft—no motor.

The action began the third night. We were pounding our ears when a terrific uproar woke us. It came from the opposite bank, forty yards distant. Something screamed. Then there was a hoarse bellow and a lot of splashing. Then screeches, the sound of blows, and a strangled drowning wail. I had never heard anything like it. We surged out of our beds, rifles in hand. We went down to the water's edge, but the mysterious strife had ceased. The star-shadowed bank was again silent.

"Well, I know one of those performers was a grizzly," Tanana said. "Come daylight we'll slip over and see if he's still around."

Sunrise touched the peaks. We poled the boat across, scouting along the alder-shaggy cutbanks. I could smell bear and blood. I felt my neck hair lift. Then Tanana halted, pointing. Six feet below us lay the carcass of a yearling black bear, partly eaten. The torn pelt was wet. In the sand were grizzly tracks—big ones. I figured the youngster had swum the river and was waylaid when it came ashore. Tanana was nervous. He scanned the alders. He started to say something. At this point, behind us, a grizzly snarled. We swiveled as one person. The bear walked out of the brush twenty yards distant. He was a blond bravo, shanty-backed, in the six-hundred-pound range. Beside me Ross's Winchester crashed. He had held on the bear's head. The brute was too close, and had to be killed quick. I saw teeth and brains fly. The cannibal fell off the bank and landed with his ruined head in the water. Bubbles rose as he died.

"Gentlemen, that was something to be excited about the rest of my life," Ross said.

The mountain grizzly isn't a separate species. He is simply a grizzly that lives in high country. I think it's his habitat that makes him so hard-boiled. With no salmon runs up there to provide easy protein, he has to kill game or subsist on vegetation. He doesn't kill often enough, so he's always meat-starved.

Consider an ornery dark grizzly I met one fall on Carpenter Creek, in the Chugaches. I was backpacking again, this time for Baldy Thomas and a pilgrim named Dave Winters. Dave shot a Dall ram toward dusk the second day. I packed the trophy and a shoulder to camp. Next morning I returned for the rest of the meat. It was on a boulder-studded brushline slope under some cliffs.

Well, I came around a pile of rocks and saw the grizzly hunkered over the meat, ninety feet distant. I told him to beat it. He showed his teeth and uttered a high-decibel roar.

With my rifle on him, I tried to bluff the character. I whistled. I cussed him out. It didn't work. He popped his jaws and started toward me. This was the moment to shoot or depart. So I departed, at my best speed. Packers don't shoot trophy grizzlies, not if they want to keep on working. When I reached camp Baldy and

Dave were there. Baldy said they had found "message tree" sign. It showed that a good-size grizzly was hanging around. Sooner or later, he said, we'd catch up with him. I said let's make it sooner, because I knew exactly where to find the animal.

Well, the grizzly wasn't in sight. We halted sixty yards downwind from the place. We surveyed it with our glasses. The bear had heaped cloudberry turf over the meat and deposited dung on top as proof of ownership. I knew he hadn't gone far. In fact, I would have bet that he was closer to the meat than we were.

We waited five minutes, then Baldy clapped his hands together. That got results. Fifty feet beyond the meat cache stood a big granite boulder. The bear walked out from behind it. I gave him 450 pounds. He snorted. He tried the wind. Then he swaggered toward us. He was plumb confident. I could practically read his mind. He didn't think we amounted to much. He had hoorawed me off the mountain, so he figured all he had to do was get tough again and the three of us would run. Dave fired. Hit in the neck, the bear died with his snout rammed against the precious cache of meat.

"You can depend on 'em," Baldy said. "They allus put on a show."

But it was the wrangling jobs that kept me wary. Twice hard-case grizzlies had made passes at the horses. The last would-be horse-killer had come close to succeeding. I was working for redoubtable old Jack Filce. We were at the headwaters of the Dog Fork, west of Tonzona River, with a pilgrim named Sam Bowers. It was September. Early the fourth morning of the hunt we climbed a butte behind our camp to check the area with our glasses. Presently we sighted the grizzly. He came pigeon-toeing out of some brilliant dwarf cottonwoods on the river-bank. He was 150 feet downwind from the grass flat on which our eleven hobbled horses were loafing. He halted and stood gazing at them. Three of the horses, including the bell mare, were lying down. The bear didn't fool around. He was an operator. We were still sizing up his pelt when, surprise, he charged hellbent at the nearest horse.

"Take him if you can," old Jack said. "I make it six hundred yards."

The bell mare was alert. She saw the grizzly coming and scrambled up. The bronze Kentucky bell hanging from her neck clanged a wild alarm. That stopped the grizzly. To him apparently it was a fearsome sound. He actually skidded as he hastily veered aside into a willow clump. The panicked horses hobble-hopped out onto an open sandbar and huddled there. I watched Sam prepare to shoot. It was a pleasure because he was an expert. I knew he was an expert because we had shot with him on the Anchorage range. The moment we spotted the bear he set the telescope sight of his Springfield sporter. He then took a prone position, using the slingstrap. He slipped the safety latch. The grizzly had left the willows and was walking slowly toward the horses, considerably less suspicious. There was no wind down there. Sam fired. The grizzly spun, fell, rolled over, and lay motionless.

"Forty years I've hunted grizzlies," Jack said, "and I still get excited."

And then there was the busy windup of an autumn hunt I made with big Frank Lee in the Talkeetnas. We were at the head of Spruce Creek. Frank was shepherding young Pete Waring. He had hired me to backpack for them. We had set out this particular morning to scout some blueberry slopes above the glacier, but the visibility was lousy. First rain, then snow squalls. Around noon we gave up and headed for camp.

Ten minutes later Pete was involved with a grizzly. We rounded a rimrock at the edge of camp, and saw that our tent was down. It had been torn down. Items of grub, gear and personal plunder were scattered everywhere. Then I saw movement behind an alder thicket a hundred feet distant. The grizzly stepped into view. In the blowing snow he looked enormous. He was a palomino, long-legged and high-humped. Between his jaws he held a slab of bacon.

Pete's Remington blasted.

The grizzly jerked back onto his haunches. He dropped the bacon and let out a bawl. I saw that his lower jaw was smashed. Whirling, he loped erratically through camp and into a small island of spruce blowdown. Pete fired again as the bear went out of sight. He didn't score. I saw the slug rip splinters off a windfall. Frank was cussing. I knew why. He had helped me pack our outfit thirty miles, and so took the bear's raid as an affront as well as an injury. Motioning us to follow, he went around to the upwind side of the blowdown. Here he made sign-talk for silence. Our scent was now blowing directly to the wounded bear. I heard the animal snarl. A minute passed. Then he gave a roar. As, I suppose, Frank had figured, the pressure was too much. Claws rattled on bark as the bear reared to peer over a windfall. He'd had to find out what we were doing. Pete shot him in the forehead.

"That mean no-good camp-wrecking S.O.B.," Frank said as we examined the kill, "sure is a first-class, eye-pleasing trophy grizzly, ain't he?"

Back to the beginning. Paul Dalton said he thought the mountain grizzly was our No. 1 trophy animal and he wanted to know if I agreed. The answer is yes. An almighty lot of hunters like the mountain grizzly's style and like the lofty country he inhabits. Of course all bears are great, but it seems to me the mountain grizzly rates superlatives. I submit that he's tops.

You Can't Beat Luck

*"You can't beat luck. Without it, gents, a man
just don't get anywhere at all."*

"**W**hatever the hell those loudmouthed wolves are chasing,
it's swung our way," said Baldy Thomas, my sourdough trapping partner, as we hastily helped bunch the eight trail-weary
Okanagan packhorses in the smother of a freak September
snowstorm. "So let's lay us an ambush where yonder point
of spruce timber sticks out, huh? With luck we oughta
bushwhack two, three of the cusses, by gosh, afore they know
what's going on."

"Pour it to 'em gents," said old Frank Lee, the contract
freighter. "Me, I'll stay here and keep the horses company.
Maybe that way I won't jinx your project too much." He
sounded plumb dispirited. I'll explain presently what his
problem was.

Baldy and I sprinted to the point of spruces. Two cow
moose came galloping downwind toward us, forty yards distant when we sighted them. Then behind the cows appeared
a wide antlered bull, with five hysterically yammering wolves
working on him. I saw at a glance that it was, as usual, a
family pack of wolves. Four long-yearlings headed by their
mother. I realized, too, that they were out for sport more
than meat. I mean, if they had been simply hungry they would
have attacked one of the cows. An easier, less dangerous target.
The boss bitch, a silver-gray beast who would weigh prob-

ably 130 pounds, was leaping at the bull's rump. She was trying to geld him, a charming practice of female wolves when in a sportive mood. Her husky offspring were busily chopping at the bull's flanks and hamstrings. Some spectacle.

I brought up my .375 magnum to deal with the frolicsome gray bitch.

This was taking place shortly after midafternoon in the Tonzona Valley, on the north slope of the Alaska Range, 150 wilderness miles southwest of Broad Pass. We had just arrived here. Old Frank had freighted us in. We brought twelve hundred pounds of grub and gear, and aimed to build a permanent headquarters and put in the winter harvesting fur—foxes, marten, and wolves. The snowstorm had struck two hours ago. It was fifteen days early, and a dire threat to old Frank because if it continued through tonight it would block the passes behind us. There was no alternate route back to Broad Pass and horses couldn't winter here. The string would starve before Christmas, if we didn't mercifully shoot them. Well, we had come down off the eastern escarpment looking for a cabin site. Baldy, mighty particular, voted against several fair locations. Then we heard the wolves' crazy blood-chorus.

Before I could let go a shot at the gray bitch, the two cow moose charged headlong into the timber thirty feet distant. Seeing us, they halted boggle-eyed, squarely in our line of fire. I got a brief look past them at the oncoming bull. His left hind leg was now dragging. If the huge dope had put up a battle in the first place, he would have been a match for the wolves. But the rutting period was in full swing, and I guess he thought he had to keep up with the fleeing cows or lose them. At any rate, he and the wolves plunged into the timber one hundred feet crosswind from us. Our cover was good. They didn't spot us. We ran after them. Half a minute later we sighted them again in a brush-rimmed glade. The bull was bucking in a circle. His mouth hung open.

Baldy's .30-06 Remington banged. A yellow yearling had its teeth set in the bull's right hamstring. Shot through the ribs, it fell to the snow, wailed, and died. The bull was executing a three-legged buckjumping turn with the gray bitch hanging on. Her lean, shaggy body was horizontal in the air. I fired a split second after Baldy. There was no chance to use the sights. I just pointed the rifle and pulled. Hair flew from the gray bitch's shoulder. Swell. But although the 300-grain softnose had exploded her heart and lungs, she held on after she was dead. Several seconds. Then her jaws opened and centrifugal force imparted by the desperately whirling bull slung her ten feet upside down against a spruce trunk. But that was too late to help the bull much. He lurched a few yards in the direction the cows had taken. Then his wolf-slashed right hind leg likewise buckling, he fell heavily.

Baldy fired again, and a brown yearling somersaulted and lay motionless. The other two were running at the edge of a willow thicket. One was coal-black, with fancy tan shoulder patches. I cut down on him. The big slug hit him at the base of his tail in the middle of a bound and boosted him, as though jet-propelled, clean out of view into the snowy thicket. The fourth member of the family had made a getaway. Baldy started to take his trail, but gave up. In this lousy visibility the odds against were too high. I thumbed replacement shells into the magnum. Then we heard scrambling sounds behind us. It was the bull. Propped on his front legs, he was trying to follow the cows.

I shot him behind the ear.

Well, the point of spruces was a first-rate headquarters site. Even Baldy liked it. There was cabin timber and beetle-killed dry snags for firewood. And a sizable spring. Presumably a view up and down the peak-fenced valley. We went back and helped old Frank bring the horses. We unpacked, pitched the 10x12 tent, and set up the Yukon stove. Then we dressed out the bull and pelted the four wolves. The bull was fat. He hadn't been chasing cows long. I estimated the wolf skins and the bounty would bring us $500. The early mountain dusk fell. We hunkered around the glowing stove, drinking coffee. It was pleasant, but the snowstorm hadn't lessened. Thus old Frank was in big trouble, whereas Baldy and I were sitting pretty. "Luck is mysterious," old Frank said sadly. "Right now I wish I didn't believe in it. But hell, that's impossible. You ever know anybody who didn't believe in luck?"

I said I knew a stalwart who had tried not to. That was my colleague Tanana Stewart. He had been wont to argue that judgment and timing were everything. Don't talk to him about luck. But he changed his mind. What caused him to change it was the fantastically lucky climax of a caribou hunt we made in the Chedolothna country, northeast of here, with a middle-aged broker type named Dan Reed, from San Francisco. I was just a kid then, wrangling horses for Tanana. . . .

A wrangler sleeps with his ears tuned for trouble. Along toward false dawn I heard a horse snort. Then hobble chains jingled, and shod hoofs clattered on the creek bars. Our string of eleven Walla Walla cayuses was hightailing it to camp. Spooked, apparently. I pulled on pants and boots, picked up my rifle, and stepped outside the tent. Tanana and the pilgrim hadn't stirred. Wind moaned through the frost-killed grass. A fat moon floated above the white crest of Mt. Foraker. We had pitched the two tents in an orchard-like stand of gnarled cottonwoods. Above us a nameless pass cut back into an east-west buttress of the range. I maneuvered for a better look up the pass and spotted the horses. They were 150 yards distant, behaving in a peculiar manner. Led by Paint, the pinto bell mare, they floundered across the creek. Then they halted to look back. Came on. Halted again to look back.

Beyond the horses the pass made a tight bend. The cliff-shadowed alder thickets there seemed to be in motion, flowing down toward camp. Equally weird in that area, moonlight had begun to reflect from many shifting bone-white surfaces. Took me a while to figure out that I was watching a mass of caribou. The great North Slope herd marching down through moonlight and shadow. Well, such is luck. We had waited here five days for the migration to show up off the west end of the buttress spur. Now it was coming in behind us. At night! Holy suffering. For millennia traveling herds had detoured around the spur. They had worn trails into solid rock there. But tonight for some reason a lead cow had broken with ancient custom to pioneer this short-cut route through the pass.

I woke up Tanana and the pilgrim.

Barefoot, clad in red underwear drawers, clutching their rifles, they hastened out of the tent. They sized up the situation, which by now was right dramatic. Proceeded by the hobble-hopping horses, three or four thousand caribou were advancing downwind through the moonlit cottonwoods. And more coming around the bend. The sounds of their pounding hoofs and clicking ankle joints, their rattling forest of antlers, blended into a roar like that of an avalanche. The trail-blaz-

ing lead cow sighted camp when she was one hundred yards
distant, and tried to turn the herd. But she didn't have room
enough. I saw that the animals were going to split around us.
Of course it was impossible in this tricky light to choose a trophy
head. Tanana didn't even try. His attention was on the horses.
I knew him well. He wasn't going to be left afoot if there
was any way to prevent it.

The guy didn't ask me to catch up a wrangling horse. Instead,
stealing my thunder, he snatched a riata from the rigging pile,
and ran to intercept Paint.

Well, the pinto mare, an expert with hobbles, was thirty yards
ahead of the other horses. I could tell that this was one time
she didn't intend to be caught. There is a strange affinity between horses and caribou. They intrigue and excite each other.
At the moment Paint was pacing the vast North Slope herd. A
wonderful experience. Maybe the high point of her life. Consequently, she had no time for us. What's more, she knew exactly how good Tanana was with a riata—barely so-so. He had
built a big California loop and was flailing it around his head.
When the mare was some twenty feet distant, he made his cast.
And missed. Paint had ducked her head and dodged. The hondo
smacked against her shoulder. The hardtwist loop fell to the
ground. But Paint had dodged blindly. With a booby trap dead
ahead, she had kept her eyes riveted on Tanana.

I yelled a warning, which was sort of dumb.

We had pitched the cook tent with fore and aft guy ropes.
Paint hit the front guy head on. She weighed eleven hundred pounds and was departing full tilt. The cotton rope parted
with a whiplash crack. The tent and its pole frame collapsed.
As for Paint, she stumbled but kept her feet and hurtled on.
Tanana should have dropped the matter right then. We had
other things to worry about. But he was bullheaded. Sema-
phoring his arms, cursing, he tried to stop Paint's ten trailmates.
But nope. They kept coming. I suppose with the North Slope
herd at their rumps, they were afraid to stop. Anyway, they
had a decision to make—run over Tanana or the fallen tent.
They chose the tent. Well, our entire commissary was under the spread of canvas. So long, outfit.

Tanana gazed at the wreckage. His lips moved, but no words
came out. Caribou were now slamming past on both sides of
us. He ignored them. At last he found his voice, or part of it.

"If you two don't mind," he said in a strained whisper, "Let's not have any baloney about bad luck. Please. We jest happened to be camped in a damned busy place tonight, that's all."

He and the pilgrim dressed. The last of the caribou drifted past. Slowpokes, cripples, and ribby old-timers. Wolfbait. I built a fire and managed to find some coffee and a kettle that would hold water. I let the coffee boil black. By the time we finished drinking it, a wild-rose dawn was silhouetting the peaks. We took out after the herd. Before we had covered a quarter-mile, we met the horses. Paint was bringing the string back to camp—surprise! But the long tilted prairie below the horses was empty. Not a caribou in sight. The herd had gone on down into the endless lowland spruce forests. Vanished. The pilgrim sighed. I felt sorry for him. He was a likable customer. But I also felt sorry for Tanana. Because if the frontier public ever heard about this episode, it would hurt. Thousands of caribou in camp, and no trophy taken. A belly laugh. A prize camp-fire gossip item.

Paint whickered.

She had halted, head high, ears pricked forward, snuffling the wind. She was looking up into the pass. We whirled as one man. Tanana gave a startled grunt. The pass was again jammed with caribou. I told myself that the age of miracles was still with us. Because this was another section of the North Slope herd. Some hazard, or error of navigation, had delayed the animals. But the lead cow was bent on following the new route. She came into view, saw us, and put on the north's most thrilling wildlife show. No matter how many times a man has seen it, it's tops. She took the herd past us at a dead run. Then she turned and brought it back, as though charging. Finally, getting our scent, she veered off. One of the point bulls carried a grand set of antlers. Tall, branchy and heavy beamed. Twin brow shovels. Tanana said, "Take him." The pilgrim knelt. His .270 Winchester crashed. The bull flinched, and fell dead.

"All right, I'm a believer," Tanana said with feeling as we headed for the kill, me leading Paint, the other horses following. "I admit that was absolutely 100 percent luck. In fact, by gad, I am gonna start carrying a rabbit's foot. Soon as I get hold of one. And I can lick the man that laughs at me. . . ."

Now Old Frank reached over and stoked the stove. It was still snowing. No sign of letup. We had eaten supper, and the horses had come to camp. They stood watching us, eyes shining in the light of a kerosene lantern I had hung inside the tent entrance. Good, honest horses. A far piece from the Okanagan hills. Not deserving the tragic fate fast shaping up for them. "Speaking of luck charms," Baldy said. "One spring over in the Wood River country I shepherded a grizzly hunter that was plumb loaded with 'em. A long-geared kid named Walt Evans. From Butte. He carried a rabbit's foot in his pocket. He sported a mule-shoe belt buckle. He wore a ring set with imitation-jade, four-leaf clovers. Boys, you never saw such a confident pilgrim. He purely figured he had luck hogtied.

"Until we met a certain whopper silvertip grizzly.

"It was a surprise meeting. We're plodding down the north bank of Cody Creek with seven Yakima packhorses. It was a purty June morning. Walt is riding beside me. Having bummed the makings, he's building a smoke. The wrangler, a Denna Injun named Tom Talkeetna, is back at the rear of the string. Suddenly my coyote-dun gelding, Pilot, gives a warning snort. About two seconds later three grizzlies bust out of some alders on our left, crosswind, heading away from us. A straw-colored yearling is in the lead. Right behind it is this monster silvertip. Behind the silvertip comes a medium-size bear the color of molasses taffy. I recognize the situation. It's a mating season squabble. You know, suitor giving junior the heave-ho so he can make time with mamma. And mamma resenting it. The oaf can't treat her junior that way. I tell Walt to take the silvertip. Drop him before he reaches cover.

"'Watch me,' he says confidently.

"Boys, it's a shame. You wouldn't think so many outrageous things could happen to a guy in such a short time. He throws away the half-made cigarette, and grabs for his .300 Weatherby Magnum. Then cusses bitterly. The wind has blown the discarded Durham back into his eyes and nose. But he's game. Sneezing, eyes watering, he tries to line the sights. The bears are two hundred feet distant, making for a blowdown tangle. The kid shoots, and misses. A gun-shy packhorse spooks. That spooks the rest of the string. Walt's steeldust bawls and comes unglued just as the kid fires a second time. I see the slug knock the top out of a spruce two hundred yards down the creek. Well, the kid is no bronco-twister. He latches onto the safety knob when the steeldust stampedes, sunfishing, amongst the packhorses. It don't help any. Tossed, he lands on his face. He staggers up. A pack pannier belts him. Down he goes again.

"The three grizzlies have disappeared into the mess of wind-thrown timber.

"Well, I hit the ground to check on the kid. He shoves me away. So I mount up and hasten to lend Tom Talkeetna needed assistance. We bunch the string and straighten a couple of packs. If the diamonds hadn't been screwed down extra tight under the corners of Humboldt pads, we'd have had outfit scattered far and wide. The kid joins us. His nose is skinned and bleeding. He's maybe gonna have a pair of black eyes. He comes up gimpy on one side. Tom Talkeetna, muttering in Denna, fetches his hat. 'Okay, so my collection of luck junk didn't work for me,' the kid growls. 'So why carry it around?' He limps down to the creek. As we watch, he throws his four-leaf clover ring, his mule-shoe belt buckle, and his rabbit foot into a riffle. Then he comes back with a hand stuck out to bum the makings. 'Now we'll see what happens,' he says. 'Which way did that silvertip go, huh?'

"We camp at the mouth of Cody Creek. Two days later we locate the taffy-colored sow bear. She's out on a Wood River bar digging Indian potatoes. By herself. She hasn't spotted us, and she's good bait. So we tie the horses and take a stand downwind of her in some willows. A half-hour passes. Twice the bear has reared up to gaze at a granite boulder forty yards out from us. Now a pair of goldeneye ducks whip down the bars, and when they reach said boulder they abruptly flare. Which is hint enough. I motion the kid to get ready. Then I bounce a rock off the boulder. Jackpot. There's a windy *whoosh*. Into view jumps our silvertip. He's been snoozing while his sow-friend foraged. He bristles. He rolls his head, sampling the wind. Then he gallops for the nearest cover—straight at us. Be doggoned if he ain't looking back over his shoulder. The kid's .300 blasts. The bear goes down fifty feet from us, finished."

We turned in. Nobody felt like talking anymore. Grim trouble on our minds. The packstring. Snow would now be drifted brisket deep in the passes. The horses were trapped. Old Frank would have to shoot them, borrow webs from us, and walk 150 miles back to Broad Pass and the railroad. At least that was the prospect. But sometime toward morning a wind gust woke me. I became aware of a drumming sound on the tent roof. Hallelujah—rain—with williwaw wind behind it. Better than a chinook, it will melt the snow in no time. Old Frank stumbled past me into the downpour. The horses were out there. When I got the lantern lit I saw that old Frank had an arm over the neck of his pet saddle mount. I heard him say:

"You can't beat luck. Without it, gents, a man just don't get anywhere at all."

Those Killer Tramp *Tigres*

"...there are two, and you have
only a few hours to kill them..."

"**F**or stock-killer *tigres*, that pair has made a mighty short run,"
I said to eighteen-year-old Jesus Bacasegua, a *yanqui* lad who
had been assigned to me as my assistant this hunt. "It must be
a trick of some kind. Maybe they figure on killing some dogs."

"Don't worry, *Señor*," the kid said. "Your old boss dog
Loba is too clever for them."

This was late of a cold, rain-threatening December afternoon near Tecolote Spring, in the Sierra Madre of southern Sonora.
We had just ridden hell-for-leather down through oak brush to
the junction of two nameless peak-shadowed valleys. My six
cat hounds were two hundred yards ahead, crosswind, bawling
that they had the *tigres* bayed. I dismounted and got out my
glasses. The dogs were bunched on the gravel floor of rock-
walled dry wash. Only one *tigre* was in sight. It stood posed
theatrically fifteen feet above the dogs at the brink of the north
rim, snarling down at them. A handsome, heavy-shouldered brute,
it obviously was the male of the outlaw pair. I gave him 240
pounds. Perhaps he sensed he was being observed. At any rate,
he suddenly crouched behind a windy fringe of *zacaton* grass.
That left only the top of his shoulders and the front half of his
head visible.

I cut down on the weaving grass, tentatively, with my .30-
30 Winchester saddle gun. Nope. It was too much of a gambling shot. I was pretty sure I couldn't make a clean kill, not

with iron sights, in a crosswind. And I sure didn't want to risk dropping the cat, wounded, amongst the dogs. But what the heck, I told myself, there was no hurry. He wasn't going anywhere. I would ride in closer and deal with him. But as I swung back into the saddle, I thought I saw a flicker of movement on the opposite—the south—rim. I raised the glasses again, to check.

What I saw was the beginning of tragedy. Loba, my veteran black *xoloitzcuintli*-bluetick pack leader, had prudently backed away from the *tigre*, clear across the forty-foot-wide wash, halting under the south wall. Loba was a first-class tactician. She had hunted all six species of Mexican cats—*tigres*, lions, ocelots, margays, bobcats and jaguarundis—and was still hale and active probably because she had always managed to keep the odds in her favor. If yonder *tigre* came soaring down off the rim, she now had room to maneuver. Her five tough young Red Walker helpers had stayed obediently on her flanks. They trusted her. They thought she was wonderful. After all, she had brought them up. But, unfortunately, this time Loba had made a grave mistake. She had underestimated the pair of cats. And so had I. When I put the glasses to my eyes, I saw the female *tigre* materialize on the grassy rim directly above the dogs.

"Santa Guadalupe de Tayopa," Jesus groaned. He hadn't needed glasses.

I didn't have a prayer of stopping the cat. She took one quick look over the rim to locate the dogs, and sprang. She landed on one Walker and snagged another with the claws of a front paw. I hated to watch, but I did. She expertly killed the first dog by biting through his neck vertebrae. Then she set her teeth in the belly of the other dog, and as he screamed and struggled, tore him open from crotch to brisket with a jerk of her head. I still couldn't shoot. Loba was slashing at the killer's rump. The remaining three Walkers were bounding in and out, trying to get past the cat's deadly paws. It was too chancy. Four-to-one I would have downed a dog. So I turned my attention to the north rim, with the idea of clobbering the male cat before he hunted cover. But he must have anticipated that. His elegant polka-dotted rear end was just disappearing into a brush clump. I never got the sights on him.

"We haven't accomplished much of anything up to now, boy," I said. "But wait."

I touched my mount with the spurs. I was riding an eleven-hundred-pound gelding—the color of a sandhill crane, with black mane, tail and ears—named Amigo. Sierra folks say that a *tigre*-hunting man is only as good as his boss dog and his saddle mount. So I was lucky. Because Amigo, like Loba, was one of the best. He grunted, and I saw the white of his eye as he glanced back at me. Then he lined out with the speed of a goosed antelope. In most parts, shooting from the back of a running horse is a lost skill. But down here, a few of us still keep in practice. The female *tigre* had fought through the dogs and was loping toward a patch of *huisache* brush below the wash. I kneed Amigo a bit to the right, so that the *tigre* was 15 degrees left of his head. I waited till we were on fairly smooth ground. Then I dropped the spliced *vaquero* reins, laid the Winchester on the cat, and fired.

Practice paid off. The 150-grain softnose wrecked the dog-killer's left front leg. But she was only a few feet from the *huisache* brush. Before I could jack another shell into the chamber, she reached the thicket and went out of view.

I skidded Amigo to a halt at the downwind edge of the brush, and stepped off. Loba came to meet me, ears flattened, moaning. She was pleading guilty. I picked her up in my arms and told her to take it easy. As for the dead Walkers, the buzzards and the ants would attend to them.

The kid came pounding up on his big-boned buckskin mule, and we surveyed the thicket. It was circular, about sixty feet across, with a sizable red lava boulder sticking up near its center. Loba and her crew had made no move to follow the cat into the brush. They knew better. But it was needful to discover the assassin's location, so I asked the kid to probe the thicket with some rocks. He began by bouncing a couple of heavy ones off the lava boulder. It was a good hunch. At his second pitch, brush shook and the cat uttered a startled roar. He must have caromed the rock smack onto her. The kid immediately followed up with a barrage of rocks. The cat couldn't take it. She screeched, and then here she came.

She wasn't charging the kid or me. It was the dogs she was after. She busted headlong out of the brush fifty feet from us, and made a three-legged bound at Loba. She missed. Loba was too fast for her. Then a Walker chopped at one of the cat's hind legs. She pivoted and struck, claw-raking the side of his face. It staggered him, but he was a warrior by instinct and breeding, and he bored in, raging. She hit him again, then got him by the throat with her teeth and shook him. Blood sprayed. Another dead Walker. I was moving toward her, waiting for an open shot. She certainly saw me, but I guess I didn't dismay her any. I got the impression that the cat knew she was doomed and only wanted to kill and mangle some more dogs before she checked out. She jumped at Loba again, and I caught her in midair, through the shoulders. She fell on her side, and when she twisted around, roaring at me, I shot her between the eyes.

Well, I thumbed shells into the Winchester, then sat on a rock and sweetened the edge of my skinning knife. The cat was big, as female *tigres* come, around 170 pounds. Her pelt, beautifully prime, had an unusual glossy sheen. The kid was carrying the Walker casualty to a busy anthill he had spotted. Thunder boomed over the peaks. Pink lightning forked down and hit an oak tree across the valley. We had a weather deadline, and time was running out.

This hunt had begun twenty-six hours ago in the town of Huatabampo, over on the Mayo River, with an urgent request from my moon-faced, two-hundred-pound friend Don Rafael Sandoval, proprietor of the vast Owl Head Ranch. I was in town loafing, giving myself, Amigo and the dogs a rest. Don Rafael had just come to my room in the Rincon del Mayo Hotel. He had the kid with him.

"*Compadre*, we have an emergency," he stated with no preamble. "This *yanqui* boy works for a bee-tree hunter, and yesterday was camped alone at Tecolote Spring. Some of my cattle were hanging around there. During the night two tramp *tigres* made a raid on them. They killed a heifer and the best white-face bull I owned. The bull's name was Pancho the Great. I paid 10,000 *pesos* for him. *Compadre*, please go to the spring at once with your dogs. Destroy those tramp *tigre cabrones*, and bring me their skins and skulls."

"How do you know they are tramp *tigres*?" I asked.

"They have to be. I was born on that range. I have lived there all my life. I personally know that there hasn't been a resident *tigre* at Tecolote Spring since 1945. Where the two tramp stock-killers came from is a mystery of *El Diablo*. But they must be killed *pronto*. You didn't hear the radio weather forecast this morning, huh? Well, we are going to have rain.

Tomorrow or the next day. You know what that means. The *tigres* will no longer be tied to water holes. Their scent will be washed out. They will simply vanish, and perhaps raid the length of the state. *Compadre*, this boy rode hard to inform me about the raid. He will return with you, as your wrangler, camp-tender, cook, whatever you want him to do. Draw on me for anything else you need, ha?"

"I just had a thought," I said. "The surest way to win popularity in this country is to own a pack of trained cat hounds."

For those who haven't hunted big cats south of the border, I'd better explain what a tramp *tigre* is. Most Mexican *tigres*, perhaps eighty percent of them, are dedicated resident homebodies. They spend their entire lives in an area of from two to three square miles. The others, the tramps, devote their lives to wandering. They cover astonishing distances. They cross deserts and mountain chains, and ford major rivers. Tramp *tigres* have been killed in California, Arizona, New Mexico, and Texas. One was shot far down on the Baja Peninsula, almost six hundred miles from the nearest *tigre* range. Inevitably, a few tramp *tigres* turn stock-killer, and due to their wide experience, are most difficult to take out of circulation. A hunt for one of them can become as complicated as a chess game.

Well, the kid and I hit the Sierra trail that afternoon, and rode straight through, arriving at Tecolote Spring shortly before sunup. The spring is situated on a cottonwood flat under a tall, dark mesa. As this was a dry year, it was the only water around. The next chance at water, a year-round seep, was in a canyon eight miles to the north, if you knew how to find it. We cooked and ate, slept three hours, then made a cast with the dogs. It was late afternoon when we jumped the *tigres*. I have told you what happened. We now skinned the female *tigre* and gutted her carcass for dog food, then headed back to the spring with our plunder.

We had, according to Sierra custom, camped two hundred feet back from the water. At dusk we brought in the saddle mounts and the four packhorses, and picketed them. I chained the Walkers, but put Loba on leash. Then we went over to the upwind side of the thirty-foot-long, grass-bordered spring pond, and took a stand with our backs against a dense scrub-oak thicket.

I had a Browning Auto 12, buckshot loaded, across my lap. Loba was stretched out beside me. She had refused to eat, grieving,

I suppose for the dead Walkers, and maybe sore at herself. At eleven o'clock a bright full moon climbed above the mesa. Lightning flashed in the northwest. I could smell rain on the wind. Our deadline was crowding us. But somewhere out there in the night the male *tigre* also had a deadline, a grim one, and was figuring his chances to survive it.

By now he was plenty thirsty. At least sixteen hours had passed since he'd had access to water. You hear a lot of campfire speculation as to how much and what kind of pressure it would take to make a *tigre* become a man-killer. It could well be, I thought, that we would learn the answer to that before morning. We didn't talk. We just sat there, *serapes* over our shoulders, and watched the moonlit pond. A few minutes after one o'clock, Loba stood up, a growl rumbling in her chest. She was staring across the pond, downwind. She had heard or seen something. I handed her leash to the kid, and walked toward the water. I was wearing moccasins. The grass underfoot made no sound. Ahead of me loomed a big wide-crowned cottonwood. I put my back against the tree and waited. I could see every foot of the pond's circumference. I figured the *tigre* was aware that I could. I heard Loba growl querulously. She thought she ought to be with me.

A half-hour passed. I was analyzing some black shadow masses across the pond when a brilliant flash of lightning illumined the scene. It gave me a split-second look at the *tigre*. He was one hundred feet beyond the water, under a gnarled silk-cotton tree, gazing straight at me, showing his teeth in a snarl. I came up fast with the Browning, but my eyes were dazzled and there was nothing left to shoot at over there, anyway. Nothing visible except inky shadows and puddles of moonlight. Some two minutes later, the *tigre* roared. A savage sound with a heap of decibels in it. The cat had swapped positions in a hurry. He was now forty yards off to my left. The Walkers set up a wild clamor. Horses snorted, and fought the picket line. Somewhere upwind I heard a buck deer take off, his antlers rattling on the brush.

I went back and sat down between the kid and Loba. The kid had been covering me, as best he could, with a .30-30 Don Rafael had loaned him. "There's no reason for being hush-hush," I said. "The *tigre* knows we are here. He's probably had us pinpointed for hours. In the circumstances, I'd be interested in hearing how the *tigres* killed Pancho the Great, and how come you were camped here alone. Don't spare the details. I need to understand that cat."

"*Pues*, as Don Rafael explained," the kid said, "I work for a bee-tree hunter. A mountain *hombre* called El Panal. Last week he runs out of tobacco. So he loads our stock of wild honey onto a packhorse, and heads for town. He says he'll be back in four days, but I know that's only talk. He'll stay in town till his money is gone. Well, the second evening I'm here alone I start feeling spooky, like I'm being watched. But I can't believe it's so, because nobody spies on a *yanqui*. Not in these mountains, anyway. I sack down, still feeling spooky, and around ten o'clock I find out what's been watching me. I am awakened by the most hair-raising sounds I ever hear. Roars, screams, screeches, grunts, yowls, and wails. Takes me a moment to realize that I'm listening to a couple of *tigres*. They are on that hillside over there under those oak trees, and they are coming toward me.

"Except for a knife, I am unarmed. We had a gun, a muzzleloader, but El Panal took it with him.

"I pull on my pants and boots, and look for a safer place. Sure, I know. Everybody says that *tigres* aren't man-killers. But maybe, I think, these *tigres* are different. Why gamble? The likeliest refuge I can see is the twenty-foot granite outcrop behind camp. So I sprint over there and climb to the top. The moon has risen, giving me a good view of the countryside. Out in the *grama* grass meadow below the spring I make out this small bunch of Don Rafael's Owl Head cattle. Around thirty head. They are on their feet, scared, moving toward the spring. The *tigres* are still sounding off, and presently I sight them. They come bounding out of the tree shadows, one chasing the other. The pursuit ends in the moonlit open space 150 feet from my perch on the outcrop. Both *tigres* crouch, screaming. Then they spring together and make wicked swipes with their paws. I figure that in about ten seconds there'll be blood and guts all over the ground.

"But surprise. It's all a noisy act. Instead of tearing each other apart, the spotted characters all at once mate. They are honeymooners. I have to sit there on the outcrop watching them perform for twenty minutes. *Señor*, if only I'd had a gun.

"Well, their mating business taken care of, the *tigres* drift down toward the meadow. I suppose the cow-brutes wind them. Anyway, the bunch panics. They snort and beller, tossing their heads. A calico steer lights out at a run for the spring. The others follow. They hit the water with an almighty splash and keep coming, up through the cottonwoods, to the opening where I'm camped. A big red bull—Pancho the Great, the ten thousand-*peso* bull—and a heifer are bringing up the rear.

"Pancho isn't in any hurry. I figure he didn't want to run in the first place, but was outvoted. The heifer, I guess, is staying behind only to keep him company. His *compañera*. But they are innocents. Because I now see the *tigres* loping through the cottonwood shadows after them, closing in fast. The female *tigre* is leading. She races alongside the heifer, and roars. The heifer tries to dodge.

"But the animal has had it. She's fifteen seconds from death. The *tigre* turns with her, and jumps onto her back. I see the cat reach forward, hook the heifer's nose, and yank her head around. At the same time she bites into the heifer's neck vertebrae. The heifer wheels over in a somersault, dead.

"Then, *Señor*, the *tigre* does something fabulous. My father told me that he once saw a *tigre* carry the carcass of a full-grown Spanish mule four hundred yards uphill to a cave. A friend of his, the famous *yanqui* tracker Buitimeo, had what seemed an even stranger story. He claimed he found sign proving that a *tigre* killed a fair-sized wild burro, one weighing maybe 350 pounds, and carried it more than a mile to its den in the side of a *barranca*. Many times I have heard our *yanqui* hunters say that if *tigres* have a choice, they always kill big animals but not bigger than they can carry. Well, this female tramp *tigre* I am watching, now takes hold of the dead heifer's neck with her teeth, heaves the carcass over her shoulders, and heads for the timber with it. The ground is rough and boulder-strewn, and the heifer weighs at least five hundred pounds, but the *tigre* hustles right along. This I am seeing with my own eyes. It must be a fact, *Señor*, that for its weight our Mexican *tigre* is the strongest beast in the animal kingdom.

"But you asked me about Pancho the Great. If Pancho had kept going and not tried to be a big-shot fighting bull, he probably would still be alive. But he sees his *compañera* heifer pulled down, and smells her blood. It makes him *loco*. He bellows and paws the ground. Then he charges the female *tigre*. But he don't get to her. The male *tigre* is standing in the shadow of that lone *chalate* tree over there at the edge of the opening. When Pancho starts his charge, the cat goes to meet him. Now I have heard people declare, *Señor*, that the domestic bull is the most dangerous animal on the continent. And of a truth, this Pancho is formidable. He weighs more than fifteen hundred pounds. He is young, active, and brave. Naturally, he is powerful. But the people who are awed by the domestic bull, *Señor*, ought to see a *tigre* in action.

"The cat streaks across the opening, lets Pancho lumber past him swinging his horns and snorting, and jumps onto the bull's back. Pancho bucks and bawls. He sunfishes like a bronco. But the *tigre* stays with him, and shoves a paw forward and claws out the bull's right eye. Then the left eye. Pancho utters a terrible groaning sound. He empties his bowels. He runs in a circle at top speed and collides with a boulder—so violently, I find later, that he tears his right horn loose from his skull.

"Crazy with pain, I guess, he throws himself to the ground, and rolls. The *tigre* jumps clear. When Pancho gets back up, the *tigre* is aboard him again. They pass me, fall into a wash, show up on the far side in a cloud of dust, and crash into another boulder. The *tigre* is now biting into the back of Pancho's neck, and clawing at the bull's throat. I see jugular blood jet in the moonlight. Pancho halts, head down, gargling, and topples over. The *tigre* watches him carefully a moment, then relaxes and begins licking the blood off his paws."

The kid pulled his *serape* closer about his chest. Cold fog was blowing through the cottonwood tops. "That's what happened to Don Rafael's ten thousand-peso bull," he said. "It was a rare thing to see. But only what one might expect, I suppose, from a stock-killer tramp *tigre*."

Our target *tigre* roared twice at five o'clock, and we didn't hear him again. When the sun topped the mesa, we returned to camp. We cooked and ate, then turned in, letting the dogs stand watch. I woke up two hours later, and shook the kid awake. It was colder. Slaty clouds filled the valley head. We saddled up. I sent Loba out to find the *tigre's* exit trail. After five minutes of scouting, she belled that she had the trail. So I released the two Walkers.

I expected the *tigre* to pull a fast one. Shucks, he had to, his life depended on it. He had now gone twenty-eight hours, to our knowledge, without water. In this climate that's close to maximum. The curious thing about the cat was that he had stayed here instead of departing in search of another water hole. Apparently he was loaded with confidence, and believed he could somehow outsmart us and resume using the spring. But that would take considerable doing. I had a couple of geniuses on my staff—Loba and Amigo. The cat's trail led north into a crooked tributary valley, then angled sharply up a steep ridge. The ridge lay between us and Tecolote Spring. It was rimrocked and wildly broken. A rain cloud hung on its summit. Loba and her crew were already well above us, out of sight.

"This may strike you as a dirty trick to play on the dogs," I said to Jesus. "But let's you and I beat it back to the spring. The ridge looks like a sucker trap to me."

I took a shortcut through a gunsight pass near the ridge's south end. We switched to the crest, and headed hellbent down the other side, dodging boulders, crashing through thickets. A hard gust of wind howled along the slope, then rain hit me in the face. Deadline rain. To the north, high above us, Loba and the Walkers were faithfully giving us position fixes. By the time we got down onto the flat, the rain had become a gullywasher. Amigo wanted to give out with all the speed he had, but I held him in so the kid's mule could keep up. As we approached the spring, the mule snorted and laid his ears back. From him that was warning enough. I reached for the Winchester. Ahead, through the driving rain, I saw movement twenty feet upon a slanting cottonwood snag. It was the *tigre*. A magnificent beast, even when soaking wet. He had now lost, but his stratagem had been sound. If we had tried to follow him over the high hump of the ridge, we'd still be blundering around up there.

Loba and the Walkers were coming across the flat, bewildered at seeing us here, I guess, and wondering how we'd done it.

"Young feller," I said to the kid, "shoot that *tigre*. Don Rafael will be forever obliged to you. In fact, if you don't want to keep on hunting bee-trees for El Panal, I guarantee the guy

133

will give you a good job riding for the Owl Head. Shucks, he may make you foreman of the spread."

The kid looked at me twice to make sure I meant it. Then he lined up the borrowed Winchester and fired. The *tigre*, heart-shot, made a grand bound off the snag at the oncoming dogs, and hit the ground dead. I saluted him. He had been a valiant outlaw to the end.

Saga of a Hunting Cayuse

Pilot was a hardnose with a simple outlook:
if it moves, fight it.

"**H**ere comes your Alaska grizzly, boy," I said to young Dale Evarts, the newest guest at Denna Lake Lodge, as the big high-humped bear charged into view. "Harvest him."

This was on a windy September morning, four miles west of the lodge. A half-dozen frustrated ravens and my hard-case Appaloosa stud, Pilot, had alerted me to the grizzly's presence. We were riding crosswind, leading three packhorses. Pilot swung his head to sniff a clump of wolf willows and bared his teeth. He snorted. He began cat-footing. I got the message. We communicated pretty good. He was telling me he had picked up hot bear scent. Apparently the other horses missed it. As for the ravens, I had been watching them. They were perched in a stand of frosted birches sixty yards upwind, *bonk-bonking* at something on the ground—which was most interesting. Yesterday afternoon Dale had killed his trophy bull moose under those birches and we were now returning to pack the meat in. We got down for a look with our glasses. At once we spotted the bear.

A mahogany-colored specimen, hog-snouted, he was crouched in an alder thicket beyond the quartered moose carcass. I gave him five hundred pounds. His pelt looked first-rate. The situation seemed to be that he had eaten as much of the meat as he could hold, and was vigilantly guarding the supply. He glanced up at the ravens and snarled.

Dale raised his .300 Weatherby Magnum but didn't shoot. The wind-whacked alders, he complained, would surely deflect a softnose. Me, I would have risked it. But anyway, a raven solved the problem. Pitching down to the meat pile, the bird snatched a chunk of kidney fat. Instantly the bear charged. The raven flapped downwind, toward us. Handicapped by its loot, it was skimming the brush tops. The bear galloped in dumb pursuit. I am sure he hadn't seen us. When he was one hundred feet distant he halted with a baffled roar. That stampeded Dale's mount and the packhorses. But Pilot stood pat. Ears flattened, he glared at the grizzly. Then I'll be doggoned if he didn't give out with his bugle-noted, boss-stallion challenge scream. It was plenty impressive. I was proud of him. The bear reared up, staring. Dale fired. Chest-shot, the bear toppled and died.

Pilot was foaled at the lodge. Roman-nosed and rangy, he was a throwback to Nez Perce buffalo horses: eleven hundred pounds, satiny pale, blue-roan coat speckled with dollar-size black Appaloosa spots; long black mane and tail; rock-hard black hoofs; intelligent dark eyes. I mean he had the showy good looks that are an asset in a dude-wrangler's mount. On top of that he was a solid pro who liked his work.

The stud made friends—for instance, Jim Harris. Jim came north for a Dall sheep hunt with us. We took him up Lynx Creek. He encountered a piece of hard luck. At dawn the first morning we sighted a ram and two ewes on the mountain above camp. Jim ran for his glasses and tripped over a spruce root, wrenching his right knee. He called it his "football knee." It immediately ballooned. Barring a minor miracle, I thought, there went the hunt. We doped the knee with liniment and applied compresses. Then we took a look at the sheep. The ram was an old-timer. With 16X glasses on him, I estimated his horns would go 15x40 inches. There were ten growth rings—a fine head. The ram was leaning against a shale turret scratching his fanny. The two ewes were on a shelf behind him. As we watched, they began sparring. The ram ignored them. He was busy abating an itch.

"Gents, I want that ram," Jim said. "It isn't far up there. Maybe with a willing, clever-footed horse. . ."

Well, it was worth trying. Our best bet was the mountain's north face, using Pilot. I talked to the stud. Then we boosted Jim aboard him and rode up onto the north shoulder. Above us now was a one-thousand-foot slope topped by cliffs. Tanana and I left our mounts on the shoulder, hobbled. I took Pilot's lead rope. We switchbacked to the cliff, then there was a dizzy ledge and a crooked chute with emptiness below it. And then the worst, a deadfall shale slide. Pilot was sweating. Jim wore a fixed grin. We went across the slide with a rush and scramble, Pilot's sharp-shod hoofs striking sparks. The rest was easy. We angled up to the summit, and saw our sheep 150 yards down the other side. The ram was being ardently nuzzled by both ewes. He looked up, and froze. I could imagine his astonishment at seeing a horse on the skyline. Jim's .30-06 Remington crashed. The ram dropped, stone dead.

Two hours later we rode into camp with the trophy head and the meat. I helped Jim dismount. He put his arms around Pilot's neck. "My friend," he said.

The Appaloosa feuded with moose. When he was a three-year-old he tried to hooraw a herd of the big animals, and nearly got killed. That was on a thirty-degree-below January morning with eight inches of snow. During the night twelve moose had moved into the lodge clearing. Our slash piles attracted them, and also we provided protection from wolves. After breakfast I let the horses out of the log barn. Pilot spotted our visitors, and gave his war beller. Dodging past me, he charged hellbent at a husky slick-headed bull. The bull stood waiting. The other adult moose began closing in. Pilot and the bull didn't fool around. No demonstrating. They reared and struck. They savaged with their teeth. My rifle was at the lodge. I sprinted for it. Then Tanana's .30-06 Winchester blasted from the kitchen window. I saw the bull's left ear buckle. He took off into the timber. The rest of the herd followed.

Pilot limped after them, but they were gone. I dabbed a loop on him and led him to the barn. Tanana brought the first-aid kit. "The whole damn bunch was gonna tackle him," Tanana said. "He wouldn't of had a chance." Probably not. The odds were scary. But anyhow, in September the stud got his revenge.

We were across the lake with a guest named Bill Baker. Bill wanted a trophy moose. We had been hunting two days. This morning we rode out to scout a cottonwood flat east of camp. We approached the timber straight upwind. Pilot tensed as antlers flashed in an opening 160 yards distant. We checked with our glasses. It was a rut-happy bull. With three cows watching, he was batting an alder bush, raking it with his antlers, striking and biting—quite a performance. But his head was skimpy.

I said forget him, let's go. To my surprise, Pilot balked. I touched him with the spurs. Mule stubborn, he refused to move. His gaze was riveted on the opening. Well, seconds later a rival bull stalked onto the scene. The newcomer had magnificent antlers, wide and massive—a heap of points. Bill hit the ground fast. His .270 spoke. The bull knelt, then fell over.

Tanana measured the head—seventy inches. Then I saw that the upper half of the bull's left ear was missing. That explained everything. This was the bull Pilot had fought. The stud had recognized him by scent and had got his revenge. I realized then that I owed this fighting horse an apology.

The Appaloosa liked action. Take an experience we had with a rogue black bear. This was in early October. I was making the round of our spike cabins, readying them for winter. Riding up to the Twin Peaks cabin, I found that it had been raided by a bear. He had ripped the weather-warped plank door off its hinges. Once inside, he had wrecked the place. I picketed Pilot in the yard. I ate some caribou jerky for supper and bedded down on the porch.

Shortly after moonrise, Pilot snorted. I sat up, the .375 magnum ready. Pilot was gazing at a patch of willows forty yards downwind. I pulled on my moccasins. I waited ten minutes. Pilot still had his eyes on the brush clump, so I walked toward the spot. The bear had good nerves, but not good enough. Halting, I whistled, and imitated the hoarse *whuf-whuf* of a panicked bruin. He wailed and fled headlong.

Well, the bear was an outlaw. When they start raiding cabins, they keep it up. Next morning I studied the sign. He was a good-size black. He had been hanging around here a week or so. Finding some clear paw prints, I memorized them. Two days later I saddled Pilot and left. I hadn't ridden a quarter-mile when I sighted a black bear.

He was three hundred yards upwind, going into an island of low scrub willows. A fat, glossy brute. I slid the .375 out of its boot. But before I could line the sights, the bear entered cover. The area around the willow island consisted of open, lawn-like, pea vine meadow. I told Pilot to get moving. He could run. As I said, he was descended from buffalo horses.

We rocketed across the open ground. I saw the bear fifty yards ahead as we plowed into the brush. I fired. Hair flew from the animal's jaw. We emerged from the other side of the island. The bear reared to fight. Pilot slammed past so close that the animal struck at him. I got a shell chambered as Pilot whirled. The bear faced us, raging. I shot him in the neck. The heavy magnum slug spun him backward. He died. Dismounting, I examined his paws. As I had believed, he was the rogue cabin-raider.

I dressed the carcass and hung it in a tree, for use when we began running our trapline through here. It was good, fat-marbled meat, smelling of blueberries. Pilot was snorty the rest of the day. He'd had a great time.

Pilot could have been a rodeo star. The one time he pitched with me, he showed real talent. He was only half-broke then. We were stormbound at the lodge this September day, an icy rain sluicing down. Our current hunter, Cliff Hodges, was dozing by the fireplace. I happened to look out the window, and saw movement a half-mile up the lakeshore. I reached for my glasses. It was a small band of caribou. They were traveling north, away from us. One of the bulls had trophy antlers. Cliff and I hastened to the barn and saddled up. I was putting on my slicker as we rode out of the yard. A wind gust caught the garment and whapped its tails against Pilot's head. Understandably he came unstuck. I don't know how I stayed up there. He was fast, strong, and tricky. The Hamley saddle sledged my rump. My neck popped. My nose bled. Finally I got rid of the slicker, and with that Pilot subsided.

We lit out after the caribou. The band had halted to browse in some dwarf birches. We cut the range to seven hundred yards, then tied the horses and went on another two hundred yards afoot.

With wind-driven rain battering us, we climbed a grassy dune. The trophy bull was now polishing his antlers on a jack-spruce snag. Cliff adjusted the scope sight of his .300 Weatherby. He rested the gun over a sand cornice. He sighted tentatively and slipped the safety latch. At last he fired—and hit the bull in the flank. I guess he had misjudged the wind. The bull humped his back and staggered in a circle. Cliff cursed. He fired again, and the bull dropped. As we headed for the kill, Tanana caught up with us. He had brought our mounts, a packhorse, and my slicker. I put the slicker on and started to board Pilot. He shied away from me, wild-eyed. I thought that over. My slicker was black. Cliff's was bright yellow. I asked the guy to swap with me. He obliged, and that was all it took. Wearing the yellow slicker, I picked up Pilot's reins. He nudged me. We were friends again. That's how I got started wearing a gaudy yellow slicker. It was Pilot's choice, not mine.

The Appaloosa had a good nose, and I made use of it. There was the time he located some meat-drunk wolves for me. This was in mid-October. I had freighted two packhorse-loads of trapping supplies to our cache on Grouse Creek, reaching there late. Snow was falling. I made camp, ate, and turned in. Somewhere to the south a wolf howled. Another answered. Around midnight the horses came hobble-hopping to camp. I spoke to Pilot. Then wolf yammer filled the snowy night. It rose from a spruce flat down the creek. I decided there were three of the shaggy thugs. Above their clamor I heard the pound of hoofs. So they were chasing a moose or a caribou. In a moment they made their kill. They were noisy about it. A lot of yipping and yowling. I figured they were young wolves. At any rate, they would get meat-drunk tonight. And there was a $50 bounty on the species.

"Come morning, we'll pay those bravos a visit," I said to Pilot.

Daylight hit the peaks. The snowfall had ceased. Saddling Pilot, I rode down the lee side of the spruce flat. There was four inches of powder snow. Suddenly the stud halted. I felt a shiver run through him. Wolf scent will do that to a horse. I turned him upwind, and gave him his head. He got the idea. We worked into an opening. There lay the remains of a moose heifer. It had been some banquet. Hair and blood everywhere. Splintered bones. Urine splashes. I could smell vomit. Fifty feet ahead I caught movement in a thicket. A yellow wolf slouched into view, gawking stupidly. Behind him two gray wolves appeared. The trio's sides bulged. Crusted snow clung to their coats. Obviously they had been sleeping, plenty meat-drunk. It was the effect of gorging. I shot the yellow wolf in the chest. The gray assassins lumbered for cover. I killed them both before they had covered one hundred feet.

I dragged the carcasses together and began skinning them. There were two males and a female. Like the heifer they had killed, they were long-yearlings, and probably litter mates. The pelts were prime. With luck we would sell them to lodge guests for at least $100 apiece. Pilot watched me work, registering disgust. He sure hated wolves.

The stud was a one-man horse, and jealous of his prerogatives. For instance, there was a dramatic episode with a mountain grizzly. This was in June. We had booked a bear hunter named Dan Masters. When the first grass showed, we loaded an outfit onto seven packhorses and rode over to Trail Creek. At timberline there, we found the valley partly blocked by a massive snowslide. The wall of ice-hard snow and assorted debris towered forty feet high. As we picked our way around the tip of the avalanche, I heard magpies quarreling on the jumbled snow cliff above us. Then I got a whiff of carrion. Pilot snorted, and began cat-footing. That was all the warning I needed. I signaled Tanana to halt the packtrain. At this instant the magpies took off, squawking. I looked up and saw a grizzly standing in a notch at the snow cliff's crest. He was a blond 450-pounder. Handsome. He peered down at us, and snarled.

I then saw the reason for all this activity. Sticking out of the snow above the bear's head were the carcasses of two Dall rams. It occurred to me they probably had started the great slide.

Dan dismounted, .30-06 Remington in hand. He fired. The bear bit at his shoulder, and stumbled off the cliff. As he fell, he bawled. That was too much for the packhorses. They fled in disorder across the valley. Tanana spurred after them. Well, the bear had landed on some uprooted alders. He now lurched back into sight, popping his jaws. Dan shot him through the head. I helped Tanana round up the packhorses, then we skinned the bear. A problem arose. Dan wanted part of the grizzly meat, and we knew none of the packhorses would carry it. The solution we came up with was to take advantage of Pilot. Bloody bear meat didn't scare him any. So we burdened him with a paint packhorse's freight plus the meat and hide. And I put my rigging on the paint. It didn't work. Jealous, Pilot attacked the pinto. I beat him off with a riata coil. I cussed him out. Then I did what was indicated.

I took Pilot's lead rope, and headed back up the valley afoot. It was a fifteen-mile hike to the lodge. "That stud is a one-man horse all right," Tanana said, laughing. "And he's gonna see to it that you stay a one-horse man."

Pilot was getting old, but it didn't show much. He was still the liveliest cayuse in our string. Consider the climax of a September moose hunt we made with Tom Morrow. We topped South Pass with the packtrain, and slanted down toward the forks of Owl Creek. Rounding a shale bastion, we saw five moose six hundred yards below us on the creek bank. A bull and four cows. We checked the bull with our glasses. He carried a trophy head. I gave it sixty-eight inches. He was trying to haze his cows across the creek. They were mutinous, and kept breaking back. Tom opted to shoot from here. Dismounting, he set the scope sight of his .270 Winchester, and rested the rifle over a boulder. He fired. I heard the slug hit. But the bull stayed on his feet. He made another lunge at the cows. This time they splashed into the creek. The bull started after them.

I didn't see what happened next. Some yellow aspen tops blocked my view. But anyhow, the bull disappeared. He wasn't with the cows when they climbed the opposite bank. Trouble. The creek was thirty feet wide and fast-flowing. Below were logjams, deep holes and brushy bends. If Tom's bull had been swept down by the current, we probably had a mean salvage job on our hands.

Stepping aboard Pilot, I told him to stir himself. He headed down the slope as though he were three years old again. He soared over washes, dodged boulders, and smashed through thickets. Then we were amongst the aspens with the creek bank swooping at us. As I reined in, I got a look over the bank. There was the bull, lying dead on the point of a bar. Lung shot, he had turned back from the ford, but hadn't quite made it. The carcass was being lifted by the current. It was almost afloat. I grabbed my riata, and jumped Pilot down onto the bar. Building a loop, I tied onto the bull's antlers as the carcass drifted free. Pilot held the strain until Tanana and Tom arrived. The three of us used our mounts to skid the carcass out onto the gravel. Tom then came over and respectfully patted Pilot's shoulder. He said that it had been a spectacular run down the mountain. He said Pilot was the greatest, and he was proud he knew him.

"I'm kind of partial to the character myself," I said, "ancient as he is."

I guess that does it. See you in an Alaska game range someday. I'd like you to meet Pilot. So long.

High-up, Way-Out
Adventures with Goats

*"Normally, the goat is peaceful. But crowd
him, and he can become a holy terror. He
doesn't wear those stiletto horns for foofaraw."*

"**O**kay, I'm thrilled," stage-whispered young Tom Logan,
my current pilgrim, as the mixed band of ten mountain
goats emerged from the alders to advance deliberately on
our cliff-brink place of concealment. "But I still don't
see my trophy billy,"

"That's him busting out of the brush. He tried to flank us,"
I said. "Take him."

That was early on a frosty August morning above the ice-
ribbed headwaters of Metal Creek in Alaska's Chugach Mountains.
We had spotted the goats from camp shortly after daybreak.
They were fifteen hundred feet above us, loafing on a scarlet
cloudberry slope. The band consisted of a boss billy, five adult
females, three kids, and a topknotted yearling. Since the rut
hadn't begun, I suppose it was a social gathering.

We put 16X glasses on the billy. He was a husky two-hundred-
pounder, his coat thick and snowy. I gave his horns nine inches,
which is good. The trophy average is eight inches. As we studied
him, he sat down like a bear. Although we were in plain sight,
none of the goats showed alarm. Probably they had never been
hunted. These peaks aren't popular with outfitters, because you
have to backpack in, and the trail up the creek is a hair-raiser.

Our stalk took forty minutes. It brought us out on an alder-fringed shelf at the mountain's brushline.

The goats were now down in some scrub alders two hundred yards upwind. I couldn't identify the trophy billy—too much brush in the way. So I resorted to a Goat-Eater Denna Indian trick. Cupping my hands at my mouth, I imitated the grunts of a panicked kid. I got action. A female trotted out of the alders and halted to stare. She was a young animal, skinny, with an ugly scar across her left eye socket. She had no kid with her, and I figured I knew why. Golden eagles probably had killed her spring kid. Trying to fight them off, she had lost an eye. The other females now came alongside her. Then I saw the billy in the brush to their left. I gave a couple more grunts. Suddenly the whole rescue squad charged. They were halfway to us when Tom's .270 Winchester banged. The billy wheeled over—finished. The rest of the goats fled up the mountain.

"This has made a goat fan of me," Tom said as we headed for the kill. "I didn't expect it, but they sure got hard-boiled."

I told him goats were especially noted for that quality and I could supply "for examples." I was remembering the horrible surprise a pack of immigrant coyotes received one November morning on Knik River when they attacked some mild-looking goats.

I was a youngster then, holding down a forty-mile trapline. Needing fresh meat, I mushed to my upper cabin with the idea of killing a fat goat. I found conditions impossible. A foot of snow had fallen, after which there had been rain followed by zero-degree temperature. The countryside was ice-sheathed. Any attempt to climb a mountain would have been suicidal. During breakfast on the fourth morning I was startled to hear coyotes yap-yapping hysterically, close upriver. This was the first time I had heard coyotes in a Chugach valley. The animals had migrated to Alaska from Canada only a few months ago. They were still cheechako—tenderfeet—and scarce.

Snatching up the .30-06 Winchester and 12X glasses, I hastened outside. The coyotes obviously were hot on the trail of something, and the chase was coming this way. Stepping into the siwash hitches of my webs, I went over to the dawn-lit river bars. Presently I saw motion at the edge of the timber three hundred yards upwind.

Three goats plodded into view. They were making for the opposite range spur, no doubt because their scanty forage had been iced under. In a moment four coyotes appeared. They were running on the glassy crust, whereas the goats were breaking through at every step. The would-be killers raced straight in. I guess they hadn't discovered that the goat is not a prey animal. Anyway, the goats turned to meet them. An instant later the coyote pack leader was impaled on a goat's horns, the goat bucking to get rid of him. Another coyote whirled out of the action with his belly ripped open, intestines dragging. I shot a dark-coated coyote, then shot a likely goat. The sole remaining coyote was departing and before I could lay sights on him, he disappeared into the timber. He had got smarted up fast. I'll bet it was the last time he tackled a goat.

The goat is a tough customer to stalk. In fact, his fans brag that he is the toughest. You climb for your billy with the odds against you. You're operating on his home mountain, and he's smart and well equipped to take care of himself. His eyes are probably about equal to 6X glasses. He has a good nose and first-rate hearing. Having spent his life on the mountain, it's a cinch he knows the location, shape and color of every terrestrial feature from brushline to summit. A camouflage suit won't help you much.

Your best bet is to put topography between yourself and him. Even then the stalk can go haywire. The wind may swap around. Marmots or parka squirrels may spot you and sound the alarm. Weather may sock the mountain in. But these hazards only add up to suspense and marvelous sport. Ask any goat hunter.

Take a stalk Pat Jarvis and I made at the headwaters of Carpenter Creek. The billy was mastheaded on a snow-patched six-thousand-foot summit across from camp. I sighted him while washing breakfast dishes. The yellowish tint of his coat gave him away. We looked him over with a 24X spotting scope. I thought his horns might go ten inches. Pat was so doggoned eager he had a case of shakes.

We began the stalk in bright sunshine, using a buttress ridge for cover. Practically everything went wrong. A bulge-bellied black cloud formed over the valley head. In the next thirty minutes it produced the full spectrum of foul weather—rain, hail, snow and crazy williwaw wind. Soaked, we battled up through one thousand feet of alders. Then we climbed two cliffs. By now marmots were heralding our presence. Finally we topped the summit in battering rain. The goat stood on a shale dump 250 yards distant, gazing at us. Pat rested his .250-3000 Savage over a boulder. He was shivering, and had a stiff crosswind to deal with. He fired. I saw the wicked 100-grain slug hit—too far back. The goat staggered to the summit's edge. Below him was a five-hundred-foot drop that certainly would shatter his horns. We didn't move. A shot would bump him into space. I was afraid the wind would blow him over. He took a long look at us. Then he lay down carefully—and died.

"Thank you, friend goat," I said.

We hurried to the kill as another sleet squall blanked the summit. I got out my steel tape. The horns measured 9¾ inches. Pat sat down and took the goat's head on his lap.

"Happiest, most rewarding stalk I ever made," he said through chattering teeth.

Goats rut in September and October. Often the beautiful animals go about it with considerable aggressiveness. For example, there was the climax of a hunt I made with Jim Carter on Carbon Creek. We scouted two days without seeing a goat. Then late the third day we sighted a billy and three females high on a peak below the glacier. I estimated the billy's horns would go close to nine inches. So we began a stalk. We didn't have enough daylight left for tactical maneuvering, so we just headed up the mountain, trusting we'd find cover. At grassline we checked on the goats. The billy was now posed atop a red rimrock seven hundred yards up the slope. Beside him stood one of the females. She was an elderly type with horns almost in the trophy class. The other two females were on a broken bench twenty feet below. The trim young matrons were sparring. Clearly they suffered from jealously.

I located a swale that angled up the pitch. We followed it on hands and knees until it petered out. We had gained sixty yards.

The next piece of good cover was a lichen-encrusted granite boulder fifty yards distant. If we reached it, I figured Jim could score. We started crawling. I expected the goats would spot us any instant, but we got a break. The two young females were still sparring. All at once the long-horned dowager bounded down off the rimrock and attacked them both. She didn't fool

around. A real battler—she had them bleeding before they could square away to defend themselves. The billy had turned to watch. That was all we needed. We scrambled to the boulder.

Five minutes had elapsed. Meanwhile, the hard-case female had given her rivals the bum's rush and was returning to the billy. Jim took a rest on the boulder with his scope-sighted .300 Weatherby Magnum and fired. I heard the slug hit. The billy fell against the oncoming female, swung his head to look our way, and died.

We climbed to the kill. Both horns measured 8½ inches. I glanced up and saw the dowager watching us from a ledge 150 yards distant. She was a hardluck character. It was her violent attempt to monopolize the billy that had made it possible for us to kill him. She looked forlorn. I waved to her, wishing her success next time.

The goat is a dramatic critter. For instance, take an August hunt I made with Jack Morrow. We had paddled a canvas canoe to the eastern shore of iceberg-dotted Lake George. Next morning at daybreak we sighted twelve goats and a black bear. The goats were scattered over a mineral mud "lick" nine hundred yards distant at the head of a wild-rose draw. We sized them up with 16X glasses. Four of the goats were adult billies. One had horns that I believed would go nine inches. With the rut still a month off, it was a tranquil scene. The billies, chewing mud, ignored one another. A gusty wind off the lake was whirling clouds of fallen rose petals through the narrow draw. As for the black bear, he was swaggering up a game trail that led to the lick. His new autumn coat shone in sunlight. I thought he would weigh at least two hundred pounds.

We made a quick stalk. Climbing through skimpy alders and devil's clubs, it took us only twenty minutes to top a ridge overlooking the wild-rose draw. The goats were now crosswind, three hundred yards below us.

I tried to spot the trophy billy and failed. All the goats had their heads down, eating mud. But in a moment that changed. The black bear pigeon-toed out of a windy thicket. At sight of the goats he halted. The goats swiveled to face him. They tossed their heads threateningly. The bear snarled. It was a classic case of animals' cussedness. The bear wouldn't detour, and the goats refused to yield right-of-way. But we had located the trophy billy. Jack cut down with his .30-06 Remington. As he did so, a tall wind-twister loaded with rose petals swooshed off the opposite hillside. I guess the spectacle rattled Jack. Anyway, he fired and missed. The goats stampeded for a graywacke cliff fifty yards up the draw. The bear fled with them. He had no choice. Jack fired again. The billy went down rolling. The bear dodged past the carcass and vanished into a brush jungle.

"Pure drama," Jack said with feeling as we hurried down the hill.

He knelt in a bank of rose petals and helped me measure the horns. The right horn went nine inches, the left horn 8½ inches.

"Man, I'm sure happy I've made the mountain goat's acquaintance," he declared.

When I was a kid roaming the coast ranges, our winter economy was based on goat hunting. The best security we knew was a limit of three fat goats hung in the meat cache. We used goat skins for bedding. Smokers carried their tobacco in goat-bladder pouches. We thought that trap scent was more effective if kept in a bone-stoppered goat horn. A little goat gall stirred into spruce-needle tea was held to be a sovereign remedy for rheumatism.

Maybe because we wished it was a fact, we pretended that goats were easy to stalk and kill. But sometimes the fiction was hard to maintain. Take a November hunt Tanana Stewart and I made in the Kashwitna Basin. We were at our timberline trapline cabin waiting for a chance to kill some sorely needed meat. A big snow wind was clobbering the basin. Finally the sky cleared, and we sighted six goats on a nearby ragged peak.

"Reckon we'd better stroll up there and harvest our meat," Tanana said, "before the damned weather gets notional again."

The goats were bunched five hundred feet below the peak's summit. We mushed a quarter-mile through the valley and climbed a ridge, which winds had blown partly clear of snow. We came out on the rim of a steep gut. The goats were two hundred yards above us. When our breathing was back to normal, we shot two of them. The carcasses rolled down almost to us.

The other goats took off across the snow-filled gut. They were wallowing badly. Then the snow moved. Tanana gave a yell of alarm. They had started a slide. Three of the goats made it out of the gut. The fourth, a yearling, didn't. As the vast tonnage of snow gathered speed, he tried to climb out on our side. He could have succeeded, but at the critical instant he looked up and saw us. Mouth open, registering terror, he turned back. The slide swept him over a cliff. We heard the mass of snow smash into a point of spruce timber. A single gust of hurricane wind struck the mountain.

"Well, anyhow, I still say it's cheaper than buying meat in a butcher shop," Tanana said, digging snow out of his ears as we went up to salvage our kills. "More eventful, too."

Goat-hunting guides have a heap of fun, but I never heard anybody claim they don't earn their money. Consider a scary predicament the Watana Kid got into over on Granite Creek. This was in August of the year I was seventeen. The kid had booked a pilgrim named Bill Howard. I was backpacking for the party. We pitched camp on that dwarf-cottonwood flat between the forks. Two mornings later we sighted a lone billy on the castellated peak above us. The sizable specimen was bedded down in a scooped-out cranny, partway up a dry waterfall course. The Kid studied him with 12X glasses and said the horns might go ten inches.

Well, it was a mean stalk. We climbed with a shoulder of the mountain for cover, then crept up a ridge until we could see into the waterfall slot. The billy, 450 yards away, was now on his feet. A half-dozen ornery magpies were swooping about him.

Because of the magpies we had no chance of getting closer. The pilgrim adjusted the scope sight of his .30-06 Winchester and took a rest over a ledge. The billy stood broadside to us. There was no wind, and at the crash of the shot, the billy reared and fell backward. He lay motionless, apparently finished.

We climbed to a conglomerate ledge, flanking the falls cliff. I sat down to wait for my pack. The Watana Kid and the pilgrim toiled on up to the hollowed-out cranny. The Kid was in the lead. Head and shoulders above the rim, he felt around for a handhold. At that point, surprise: the goat stood up! Assorted things happened. Weaving on his feet, blood trickling from a neck wound, the goat lurched forward. The Kid tried to duck. I couldn't shoot, because he was in my line of fire. The billy stabbed at the Kid's face. But, dying, he was slow. The Kid stuck his free hand out, grabbed a horn, and hung on. They struggled, then the billy coughed blood and collapsed. Well, the Kid was a stolid soul. Without comment, he muscled himself up into the cranny and helped the pilgrim over the rim. He got busy with his knife, and soon he tumbled the dressed-goat carcass down to me.

"That gets you gents a twenty percent bonus," the pilgrim said when they came off the cliff. He measured his trophy again. The left horn went ten inches, the right horn 9½ inches. "I figure the Kid just earned it for both of you," he said.

Goat hunting combines sport and adventure. For example, there was a late-September hunt I made with Walt Beecham in the isolated and goat-haunted Blue Hole, across Knik Glacier.

We camped one night on the ice. Arriving at the hole the next day, we found it two-thirds full of churning cloud mist. Nevertheless we sighted eighteen goats. Most of the wonderful animals were watching us but didn't appear disturbed. So far as I knew, the place had been hunted only once before—five years earlier. I made out several trophy billies. The likeliest one was on a striped sandstone ridge eight hundred yards distant, at cloudline. His horns were better than the trophy average—close to nine inches. With him was a fluffy coated female, and they were rut-preoccupied, nuzzling and frisking each other. Thirty yards down the ridge stood a non-trophy billy, intently watching them. The three were high-humped and had immaculately white pelts. I was recalling that these animals actually were a variety of antelope. And that the buckskin mountain men called them snow buffalo. Admiring the beasts, we began figuring out a stalk.

A tilted wolf-willow jungle offered cover. An ancient goat trail ran through it. The bordering bushes hung with silky tufts of shed hair. Crouching to keep our heads below the brush tops, we headed for the ridge. When I thought we had cut the range to four hundred yards, we risked a look.

Cloudline had moved down one hundred feet. The trophy billy and the female were now mere shadow forms in a drift of blowing mist. I could just barely distinguish the two. Walt rested his .270 Winchester over an outcrop. Before he could fire, drama occurred. The female decided to change partners. One moment she was frolicking with the billy. The next she struck him with her front hoofs and went trotting down the ridge. The other billy came to meet her. But he didn't get opportunity to pursue his luck. They met and touched noses. Then the trophy billy slammed down at them. He belted the short-horned billy off his feet and stabbed him in the rump as he was getting up. The two reared, hacking at each other's throats. They separated and feinted for advantage. Then Walt fired. The trophy billy dropped. The interloping Romeo and the female beat it.

We went up to the kill. As tatters of mist swirled about us, I measured the trophy. Each horn went 8¾ inches. Walt patted the billy's shoulder.

"They are a truly great game species," he said.

Back to the beginning—Tom Logan remarked that he hadn't realized goats were so hard-boiled. I told him he ought to put in a couple of decades hunting and observing the animals. Normally, of course, the goat is peaceful. But crowd him, and as I have described, he can become a holy terror. He doesn't wear those stiletto horns for foofaraw. In fact, a goat is the only animal known to have killed an adult mountain grizzly and been able to walk away from the scene. The authority for that is the zoologist William Hornaday.

Well, we dragged Tom's goat carcass off the mountain. We cooled the meat in a permanent snowdrift. Toward dust we spitted the saddle on a green pole and barbecued it over cottonwood-bark coals. Fat dripped on the coals and flared. The mountain stars came out. When the meat was ready, we ate slabs of it with brown beans and bannock bread. For dessert we had sugared blueberries. The coffee was hot and strong.

"I am a goat fan forever," Tom said, lighting his pipe.

Believe It ...
Black Bears Attack

*Angry, charging bears convinced me. It's a die-hard
myth that all blackies are non-agressive.*

"**N**ow that's my idea of a trophy black bear," said young Hank
Peters, as we backed toward our rifles. The bear stood one hundred
feet distant across the timberline meadow we had picked for
tonight's campsite. Mane bristled, showing his fighting teeth.
"Just look at that clown. Some act he's putting on, huh?"

"Don't be fooled. It's no act," I said.

It was late in a snow-spitting September afternoon under
Mt. Dall, on the wild north slope of the Alaska Range. I was
guiding Hank on a sheep and grizzly hunt in the Rainy Pass country.
We had 350 packtrain miles under our belts. The bear had appeared while we were rustling squaw wood for our supper fire.
Shouldering out of some wolf willows, he gave a hoarse *whowf-
whowf* and popped his jaws. Perhaps, I thought, he had meat
cached here. A mob of magpies indicated as much. Or maybe
he just hated humans. Anyway, he was working up nerve to
get tough. And our rifles were fifty feet yonder at the rigging
pile. Plenty big as mountain black bears go, he'd weigh at least
two hundred pounds. His thick autumn coat looked good. Under
a dusting of snow on the guard hairs, it was pure jet. Hank
hadn't taken a black bear. He had been holding out for an
unusually fine specimen, such as this one.

So the kid was thrilled. But I saw that he still didn't believe the bear meant it. He had bought the diehard myth that all black bears were strictly non-aggressive. You could hooraw them with a club, and so on.

Me, I was in a sweat to lay hands on my rifle. But I didn't want to risk any quick moves. The bear raged, foam dripping from his jowls. He swung his head and bit off a willow branch. He crouched as though to spring. I mean he was having himself a swell tantrum. Then he made a twenty-foot rush at us and that convinced Hank. Dropping his armload of wood, the kid sprinted for his rifle. Well, up to then we'd had the bear bluffed. But now I guess he thought Hank was fleeing. Anyway, with a buzz-saw snarl, he charged. I yelled, sailed my hat at him, and fumbled for my knife. The bear dodged around me, losing a couple of seconds. Hank reached the rigging pile and snatched up his .270 Winchester. The weapon was chamber-loaded. Lining the open sights, Hank fired. Blood and brains splattered. The bear fell, skidded, and lay motionless, fifteen feet from the kid.

"Okay, he meant it," Hank said as we lit cigarettes. "Man, that was the highlight of my long hunt."

I thought we would soon learn why the bear had been hostile. Most black bears, of course, would rather run than fight. It's the odd hard case that provides drama and slam-bang action. Take the windup of a black bear and moose hunt I made with Dale Evarts on upper Montana Creek, in the Talkeetna Mountains. Dale killed his bull the third day. The bear was easier. We didn't have to hunt him. We had bivouacked in a dugout cabin on Ptarmigan Bench. Late that night the savage sounds of a bear fight woke us. Dressing hastily, we stepped outside. The bears were battling in a wild-rose patch down near the spring, forty yards distant. Roaring. Tumbling like cats. We had a misty moon. I could see that the animals were blacks—sizable warriors. Dale raised his .300 Weatherby Magnum. He sighted, then whispered, "Nope." He needed a better chance.

At this point I had a hunch. Last evening I had hung Dale's moose cape over an aspen limb behind the cabin. I now trotted over there. The cape was gone. That explained the bear fight. The bandits were deciding who owned the loot.

We eased down the hillslope. The bears were in deep shadow under a birch. Suddenly the action stopped. I suppose the animals had seen us. Then one of them fled, crashing into a thicket. The other loped out across an open space. He was dragging something—the moose cape. Dale brought up the .300 again but still didn't shoot. In the thin moonglow his receiver sight was a handicap. The bear had covered only a few yards when apparently he stepped on the cape and tripped himself. Anyhow, he fell. Bounding up with a roar, he took off again, and the same thing happened. Dale walked toward him. Nine out of ten black bears would have beat it. This one stood his ground, snarling. I could practically read his mind. He had fought for the cape. He figured it was his. If he had to fight us too, he was ready. Dale took another step. The bear charged. Dale fired and the animal went down, finished.

"He sold me," Dale said as I ignited a twist of birchbark. The bear was a 180-pounder, smelling of blueberries. Except for gashes on his head and neck, his pelt was first class. "I'll be back next year, for sure."

Opening the carcass I remembered another guy who had been delighted by a black bear's attack—Tom Talkeetna, a Denna Indian. "It was something," Tom told me. "I've got bad troubles and this reckless bear solves them. It happened at Lynx Lake, near the end of May. I'm lying in a little cottonwood bark lean-to, listening to chinook wind. My eyes are bandaged with socks. That's on account of three days ago I go snow blind. It scares me. Because I'm snow blind once before and the Doc said let it be the last time. So now I'm afraid to lift the bandage. Well, I hear the bear snort. He's under my meat cache, thirty yards downwind. I don't move. He's got a horrible surprise coming. It's just a siwash cache—poles lashed between two spruces. But I have tied porky skins around the spruces. They oughta stop anything. The bear paces, growling. I figure he's plumb desp'rit hungry. Or batty in the head.

"I sit up and check the chamber load of my .30-06 Remington. I sure could use the bear. My meat supply is down to two beaver carcasses. Lift that bandage, I tell myself.

"But I stall. I'm scared I'll see blank darkness. Then I hear a new sound through the moan of the chinook. It's the bear's claws rattling on spruce bark. He's climbing. He's gonna try for the beaver carcasses, come whatever. I hear him grunt.

Then he gives a *wha-a-a* you could hear a half-mile. He's reached the porky skins. Well, the sonofagun has guts. He tries to keep climbing. But it's too rough. He has to let go. He lands in the foot of wet snow with a *whump* and gets up roaring. I yank the bandage off. Daylight smashes at my eyes. But I can see. The bear is a whopping black. A 250-pounder. He's facing me. His chest and legs are stuck full of quills. He's chewing a mouthful of porky hide. I raise the Remington and that does it. Here he comes. I shoot him in the chest. He goes down coughing blood and quills, but staggers up. So I put a finisher through his head.

"Boy, I am all-out happy. I go over and talk to the bear, Injun fashion. He's been traveling some. His soft winter paw-pads are bloody. I guess the chinook thaw flooded his den. Most likely he ain't et for seven months. I tell him he had good reasons for getting ornery. And I thank him."

Despite their banditry, black bears were important in our frontier economy. They supplied meat and skins. They helped bring sportsmen into the country. Every fall at my Toonakloot homestead I killed a couple of fat blueberry-fed black bears. We slow-smoked the side meat and quarters. We rendered out the fat. To my taste you can't beat good black bear ham and bacon. And the lard is equal to the best sold in stores. If we had time, we tanned the skins ourselves with yellow laundry soap. If not, we hired Indian women to tan them. We used the skins for bunk covers and sled robes. Since sportsmen are partial to black bears, the animals were a financial asset. We booked fly-in hunters. They landed at the creek mouth, and we hosted them at $25 apiece per day. Thus we were considerably indebted to the Toonakloot black bears, if we did cuss them.

There was a big hard-boiled black bear Pat Jarvis and I met one spring in the Wood River country. We had finished a griz-zly hunt and were camped on lower Cody Creek. I had shoved our ten cayuses, hobbled, onto a pea vine meadow one hundred yards downstream. Just before dusk we saw them crowd around something, excited. We went down to investigate. It was a moose calf. It stood between the bell mare's legs, hunting milk. I scanned the timber for mamma. No mamma in sight. Well, I didn't want to take the calf to camp. That never helps. Besides, mamma might show up hostile and tear hell out of things. I decided the bell mare was the best bet. She had her head craned around, nuzzling the calf. Friends already. So I told her to take cover.

Maybe, with us out of the way, mamma would come in and claim the youngster.

We ate supper and sacked down. An hour or so later, at moonrise, a wild jangling of the mare's Kentucky bell woke me. I reached for my moccasins and rifle. Then the string pounded into camp, without the calf. Obviously, I concluded, mamma had come for it. Great. I told the mare to relax, and went back to bed.

Next morning we checked for sign to make sure. Cold fog hung over the creek. Instead of cow moose tracks, we cut the paw prints of a black bear. Then we found blood and calf hair. So long, youngster. Pat cursed. I took the bear's trail as a pair of ravens circled us. The trail led into fog-shrouded willow thickets. I got the smell of a kill. It proved to be the bear's cache. He had eaten part of the calf and covered the rest with turf. The two ravens now alighted in a snag twenty yards distant. I watched them. Pro hunter's sixth sense told me the bear was close. But the ravens seemed to be eying only us. I let five minutes pass. Then I took hold of the carcass remnant and started away with it. At once an impressive snarl sounded—behind us—which explained the ravens' gaze. The bear came busting out of a thicket. Pat's .270 Winchester blasted. Heart-shot, the calf-killer somersaulted and died.

"Well, he was an S.O.B.," Pat said when we had examined the kill—160 pounds, with a beautiful pelt. "But an exciting S.O.B."

Black bears give good sport anywhere. But personally I like to hunt them in the Chugach, Talkeetna, and Alaska Range timberline berry patches after the first frost. It's open country. Usually the weather is perfect. You locate your black bear and size him up with glasses. Then you have the fun of a stalk with the bear continuously in view. Often, if it's a good berry year, the animals are abundant. I once saw twenty-six black bears stuffing themselves with blueberries on the north slope of Susitna Mountain. That same autumn, scouting a serviceberry patch at the head of Knik River, I saw eighteen. Many visiting hunters take their black-bear trophies as a bonus during sheep, goat and moose hunts. It makes for busy hunting, also drama. Because peaceful or ornery, the black bear is an action animal. He may not always get full credit, but he enlivens plenty of hunts.

A wounded black bear rates total respect. Consider, for example, what one did to Kobuk Jones in the midst of the Metal Creek gold stampede, back when I was a kid.

Six of us had arrived at Cottonwood Flat on a pretty June morning and staked our claims. We were ahead of the main stampede because we had traveled light. But there was a penalty—we were about out of grub. Kobuk spotted the black bear. The animal had materialized on a snow-patched slope eight hundred yards above us. Jubilant, Kobuk took a look with 12X glasses. Our medicine, he said, got better. The bear would go anyhow two hundred pounds, and was royal fat. A lot of fine eating, by gosh. Grabbing his .30-06 Springfield, Kobuk asked me to accompany him as packer. We went up through a mess of alders. When we next saw the bear he was four hundred yards distant, climbing. Not spooked, just moving. Well, Kobuk needed to get his wind back. But this was an emergency, so he cut down with the Springfield. He did all right. The 220-grain softnose hit with an audible *whoomp*. The bear half-turned and came rolling.

"Ain't that purty?" Kobuk said while our meat-hungry associates down on the flat cheered and waved their hats. "He's gonna roll plumb into camp."

But he didn't. He lodged in a clump of alders on a six-foot shale rim fifty yards above us. We toiled up to the place. Kobuk, standing on tiptoe, tried to yank the carcass free. I heard a gurgling sound. Then the bear, suddenly un-dead, kicked Kobuk in the face with both hind feet and fell on top of him. Well, Kobuk was a roughneck frontiersman. He let out a startled yell. But at the same instant he took a scissors and strangle hold on the bear from behind. His knife flashed. The bear reared and toppled backward, bellering. The two rolled. I was out of it. I hadn't brought my rifle and Kobuk had the Springfield slung over his shoulder. They came to a halt in some alders. Kobuk made another pass with his knife. Then he sat up and spit out several teeth. His nose was flattened and he had lost part of an ear. As for the bear, it was really dead this time. I noted that it had been shot through the muzzle.

"My fault," Kobuk said with a bloody grin. "Anybody that takes fool chances with a black bear deserves to get kicked in the face."

The black bear is a genius at survival. He's had to be. While the grizzly and brown bears have been carefully managed, he suffered varmint status for years. Nobody championed him. He was a free-for-all target. No closed season on him most places and no bag limit. Spoiler types hunted and trapped him for his skin and fat. He was slated for near extinction. But he fooled everybody. Incredibly, he flourished. Smarter than the glamor bears, he adapted to civilization's advance. He learned to use cover. He became a master thief. He was able to match tricks with hunters. Today he has a slew of things going for him. Sportsmen like his style. Public sentiment belatedly is with him. He's protected. His tribe is healthy. Since the cubs climb like squirrels, the wolves and grizzlies seldom score on them. Any way you figure the black bear, he has a sporting stake in the future.

Most black-bear attacks are a surprise because we are conditioned to peaceful black bears. Take an experience Bill Baker and I had one wind-whacked noon on Kashwitna River. We were en route to the headwaters for a goat hunt, lining a fourteen-foot freight skiff.

We sighted the black bear and two coyotes seven hundred yards ahead, at the mouth of Slide Creek. They were blurred shapes in blowing sand. But you could see that a heap of activity was going on. Leaning against the towline's loop, I got out my 16X glasses. The big prisms cut through the sand. I saw that the bear was guarding a white-pelted carcass of some kind. Typically, the coyotes were giving him the old razzle-dazzle. One would sucker him into chasing it, while the other snatched bites from the carcass. The bear looked okay. Even in this wan sandstorm light his coat had gloss. Bill said he wanted him. Swell. But it was going to take luck. There was no cover, and no place to tie the skiff, just a long reach of flat fireweed river bar. And if the wind shifted 10 degrees left, the bear would surely get our scent.

Taking the towline over our shoulders, we plodded on. The bear and the coyotes were busy with their skirmishing. We had covered one hundred yards when the wind hauled left.

I saw the bear wind us. He and the coyotes whirled, staring. Then they fled crosswind amongst high-piled rows of drift. We went on. Ten minutes later we reached the creek mouth. The carcass was that of a six-year-old Dall ram, shot through the ribs. I assume it had washed down the river. Well, close upstream lay a spruce drift-log we could tie to. We headed for it. The skiff had been thirty feet out in a steep riffle, held there by the wind. Now, between sand-filled gusts, a current slant swung it inshore. Wallowing, it grounded alongside the carcass. We heard a bawl. The bear had emerged from behind a drift pile. Bristled, he was watching the skiff. I guess he thought it was about to make off with his sheep carcass. He bawled again. Then he charged the craft. Some hard case. Bill's .300 Weatherby Magnum banged. The bear, lung-shot, fell at the skiff's stern.

Indian hunters have an unusual lot of trouble with black bears. One day Googla Second-Chief told me why—shortly after he himself had been worked over by a black bear. I was visiting the guy at Eklutna Indian Hospital.

"I ask for it," Googla said. "I'm trying to be a dumb Injun hero. The bear is denned up under that pink sandstone cliff a mile south of my Chickaloon cabin. The sled dogs find him. Well, I need meat. So I shovel the snow away and go in after him. I've got a lighted candle in one hand and my .30-06 Winchester in the other. The bear is curled up at the end of the tunnel he's dug. I should have shot him then. Instead I think it'll be smart to kill him with my knife. But just as I'm gonna stick the knife into him, he rolls over and gets up. He growls. Well, I only got two hands. I drop the knife into him, he rolls over and gets up. He growls. Well, I only got two hands. I drop the knife and reach for the rifle. The bear jumps at me. I shoot him in the neck, but it don't stop him. We rassle around in there it must be a half-minute before he dies. He bites me two, three times. He claws me some. It's a lesson.

"Because, if you ain't figured it out, one reason Injuns have black-bear trouble is we like to brag. We sit around a fire and tell yarns about how we usually kill black bears with a knife or an ax or maybe with a club. Big windies. Then the next time we meet a black bear close we think we gotta live up to our stories. And maybe we get hurt. Like I did."

Back to the beginning and Hank Peters. I skinned and dressed Hank's bear. Snow was coming down good now. We toted the carcass over to a cottonwood that had a convenient hangman's limb. Under the tree we found a mound of blueberry turf with a caribou antler sticking out of it. So that was why the bear had been so tough. Digging into the heap, we exposed the carcass of an elderly bull. Of course it was the bear's kill. He'd needed it. With winter coming on, he'd have been putting on all the fat he could. He had tried to chase us away, or perhaps kill us, because he thought we aimed to hijack the meat.

"He was wonderful," Hank said. "I learned about black bears from him. Unpeaceful ones are best."

1,000 Pounds of Trouble

"I try to see through the high grass,"
said the Watana Kid.
"Then a bear whooshes, practically in my face.
He towers above me. He's a 1,000 pounder.
I'm in trouble."

"**O**kay, there's your Alaska trophy brown bear," I said to Bill
Baker, my current hunter, when we spotted the bruin giant
and his mate in a snow line drift 120 yards above us. "An-
chor him, boy."

"He's fantastic," Bill said.

This was early in a crystal May afternoon above Chinitna
Bay, on the west coast of Cook Inlet. We had first sighted the
bears thirty minutes earlier. They were disporting themselves
in a snowy swale partway up the mountain. Rolling and tumbling. Chasing each other. We looked them over with 16X glasses.
The male was a likely brute. He had an unusual copper-tinted
coat. He would go around nine hundred pounds. Bill was so
excited his eyes bugged. We made our stalk up a narrow creek
ravine. Due to overhanging alders we had to climb blind for
eight hundred yards. Williwaw wind gusts were blowing from
every direction. Then the ravine widened. We saw the bears
reared on the snow-patched slope to our left. I suppose the erratic
wind had alerted them. They were trying hard to locate us.

Bill brought up his .30-06 Winchester. He was out of
breath. He had poor footing. There was sun glare in his eyes.
But it was a case of shoot now or lose an advantage. I heard

163

the 220-grain softnose hit. The trophy male flailed the air and toppled forward.

He slid thirty feet into some alders. I saw that he wasn't dead. His ribs were heaving. A moment later he lurched up. One side of his face was bloody. It looked as if the heavy slug had gone in his mouth and wrecked his jaw. But he could have made a getaway. There was cover a few feet distant. Instead he gave us a display of brown-bear courage. With a bawl he came smashing down through the belt of brush. He halted in the open, swinging his massive head. He wanted to fight. Beside me Bill's rifle banged again. I saw hair fly from the bear's brisket. He fell rolling. The rest of the slope was rimrocked. The bear pinwheeled, bounced and soared, to bust through an alder thicket onto the creek bars—forty feet from us. We went over to him.

The slug had scrapped his heart.

"Mister, that was hair-raising," Bill said in a voice that didn't sound like his. "It surprised the hell out of me."

I told him that brown-bear hunting was full of surprises. As I got out my skinning knife, I remembered the climax of a June hunt I had made with Pat Jarvis at Redoubt Bay. We were camped alongside Red Olson's salmon gill-netting station. In three days of hunting we hadn't sighted a bear. The fourth morning our luck changed. We were awakened by a splashing and slapping out on the mud flat. I recognized the sounds. They were made by netted salmon being grounded by the ebb tide. But then we heard a brown bear snarl. Dressing, we hastened to the beach line. The bear was one hundred yards distant, at the water's edge. An enormous beast, he was trying to pull a salmon out of Olson's net. He had lost his temper. As we watched, he gave a mighty tug, slipped, and fell sprawling. He bounded up, roaring.

Sounding off like a crazy animal, the bear attacked the net. He took a cork float in his mouth and savaged it. He bit through the lead line. Then he snatched up another salmon. Finding it also fouled in the linen meshes, he ripped it to shreds. He was an awesome example of frustration. I guess he knew he'd better get off the mud flat, but was too stubborn to leave without a salmon. He pounced on still another king and did better. He bit the salmon's head off, freeing it. With the big fish between his jaws, he galloped for the nearest timber—straight at us. Pat waited till the bear was one hundred feet distant. Then he stepped into the open. The bear skidded to a halt. Pat fired. The magnum slug hit the animal in the throat. He fell over and rolled once, hanging onto the salmon, and died. He was a fine trophy animal. About eight hundred pounds, with a rusty brown pelt.

"A berserker," Pat said. "No other animal in the world would have put on that show."

The brown bear is a slippery character to stalk. His eyesight lets him down, but he has sharp hearing and a first-class nose. He also appears to possess a kind of radar sense that warns him of danger. You'll spot a bear lying apparently asleep on a mountainside. You begin your stalk, with good cover and the wind in your favor. You don't make a sound. But suddenly the bear surges up and takes off, inexplicably spooked. Then there's the animals' restlessness. They roam seemingly without purpose or direction. You may follow a bear for hours before getting a shot or losing track of him. But it's marvelous sport, loaded with suspense. Most successful stalks are made on mountainsides or at creek mouths where the bears fish salmon and hooligan and hunt seals.

When I was a lad on this wild coast, we lived amongst the brown bears. Every move we made was conditioned by their presence. Our cabins and catches had to be proofed against them. We carried a bear rifle wherever we went. Even to the privy. The weight was bothersome when you were backpacking, but you endured it. You figured that if you left the weapon in camp just once, sure as hell you'd get fouled up with an ornery brown bear. On non-hunting forays up the salmon creeks, a man would pound on his frying pan to warn the bears he was coming or else sing in his loudest voice. The bears were good for us. They kept us on the ball. And they attracted golden pilgrimages of trophy-seekers. Now and then, of course, a man got mauled or killed. But usually it was his own fault.

The Watana Kid provides an example. The Kid had been guiding brown-bear parties since black-powder days. He was cautious. He understood the animals as well as any man living. But one August afternoon the law of averages or something caught up with him.

"I almost stumbled over the bear," the Kid related afterward. "You couldn't blame him for being sore. I'm heading up Drift River to establish a spike camp. I've been on the trail seven hours, toting ninety-five pounds. You know how it is when you're dog tired. You aim to make enough noise so the bears will get outta your way. You intend to keep a sharp lookout. But too often you don't do either. Well, I come to Telai Creek Flat. The grass here is chest tall. Suddenly I smell rotten salmon. Then I see a cloud of blowflies. I realize I have blundered onto a bear's salmon cache. When they can, they allus let their fish spoil. I thumb the safety latch of my .30-06 Remington. I listen. All I hear is creek sounds. Sidestepping, I try to see through the high grass. I see some movement. A bear *whooshes*, practically in my face.

"The bear rears up. He towers above me. He's a one-thousand-pounder. A shaggy dark so-and-so with yellow ears. I guess the creek's racket kept him from hearing me. Or maybe he was asleep.

"I drop my pack. The bear makes a swell target. But as I bring up my rifle I stagger like a drunk. Shedding the pack was dumb. That allus leaves you off balance. Well, the bear snarls, and I shoot. Blood mist jets from his shoulder. He jumps at me. I dodge and fall over the pack. Instinct takes over. I latch onto the pack and roll to get it on top of me. The bear slugs the pack. He bites off one of the packboard's wooden horns. He shakes the pack with me hanging onto it and belts it again. His blood is pouring onto my face. Then, as though in a terrific hurry, he lopes three-legged out toward the creek. I sit up and work the rifle's action. The bear is now sixty feet distant. The grass between us has been trampled flat. I hold [sight] on his stub tail, and pull. He goes down with a windy grunt, but gets up. I shoot him through the head. That one does it.

"Well, I take stock," the Kid said. "I find the bear has beat me up some, but I ain't complaining. I'm plumb delighted to be alive. Especially since the whole thing is my fault."

Brown bears are talented grub thieves. Take the windup of a May hunt I made with Tom Logan at the mouth of Big River. It was a still moonlit night. We were bedded down under a wide Sitka spruce. Pro-hunter's sixth sense must have awakened me. I opened my eyes but didn't move. Forty feet distant in the camp opening stood a trophy brown bear. A blond eight-hundred-pounder. He was gazing at our meat cache. The cache consisted of some bacon and the carcass of a fat black bear suspended from a cottonwood limb with net twine. Tom was snoring. I didn't have a prayer of waking him without spooking the bear. So I waited. The bear drifted over to the cache. It was eerie seeing an animal that big move silently as a lynx. Tom muttered. The bear froze, staring at him. A half-minute passed. Then the bear reared, set his teeth in our meat carcass, and yanked. The twine broke.

Carrying the one-hundred-pound carcass as though it were a rabbit, the bear faded into the moonlit timber. The only sound had been the pop of the twine. I woke Tom and told him what had happened. "We'll never catch up with him," he said.

We were lucky. The bear had ghosted toward the beach. As we scouted after him, a cub squalled ahead of us. There was a snarl, a crashing in the willow brush. Some kind of bruin drama was developing. We went on with due caution. The moon-silvered beach was bright as day. I saw movement fifty yards upwind. It was a huge dark sow and two cubs. They were facing away from us, looking up at the grassy top of a twenty-foot dune. I caught the flash of eyes up there. Then we heard the sound of heavy jaws crunching bone. We had located the clever cache-raiding trophy bear. He was hunkered behind a screen of dune grass, stuffing himself. I guess the audible feeding was too much for the sow. Anyway, she started climbing the dune. The trophy bear stood up. He bellowed at her. Silhouetted against the sky, he made a fair target. Tom knelt. His .300 Weatherby Magnum crashed.

Pitching forward off the dune, the bear lay motionless. "Man, what a cache-robber," Tom said in awed tones.

The brown bear's survival quotient has improved lately. It's been a long effort. When I was a kid, nesters at Kodiak agitated for a federal bounty on the animal. They argued that he was dangerous, and therefore an obstacle to progress. And boy, progress was a sacred subject. I knew Cook Inlet coaster types who never passed up a chance to kill a brown bear. But it's different now. The theme in Alaska today is: Preserve the brown bear, he's unique; also he's a state asset. Credit for this is due mainly to the militant new conservationists. I mean the kids have accomplished what legislators and enforcement officers maybe never could have. They have sold the Alaska public. They are getting solid cooperation. As a result, apparently the brown bear is safe.

Even when clowning, the monster bears are impressive. For instance, there was a performance Jack Benton and I witnessed one June morning below the mouth of Redoubt Creek.

We sighted the two bears at sunup. Hours earlier we had sailed a dory into the creek and sacked down on the bank. With no noise. No fire. Birds screaming out front woke us. Dressing, we headed for the beach. The forty-foot inlet tide was halfway in. We pushed through dew-wet willow brush and saw the bears. They were three hundred feet distant in the first waves, bounding about mysteriously. Above them circled a canopy of gulls, terns and other seabirds. One of the bears was special. I had 12X glasses on him. His long spring pelt was mahogany-colored. No rubbed spots. He would go 950 pounds. Both bears were grabbing at something in the water. A gull dived beside them, to surface with a silvery ten-inch fish in its beak. That explained the action. The annual horde of hooligan (eulachon) had arrived to spawn. Jack raised his .375 Winchester Magnum. I told him to take it easy.

If he killed the bear out there, we wouldn't be able to skin it until the tide ebbed. We'd have to moor the carcass to a stake. Maybe it would still be there when the beach was exposed again and maybe not. Some killer whales were hanging around.

Presently the trophy bear caught a hooligan and galloped ashore with it. He frisked ponderously, clowning. It really was funny. The fish weighed perhaps ten ounces. He had it by the tail. As he cavorted, the mob of seabirds swooped down at him. They eddied and dived, trying to snatch the hooligan. The bear reared, striking at them. Then the other bear came ashore and made a pass at the fish. This bear was smaller, with a straw-colored coat. Clearly it was the trophy bear's mate. They collided. They wrestled, rolling on the mud. The trophy bear dropped his hooligan. A kittiwake scooped the fish up and streaked downwind, with its wingmates pursuing. The bears stopped wrestling. They searched for the fish. Then they swaggered up off the beach, crosswind. At high-tide mark they got our scent and halted. Jack fired. The trophy bear spun, bawling, and fell over. Finished.

As I was saying, the brown bear is a difficult animal to stalk, but there's no finer sport. Take an eventful stalk Dave Winters and I made one windy May morning above Kahona Rapids. We sighted the bear catching trout.

He was seven hundred yards above us, on a wild celery bench. We sized him up with our glasses. A baldface, he had a striking reddish-brown coat. I thought he would go nine hundred

pounds. We climbed for him, through tangled alders. Fifteen minutes later we got our next look at him. He was at brush-line, scratching his rump on an outcrop. A bad thing to see. When the bears emerge from hibernation I guess their winter coats are almighty hot. Anyway, they get busy thinning them. They rub against trees and rocks. They pull out hair with their teeth. They slide down snowslopes. Well, our baldface stopped damaging his pelt and prowled west around the mountain. We followed, trying to get close enough for a shot. He turned east. We tagged along, sweating. Then he went out on a long snow stringer. He lay down there and rolled, squirming luxuriously. His mouth hung open, grunting with pleasure.

We had cut the range to five hundred yards. Dave set the scope sight of his .30-06 Winchester. He rested the gun over a ledge. Just then the bear stood up, took a running start, and launched himself down the snow stringer.

It was spectacular. He covered eighty yards at astonishing speed. Then the stringer ended in a patch of alders. He plowed end-over-end into the brush tops, out of sight. Bears keep doing it, so it must be fun. We worked crosswind down the steep pitch. The alders were thick. The ankle-deep brittle mat of last year's redtop grass was noisy. But the wind covered for us. We saw the shine of snow ahead, then saw the bear. He was on the far side of an alder clump two hundred feet distant, scratching his ribs against a boulder. Whuffing and grunting. Dave sighted through the brush. He fired. The softnose slug clipped off an alder branch and knocked the bear down. With a choking bawl the animal lurched up. He bit at his left side and charged. It was a blind charge, 30 degrees off. Dave had chambered another shell. He fired as the bear showed in an opening. Hit in the forehead, the bear fell stone dead.

"A wonderful brute," Dave said. "And his handsome pelt is still unblemished."

Back to the beginning. I finished skinning Bill's bear and lashed the hide and skull on my packboard. Bill said he wanted to try some of the meat. So I cut out the bear's tenderloins and added them to the pack. At camp we cooled the meat on a block of sea ice. Later we seasoned several steaks with salt, pepper, and powdered garlic, and broiled them over driftwood coals. I won't claim they were gourmet fare, but it's a fact I've eaten worse steaks in high-toned restaurants. At sunset we sighted a brown bear coming over a snowy ridge to the north. He was wallowing. When he reached bare ground, he stood gazing down toward the rapids. We put glasses on him. He looked good. He had a light brown coat that shaded to mahogany on his legs. I gave him eight hundred pounds. A legion of hunters, I told myself, were dreaming about bears like him. I sent them this thought: *They're the world's greatest gents.*

Grizzlies with Short Fuses

Adventures with bears
that declined to run away.

"Man, look at those spooky cayuses. They don't trust a grizzly even after it's dead," twenty-year-old Walt Davis, Jr. said as I began skinning his mountain baldface. "Just look at 'em."

"I'm looking," I said. "Check your chamber load, boy."

This was at timberline on Wood River, in the Alaska Range. A pretty June morning. Fifteen minutes ago we had been riding upriver, scouting. I heard a bear snort. Then two blond grizzlies loped out of some willows eighty yards ahead. I whistled. The larger of the pair, a five-hundred-pound baldface, halted. Walt had hit the ground fast. His .300 Weatherby blasted. The bear spun and fell over dead. It was an efficient kill and I congratulated the kid. We led the horses to a snag thirty feet from the carcass and tied them. They stood like statues. They were sourdough hunting cayuses. The smell of grizzly blood didn't faze them any. I rolled the carcass onto its back. The pelt was taffy-colored, beautifully prime. I got out my knife. Then Red, my sorrel gelding, blew sharply.

Both horses were staring past me, crosswind, ears cocked, nostrils flared. Red struck the ground with a front hoof. I took a careful look over my shoulder. Nothing there but sixty feet of open mossy ground and then a wall of burgeoning willows. But I felt my neck hair lift. At this point Walt commented on the horses' behavior. I stood up and started systematically taking the willows apart.

There was a shadow that didn't belong. It wasn't moving with the wind. I took a step forward. Willow tops bent and shook. The shadow became a blond grizzly. I am sure it was the mate of the bear Walt had shot. She humped her back and urinated. She grunted. Then she swaggered toward us, showing her teeth, pigeon-toeing, rolling her shoulders. Clearly she had returned looking for the boyfriend. The rut was in full swing, and I guess she had it bad. Plenty of hunters would have killed her. She had declared herself. As a result, she was one of the most dangerous animals on earth. But Walt took a chance. He put a slug between her front paws. Gravel sprayed her. She buck-jumped sideways, roaring. Then abruptly she lost her nerve and fled.

"Some arrogant sow grizzly," Walt said sort of breathlessly. "She acted as though she owned the countryside and we were lowdown trespassers."

That's a grizzly characteristic. It's part of what makes the species great. Also it's the basis of most grizzly trouble. For another example, take an experience Baldy Thomas and I had one spring afternoon in the Talkeetnas. Baldy and I were urgently fish hungry. Since freeze-up we had been on a trapline diet of moose meat, beans and bannock bread. Consequently we had begun daydreaming about sumptuous feasts of broiled trout and spring greens.

The ice had gone out. Bare ground was showing on the birch ridges. Then one morning the first robins yelped in the clearing, and Baldy declared it was time we made our annual spring pilgrimage. He meant hike up through the foothills to Lynx Lake and do some fishing. Lynx Lake is special. When its outlet creek opens, hordes of gaudily colored Dolly Varden trout gather on the upper two or three riffles. They'll hit recklessly. I said I'd be ready in ten minutes.

It was a six-hour jaunt, using webs. At the lake we cut a grizzly's deep-wallowed trail but didn't try to locate the animal. Our minds were on fish. Thick shelf ice overhung the outlet creek. As we went out onto it, I heard a heavy splashing. An instant later we saw the grizzly. He was in the creek, twenty feet distant, five feet below us. He had caught a nice Dolly Varden, and was about to jump up onto the opposite ice rim. There are handsome grizzlies and ugly ones. This specimen was ugly. His shaggy coat was tobacco brown. He had a

174

hog snout. He would weigh about 450 pounds, and most of it was in his slab shoulders. Well, I suppose he winded us. Anyway, he whirled with a muffled *whowf-whowf.* Baldy and I shed our packs. It was up to the grizzly. He could beat it in peace if he wanted to. We sure didn't need him. The ugly oaf glared. Suddenly he opted to fight.

Baldy had stepped ahead of me. The bear dropped his trout, bawled, and came across the creek in two bounds. He jumped for the ice shelf we were on and would have made it easy but Baldy's .30-06 Remington banged. Hit in the chest, the bear landed short and clawed the ice for pawholds. He was looking me in the eye as he tried to muscle himself up onto the shelf.

Three feet of the ice caved. The bear fell back into the creek. The mass of ice came down on top of him, driving him under. He fought clear of the ice and stood up. He was coughing blood and water. I saw that his right leg wasn't working but he started for us again. Baldy let go another shot. The 220-grain softnose smashed the bear's muzzle and went through the neck. He fell but lurched back up, bawling. He was still trying to attack. Baldy shot him between the eyes.

Well, you've got to admire such an animal. Obviously he had regarded the riffle as his private fishing spot. And he figured he was big and tough enough to hold it. Give him credit, I thought, for a sound frontier attitude. Then Baldy growled, "Damn it, he's fouled us up good. It's late, there ain't much daylight left. And instead of us catching a mess of Dolly Vardens for supper, we now gotta slide down there and skin the ornery sonofagun."

The grizzly has a heap of glamor. He is probably the country's No. 1 trophy bear. Naturally frontier folks respect him, but he makes a lousy neighbor. One reason is he's larcenous; every stilt-legged "siwash" cache in Alaska is a monument to his aggressive thievery. You can proof a log cabin against black bears and wolverines. Nothing to it—just wedge the door shut and spike pole shutters over the windows. But you can't proof a cabin against the grizzly. If he wants to break in, he will dig through the sod roof or maybe dismantle a wall by heaving the logs off their corner notches. The solution, of course, is a cache. A tall one with tin sheathing bands on the legs. But some of us maintained up to half-a-dozen trapline and hunting cabins.

We never got around to building caches at all of them. So we were vulnerable. And the bandit grizzlies raided us.

I sojourned for years amongst grizzly populations. Fifteen years in one fine grizzly range and nearly that long in another. Some seasons I encountered a lot more grizzlies than humans. The worst troubles I had with the animals were over meat at camps without caches. A grizzly goes haywire when he scents a fresh carcass. If he gets a chance to take possession, four times out of five you've got to kill him. For example, there was an episode that occurred during a September moose hunt I made with Bill Harris at Erickson Lake in the Susitna Valley.

Bill killed his trophy bull a mile from the cabin. It was late afternoon. We packed the antlers, the cape and a rack of ribs to camp. Next morning we went back to finish the job. A grizzly was at the carcass. First we heard ravens bonk-bonking eight hundred yards ahead. I could tell they were circling the meat pile. We got out our glasses. The bear stood fifty feet downwind from the meat. He was a whopper silvertip, close to six hundred pounds and plenty hostile about something. His mane had bristled. I saw him snarl. He made a fake rush at the meat. Now I understood. Yesterday, to reduce weight, Bill had taken the canvas sack off his packboard and hung it on a birch limb above the meat. It was swaying in the wind and presumably the bear thought it was alive. As we watched, he let out a bellow and charged hellbent. Batting the sack down, he began savaging it. Some tough grizzly.

I asked Bill if he wanted the animal. He replied, "Hell, yes." So we commenced a hasty stalk. But the wind shifted just enough. We were still out of range. I saw the bear get our scent. He started to leave but changed his mind and returned to the meat. He paced nervously. He stood up, snuffling the wind. Finally, with visible reluctance, he took off. Well, we got busy packing the meat to camp. There were seven packs. Because of the bear, we made short relays and kept the two meat piles always in sight.

Experience and a pro hunter's sixth sense told me the bear was somewhere downwind monitoring our operation, but we didn't get a glimpse of him. He knew how to use cover. It was dark when we reached camp with the last two packs. I figured the bear would give us trouble before morning. Since he had taken possession of the meat once, he would consider that he owned it.

The bear was a local. I knew him. I knew his parents and his litter brother. They were all determined thieves. Bill, wearied by the packing chore, turned in early. I stretched out with my clothes on. I had no cache at this cabin. We had simply hung the meat from a pole lashed between two dooryard spruces. Shortly after moonrise I heard a thud out there. I shook Bill awake, eased the plank door open, and handed him his .30-06. The grizzly was reared at the meat pole and had pulled down a hind quarter. He now took hold of a shoulder and yanked. The babiche tie-thong snapped. The grizzly let the shoulder fall. Bill raised his rifle. Something warned the bear. He whirled with a hoarse *whoof*. Bill fired. The bear made two bounds at us and went down. He was popping his jaws. So Bill gave him a make-sure shot.

"Okay, they are bandits. But they're wonderful bandits," Bill said when I had brought a lantern and we were admiring the silvertip pelt. "It's mighty easy to forgive them."

Grizzlies that won't run dominate campfire talk sessions up here. One night in Broad Pass, for instance, I heard three sourdough grizzly specialists hold forth on the subject. Frank Lee, Tanana Stewart, and Jack Filce. They had hunted grizzlies from the Sierra Madre to the Endicotts. Collectively they could claim nearly a century of experience with the short-fused glamour bears.

"Some of the real goshawful troubles I have had with grizzlies," said Frank Lee, "were started by cheechako sportsmen. Take the windup of a June grizzly hunt I made in the Yanert country with young Howie Hawkins.

"The trouble begins at Ptarmigan Ford, early of a foggy morning. I lead the ten-horse packtrain into the belly-deep fast water. Howie is riding up front with me. When we're halfway across the fog lifts a little and gives us a look at the opposite bank. It also shows us two blond Toklat-type grizzlies. The bears are hunkered on a windthrown cottonwood, ten feet above the ground. They're eating buds.

"I give each of them four hundred pounds. Their coats are straw-colored and they're first-class trophy bears. But this is a bad time to sight them. I tell Howie to take it easy and wait. Just then the bears get interested in us. One of them jumps down into a thicket. That makes the cottonwood bounce like a seesaw. The other bear rides it standing up, hanging onto a limb.

177

It's a spectacle that boogers the horses. My roan stud snorts. I hear the packhorses halt.

"Tom Owl, my Denna wrangler, yells at the horses. He slaps with his riata. Good. Let the bouncing show-off grizzly spook. There are plenty of grizzlies around. The important thing is to get the packhorses moving. If we don't, they'll lose their footing. The river will roll them and so long, outfit. I touch the roan with my spurs.

"He's a savvy cayuse. He lunges ahead, quartering into the current. The packhorses stall a moment longer, then decide to follow. I tell myself we're lucky. But Howie changes that. Maybe he didn't understand when I said to wait. Anyway, unnoticed by me, he has hauled his .375 Winchester out of its boot. He fires. In the fog the big magnum sounds like a cannon. I'm watching the bear. The bouncing character bawls and either jumps or falls off the cottonwood. Well, that does it. The packhorses, scared silly now, turn downstream into the fog.

"'Did I hit him?'" Howie asks excitedly.

"I don't answer. Instead I grab the kid's bridle and head downstream. We go off the ford into swimming water and catch up with the packhorses. They have grounded on a sandbar. Tom Owl is with them. As we splash ashore the roan stiffens, gazing across the foggy bar. He walls an eye at me. I get the message. The bears are over there.

"I tell Howie the score. We dismount and hurry to the far side of the bar. We halt behind a pile of drift. After a minute or so, I see movement in a foggy thicket. The two grizzlies come into sight, walking. One of them has a red gash across his forehead. I guess the pair figure they have left us behind at the ford and are plumb safe. Howie brings up the .375 and fires. It's a clean kill. The show-off grizzly coughs and falls over. I salute the kid. I tell him he is a genius because he certainly outperformed the grizzly."

There was laughter around the fire. Then Tanana Stewart began talking.

"Normal grizzlies understand about high-powered riles," he said. "You can predict their actions pretty well. Most of them would a heap rather run than face gunfire. But now and then you meet a rogue grizzly. They are something else. They're crazy. You can't figure them at all. I tangled with a big roach-backed rogue over on the Kahiltna one spring when I was a kid and it still gives me the creeps.

"I'm hand-sledding an outfit in on the May snowcrust. The first thing I do is set some beaver traps. Next morning I run them. I take a fine blanket beaver out of an open-water pond set and pelt the carcass. But as I'm resetting the No. 4 jump trap I get the sudden feeling I'm being watched. Then I hear snow crunch behind me. My .30-06 is standing against a birch ten feet away. I don't hesitate—I dive for the gun. *Wagh-h,* a grizzly roars.

"I snatch the rifle and roll over, thumbing the safety. Well, the grizzly is departing. Before I can lay sights on him, he goes into a belt of alders. But I saw that he was sizable and dark, with a fancy yellow mane. A so-called roach back. I check the marks his long winter claws made in the crust. He was stalking me, straight upwind. I suppose he wanted the beaver carcass. Anyway, he was only thirty-five feet away when I made the dive for my rifle.

"It's scary. I keep a sharp watch all day. No bear. But that night he runs my line. I go over the sign carefully at daybreak. I find where two trapped beavers climbed out onto the creek bank. The bear ate one and carried the other away, minus a hind leg he bit off and left in the trap. By now I know I'm up against a rogue raider.

"The next trap set is at a boulder-rimmed pond. As I angle down to it I see blood on the snow. Then I spot a trapped beaver lying dead under the pond bank. It's been ripped open. I shuck my right mitten and take a searching look around. The bear has got to be close. Fifty feet to my left there's a snow-hooded boulder. I see claw marks leading to it. I walk that way. I cover twenty-five feet. Then the roach back comes out from behind the boulder. He's slobbering as he jumps at me. I put a softnose through his skull. End of a rogue grizzly."

Jack Filce spoke up next.

"One August morning at the head of Metal Creek, in the Chugaches, a shanty-backed yellowtip grizzly ruined me financially. I'm prospecting. I have struck a little fireweed bar that's bonanza rich and build me a sluice box. I get busy shoveling pay gravel. Nuggets and dust collect behind the box's riffles. Ten days later I'm nearing the end of the bar, and I know I'm a rich man. Then the damned grizzly shows up. My camp is on a cottonwood bench 150 yards away. I'm cleaning some bedrock when I hear a tinny crash. Something has knocked the tent stove over.

"Picking up my .30-06, I run to investigate. I'm forty feet from the tent when this grizzly bounds through the flaps with a slab of bacon between his jaws. As he slams past me heading for the brushy bench rim, he gives a threatening snarl.

"I let go a shot. The bear bawls and drops the bacon. But he ain't hit hard. I saw hair fly from the top of his hump. Two inches too high. Putting on speed, he smashes down through alder thickets into a mess of windfalls. So all right. When he leaves there, he'll have to cross open ground. Then I'll kill him. I'm gonna need the meat because it's a cinch he has either eaten or scattered what little grub I had.

"Watching close, I see brush move in the windfalls. I rest the .30-06 over a snag. Then the bear busts into the open, galloping down the narrow creek margin. My sluice box is set up crosswise of the worked-out bar. The bear will have to hurdle it if I don't drop him first.

"He's now running in low willow brush. I fire and he somersaults. But he gets up and sprints on. He's only a few yards from the sluice box. I find him in the sights and pull. I hear the hit but he keeps going. I figure he's dead but won't admit it. Anyway, he tries to duck under the sluice box instead of jumping over it. A mistake. He's too tall. He hits it traveling maybe thirty miles an hour.

"The box topples. One end skids into the creek. The stiff current grabs it—and there goes my gold. The last I see of the loaded sluice box, it's whirling through a rapids. As for the yellowtip, he's down, not moving. Well, I tell myself he got the worst of it. But that don't help much. Me, I never could hold a grudge against grizzlies, no matter what."

I thanked the three sourdoughs. I said I would remember their experiences. And so I have.

Grizzlies can be tricky. For instance, there was an educational stunt pulled by a giant grizzly that used to come past my Susitna Valley homestead every fall at freeze-up. He had a set routine. Within twenty-four hours after mush ice clogged the creek, I would find his huge tracks on the bars out front. I had never sighted the solitary monster. He laid off me, and I returned the favor.

But then I told Hank Peters about him during a moose hunt. Hank was fascinated. He said it was a challenge—a special hunt for one particular traveling grizzly. Just the kind of odds-against hunt he enjoyed. So deal him in. He would wait over. Well, he waited twelve days. Then one snowy night we heard the mush ice. Next morning we looked for tracks. No tracks. But I assured Hank the bear would soon arrive. He was a punctual animal, I explained again.

We laid an ambush. It was on a hillside below the cabin where we could watch a hundred yards of the creek. We huddled there three hours. Snow was coming down thick now. Dry winter flakes. I felt embarrassed. This was the first time in five years the big grizzly had failed to ghost past on freeze-up morning. Then we heard magpies squawking up at the cabin. I had a hunch. I told Hank I thought the bear had bypassed us and to come on. We headed for the cabin at a run.

My hunch was good. We found a line of platter-size bear tracks. Then we saw that one side of the canvas-walled smokehouse had been ripped off. Salmon fillets and slabs of black bear bacon were strewn over the snow. Hank grinned, pointing. Directly in front of the cabin door, fresh and steaming, was a signature pile of dung. I guess maybe it *was* funny at that.

We took the bear's trail, running. He had followed the creek. We shortcut across a bend. We got ahead of him. Presently here he came. He was dark-coated, almost black in the swirling snow; a high-humped, one-thousand-pound apparition with a massive blunt-snouted head. When he was thirty-five yards away, I spoke to him. He stared and reared to his full height. A growl rumbled in his chest. I suppose it was an invitation to fight. Hank's .300 Weatherby hammered. Head shot, the enormous grizzly pitched forward, dead.

"Terrific," Hank said. "End of grizzly trouble. For now."

Adventures with Rut-Crazy Moose

Never a tacit animal,
the majestic moose can turn into a whirlwind
of killer speed, bone-crushing power and
fire-in-the-eye fury during the early
fall mating season.

"**M**ister, I sure want that crazy bull moose. He's magnificent. A wonder-antlered warrior with style," my client Hank Peters stated urgently as, with 12X glasses, we watched the rambunctious trophy animal perform six hundred yards upwind from our position atop a grassy spruce knoll. "But I can't hit him to hell-and-gone over there."

"Don't let that worry you. Here he comes," I said.

We were on the game-rich Dog Fork of Alaska's Kuskokwim River, five days' ride west of civilization. It was a bright September morning featuring moose-mating rituals. Our target bull had been out front in a timberline burn, sham-battling an alder bush. Eighty yards crosswind from him another bull had a cow backed against some high-piled blowdown. The eager oaf acted as though he believed she wanted to escape. Shucks, if she'd been unwilling she could have dodged clear anytime. Apparently neither bull was aware of the other's presence, but I saw the cow's big ears signaling. I guess she knew that another prospect was nearby. To further complicate the setup, small bands of barren ground caribou were drifting downvalley. One bunch had halted between us and the moose. It would be difficult to move without being spotted by them, and if they spooked, the moose would too.

So we stayed put. Our trophy bull was again attacking the alder bush. He feinted. He bounded sideways. He bored in, head down, and antler-whacked the bush with a combination left, right, left. Then he made a couple of buck-jumps and swapped ends.

He was plumb loaded with stuff and vinegar this morning. He turned toward us, testing the wind. I gave his head sixty-seven inches. The palms were wide and flat. I counted twenty-six points. The brow development was massive. He had no "bell." Instead a shaggy "muff" appendage decorated his throat. I estimated he would weigh about 1,250 pounds. He now humped his back and uttered a series of war grunts—deep, thudding sounds, clearly audible at our distance. At once, the other bull answered. Our bull froze, listening. His mane bristled, then he headed for the pile of windfalls at a fast trot.

Well, he busted through a thicket, and there stood the caribou—about 150 of them—alert and watching him. He shook his antlers and jumped at them. The fleet caribou took off. Gazing after them, he gave a loud snort, and antler-scythed a willow clump. The character had style, all right.

The other bull and his cow walked around the windfalls, and our bull attacked immediately with no preliminaries. The two crashed together and fought, head-to-head, for five minutes. The other bull went to his knees. His tongue hung out, while blood spilled from his nose. Still down, he took two antler-thrusts in the ribs, then managed to lurch up and flee. Our bull didn't pursue. The cow was trotting across the burn, and he galloped after her. She laid her ears back and squealed. He belted her rump with an antler blade. She halted then, submissive. So he had it made. She was his cow.

He had chased her two hundred yards, into easy rifle range. Hank rested his scope-sighted .30-06 Winchester over a bunchgrass hummock. He fired. The 220-grain softnose chugged home. Shoulder shot, the bull made one bound away from us and fell. We hurried to the kill. Hank patted the bull's scarred muzzle. "The fightingest Romeos in the wilds," he declared.

It's a fact. If the notion strikes a rutting bull moose, he'll fight anything—or try to. There was the suicidal, valiant bull that trotted through Talkeetna Village one autumn evening. A freight train was pulling in. The bull planted himself in the middle of the track. Brakeshoes screeched, and the whistle wailed. The bull charged. He slammed head-on into the engine, and was slashing with his antlers when he went under the drivers. At the headwaters of Montana Creek, a rutting bull chased my six pack dogs into a riffle and was stomping them when I shot him. Over on Kahiltna River a rut-wacky bull attacked a moored floatplane, wrecking its tail section. At my Toonakloot homestead on the Susitna, a screwball bull invaded the strawberry patch one starlit autumn night and demolished a scarecrow I had placed there to discourage larcenous robins. In short, the ornery brutes simply don't give a damn.

You can't "expert" rutting bulls because they are too erratic. Take the surprise climax of a moose hunt I made with Pat Jarvis in the Tonzona Basin. First, we happened on a mating scene. It was a chill September morning, and we were bringing our eight-horse packtrain up the timbered west bank of the river. We sighted the two moose four hundred yards upwind on the open east bank, so I got out the 16X glasses. The rut-smitten pair was plenty busy, so busy you'd have thought they'd be off-guard. But I'll be doggone if the chunky, young cow didn't have her head craned our way. We had good cover, and the river was making so much racket she couldn't have heard us. I guess sixth sense must have warned her. When the bull gave her the opportunity, she tried to sneak away. He blocked her. She tried again, and he got tough. He swung his head and hit her a good one. The blow staggered her. She gave up, for the moment.

Pat knelt, and sighted his .300 Weatherby Magnum. I still hadn't gotten a front or rear look at the bull's head. He stood quartering away from us, closely watching the cow. He was a rawboned giant—maybe fourteen hundred pounds. His antlers showed that he had passed prime age: The blades were long but narrow, and there was an array of freak points; some forked, others stuck out at queer angles. If the head had width, it would make a fine trophy.

The bull now pawed the ground, and grunted. He swaggered toward the cow, obviously with romance on his mind again, but the cow fooled him. She let him nuzzle her flank. Then, she sidestepped and lit out like an antelope for the timber. The bull pounded after her, and just as he reached the spruces, I got a good rear view of his head. It was okay—sixty-nine inches anyhow. I told Pat to take him, seconds too late. Before he could shoot, the bull went into cover.

Next morning at sunup, something spooked the horses. They came hobble-hopping pell-mell to camp. Pat and I hastily investigated. Forty yards from the tent, we beheld a bizarre sight. We had taken our wet saddle blankets out to a beaver clearing and hung them on bushes to dry. There, performing in the midst of them, was the elderly Romeo bull. He had a red blanket speared

on an antler tip. Whirling and lunging, grunting, he was battling the blanket to a finish. The chunky young cow was across the clearing, a spectator. Pat's .300 blasted. The bull, heart shot, dropped.

"Rutting bull moose," Pat said, grinning as he admired the freaky head, "seem to be where you find them, no matter how expert you get."

The colorful bravos will attack humans, but they sure don't make a practice of it. I hunted and trapped for many years in the three great moose ranges; the Kenai, Susitna, and Kuskokwim ranges. I had entire moose populations for close neighbors. We shared trails, the moose hung around my clearings, yet I was attacked only twice.

Of course, I never took any chances with the animals. I had learned my lesson at an early age from a scary episode which took place when Anchorage was still a tent-and-log-cabin town. I had a line of rabbit snares on the jack-spruce bench across Ship Creek. Meat was scarce in town, and mighty expensive, so I needed the rabbits I caught. While running the snares one late-autumn morning, I heard a rutting cow sound off ahead. After a moment, I spotted her. She was seventy yards crosswind in a grass flat.

I got down to hide behind a Hudson Bay tea bush. The cow was facing away from me. She tried the wind carefully, listening and waggling her sail ears. Then, she stretched out her neck and broadcast another invitation. It was a weird kind of yodeling, alto moan, full of impatience, and this time we both listened. If there was a bull around, I wanted him. I was plenty tired of rabbit meat. With a moose carcass hung up, I'd be set for the winter. Even the sourdoughs would envy me. They were boating moose meat from the Kenai. The cow worked her nose and ears a couple of minutes, then she started walking away. That dismayed me. I had confidence in her ability to summon a bull if there was one in the area, so I stopped her. I didn't have time to think and simply acted on impulse. I hid carefully and faked a bull's chesty challenge grunt.

The cow pivoted and took several steps toward me. Her ears were plumb rigid. She relaxed, snapping off some willow twigs, and began chewing them. She was pretending indifference. The poor dope really believed there was a bull calling to her. I was wondering how to handle the situation when I heard a curious sound behind me. I glanced over my shoulder. There stood a bull, 120 feet away, gritting his teeth. He was young and still fat, so he hadn't been chasing cows long. He had a ten-inch bell, and his neck was rut-swollen. He would weigh about eleven hundred pounds. And he was on the warpath. Maybe he didn't know what I was. Anyway, he gave a grunt and started for me. I shot him in the chest with my .30-06. He stumbled but kept coming. I put another slug into his chest, and dropped him fifteen feet from me.

These big critters were a great frontier asset. We owed them a lot. One fall afternoon on the Kashwitna trail, I added up my current debt to the species. I had halted to watch a bull up ahead of me on a burnt ridge, cleaning velvet off his antlers by rubbing them against a little dog-tail spruce snag. Rough and in a hurry, he pushed the snag over then chose another and pushed it over and another. It looked like he might run out of snags before he got his antlers cleaned.

I felt a surge of affection for the mean-tempered beast. I was wearing moose-hock moccasins and a moose-hide jacket, carrying moose-sinew thread for repairing them. I was on an eighty-five percent moose-meat diet, my cabins were lighted with tin-can lamps burning moose tallow. My snowshoes had moose-babiche webbing, I slept on a moose-hide bunk cover, and the only money I possessed had been earned guiding a cheechako moose hunter.

"Happy mating moon, friend," I hollered at the bull as he pushed over another snag. "May your tribe increase."

Rut-bewitched moose put on some of the best action shows in nature, and Alaska provides dramatic settings for them. Take a drama Dale Evarts and I witnessed one fall night at the Toonakloot homestead. The sound of hoofs woke me. I went to the north window for a look. There was an inch of snow on the ground. Colored aurora fires blazed in the sky, dimming the stars. Presently, a trim moose cow trotted into the clearing. I recognized her. She was a homestead guest, name of Judy. She had shown up last year, wolf-spooked, and stayed on. I was about to open the window and say hello when a bull loped into view, following her. He wasn't much, just a husky mulligan bull, with so-so antlers. But then I saw movement off to his right. It was another bull, a huge specimen, likewise pursuing our Judy. Red aurora light glanced from his antlers. They had spread. They looked good.

I shook Dale awake and briefed him. We pulled on pants and packs while Dale picked up his rifle, and I eased the cabin door open. The bulls had halted in the center of the clearing fifty feet apart. They grunted dire threats. They bragged about how ferocious they were. The cow stood beyond them in the shadow of a birch, looking straight at us. Dale nudged me, excited. This was the third day of his hunt, and he had expected to score out on the foothills. He had been resigned to the onerous chore of backpacking antlers and meat two or three miles—now we had a pair of candidates right in the dooryard. I motioned him to take it easy. I wanted a better look at the second bull's head. Besides, I didn't believe Dale had a good shot. The animal was ninety yards away, and aurora light is tricky. You think you can see okay, when actually you can't.

The bulls got through grunting. They closed, their antlers banging together. They began straining to break each other's neck. As they fought, the light improved. A band of pulsing neon blue had formed across the sky. The mulligan bull abruptly lost. Shoved backward, he tripped over a sawlog, and went to a sitting position. The big bull hooked him in the belly, threw him, then stomped him. That was plenty. The loser struggled up and, wheezing, limped for the timber. A fiery orange cloud was now drifting overhead, making more light. Our cow trotted toward the creek-flat birches, looking back. The big bull followed. I guess the cow figured she was taking over, but she made a mistake. She knew we were there, and she led the bull past us. His head would go about sixty-six inches. A nice trophy. Dale's .375 Winchester Magnum bellowed. The bull, hit high in the shoulder, fell sixty feet from the meathouse.

The bull moose is one of evolution's pets, superbly equipped for survival. He'll weigh up to sixteen hundred pounds. He is powerfully built, deep-chested, slab-shouldered, and short-coupled. His splay hoofs are made to order for Alaska's quaggy spaghnum-moss tundras. As the old-timers used to say, he roams where a saddle blanket would bog. His outsize ears are probably the sharpest in the wilds. Break a match-sized twig, and he'll hear it at 150 yards. A bull's nose is equally keen. He'll pick up a cow's body scent and trail her at a gallop, on long legs which also enable him to travel in the big snows while a thick hollow-haired coat insulates him against the cold. I have seen moose feeding at 60 degrees below zero. Of course it's his antlers that set him apart. They are the world's heaviest, and he grows them exclusively for rut-season fighting. He's a part-time mayhem expert, one of evolution's autumn-hardcase protégés.

You occasionally see cows fight and bulls could learn from them. They are fast and crafty. They go for broke.

Bill Baker and I watched two rival cows battle one early autumn noon at the forks of Montana Creek. We had been camped in the area three days waiting for the annual Moose Wind. It was impossible to hunt. The frosted birch forest was too noisy, and fallen leaves lay ankle deep. You'd spook more moose than you'd see. But today I figured we'd get wind and action. Clouds were piled in the south. The sun was hazy. So we anticipated and headed for this moose-pasture burn at the forks. I wanted to be ready.

Around noon a breeze stirred the treetops, and yellow leaves showered down. We rounded another creek bend. The burn was seven hundred yards ahead. I saw a bull's antlers flash there. I got out my glasses. The bull was busy pawing a hole in the ground. He sported a rare trophy head.

The bull was big. I thought he would weigh 1,350 pounds. His antlers would go about sixty-eight inches. Each palm had a matching wave in it near the tip. I noted a fine lot of points, but couldn't count them; the bull wouldn't stand still long enough.

A hard wind gust now whistled down the creek, bringing a golden blizzard of birch leaves. The bull squatted over the hole he had dug, and urinated. Suddenly he jerked his head up. Two fat cows had walked out of the bordering alders. They halted thirty feet apart, glaring at each other. Their manes bristled while the bull tossed his antlers and pranced for them. He had a project, so we started our stalk. The Moose Wind was blowing steadily now, and gaudy leaves filled the air. I saw the bull rearing, rut-happy and wind-drunk. But the plump cows ignored him. They had opted for trouble.

We sprinted two hundred yards. There wasn't much need for caution. The roaring Moose Wind and the clouds of bright leaves made it an easy stalk. The hostile cows had begun fighting. Like fat furies, they stood on their hind legs and struck and bit: They didn't need antlers. Their edged hoofs dealt sledgehammer blows. Their powerful jaws could kill. They slammed together in a sort of clinch, and one bit off half of the other's left ear. They kept wailing away without pause. A cow fell. The other jumped on her. There was a tangle of legs, and then they were both down. They bounced up and closed again. The bull just watched.

Bill rested his .30-06 over a spruce limb. He fired through level-blowing leaves, and missed—or maybe the bullet was deflected. The three moose swiveled to face us. Bill fired again, and the bull knelt, then fell over.

"Hooray for moose. I'm proud to be their fan," Bill said as the cows lit out upstream.

I favor timberline moose hunts. I believe they are the most rewarding. The open parks give you visibility, providing a chance to compare heads. You get selection.

Today, the eastern Kuskokwim valleys offer some of the best timberline moose hunting. They are high and "parky," fenced by Alaska Range snowpeaks. It's beautiful country—packtrain country without a village or a foot of road in it. You camp on a lookout rim, panning with your glasses. There are gangs of moose like you used to see on the Kenai, and they haven't been hunted much. I once saw four trophy bulls in the same quarter-acre dwarf-willow patch.

These hunts let you show off your stalking skill. Because you'll probably want close looks at a number of bulls, each stalk will present fascinating problems. Also it will sharpen your ability to judge a trophy head. It's grand sport.

Rutting bulls are hostile toward horses, and horses don't like them either. For example, consider a hunt Walt Davis and I made over in the Steep Fork Valley. We first sighted Walt's bull on a cottonwood bench. It was late afternoon, and raining. I had decided to call it a day when I saw the pale shine of the bull's antlers 650 yards upwind. I put my glasses on the animal. He was sizable—maybe thirteen hundred pounds. I thought his head might go seventy inches. He had a stubby bell, and his neck was grotesquely swollen. One of his brow tines stuck out like a bayonet. I couldn't count points—too much rain battering down. The bull had a cow with him. She was an elderly type, with notions. She had crowded against him. She licked his neck. She bit a tatter of velvet off his near antler. He paid no attention to her. He was watching something down in the valley. He shook his head. I saw his mane lift.

Walt said he couldn't score at this range. The rain was turning to hail, and I guess it looked like boulders in his scope sight. We began a stalk. I now saw what had made the bull angry—our ten cayuses. They were down in the timber, hobble-galloping, hellbent for camp, hail pounding their ears flat. As they tore past, the bull had a tantrum. He antler-whapped a raspberry bush. He crow-hopped. He pawed the ground. The cow shied away from him. Clearly she'd had experience. The bull took another mean cut at the raspberry bush, then trotted over the bench rim. I suppose he wanted to get the horses' scent. Anyway, there went our stalk. Half-inch hailstones were now whanging down. We huddled under a skinny cottonwood. When the storm ended five minutes later, the bull and the cow had disappeared. It was too late to track the pair, but I was sure we'd locate them again.

We did. Sooner than I expected. Early next morning we heard a bull grunt between camp and the river. Then a horse squealed. Walt grabbed his rifle, and we headed that way at a run.

I had a hunch that proved good. We climbed over a windfall and spotted the bull and his cow, slobbering as they pirated some rock salt I had put out for the horses. They had their heads angled away from us. The horses were bunched fifty feet beyond them, in Walt's line of fire. As we maneuvered for a safe shot, action developed.

My roan saddle gelding, Red, challenged the bull. Red was proud cut. He thought he was a stallion. Teeth bared, he danced in at the bull, but the bull met him halfway. Red struck, and missed. The bull raked Red's ribs with an antler tip. I told Walt to take a chance before I lost a good horse. He knelt. His .30-06 banged, and the bull, lung shot, jumped at the other horses. Walt shot him again, in the shoulders. That did it.

"Man, what an operator he was," Walt said. "Fantastic."

Moose are wary and elusive most of the year. They don't have time for exhibitionist activities. The grim business of survival keeps them busy. In winter, they battle deep snows, cold, hunger, wolves, and treacherous ice. Usually, they avoid trouble with other moose, but human scent will panic most of them.

192

Skeleton-thin in spring, they spend the summer putting on fat. The cows rear their calves. The bulls grow antlers. Naturally, by the time autumn and the rut comes, they are ready for a spree. That's the way they behave. Their abandon amazes visiting hunters. I remember a dialogue that took place between old Tex Cobb and a cheechako moose hunter he was guiding.

"That crazy slam-bang rut season fighting must take plenty out of the bulls," the hunter said. "It's a wonder they aren't all wrecks."

"Mister, the fighting," Tex replied deadpan, "is jist incidental."

Grizzly Fever

The epitome of big game in North America,
the grizzly is as unpredictable as he is cunning—
with legends as great as the land he roams.

"Oh, man, what a grizzly," my client Sam Lowry said, jerking his rifle out of its saddle boot, when he saw the big mountain silvertip on a morainal crest two hundred feet above us. "Oh, man, look at that beautiful pelt."

"Damn it, dismount." Unfortunately, I said this a split second too late for him to react.

The location was the headwaters of Healy River, deep in the Alaska Range. A crystal June morning. We had ridden out early to check the narrow east fork. The prospects looked mighty good. A sizable grizzly had passed this way, feeding on fiddlehead fern sprouts, after the dew stopped falling. His front paw tracks in the granite sand were six inches across. As we followed him up the bars, we found where he had halted to scratch himself on a mossy boulder. I reached down and picked some hairs off the moss. They were two inches long and silky. I pulled a couple of them across my thumbnail. They weren't sun-kinked, so the bear was still prime. Ace, my sorrel stud, had been snuffing the wind. He now laid his ears back to let me know we were getting close. He was gazing at the ridge summit directly above us on our left.

I scanned the crest. Nothing. Then I saw movement in a jumble of boulders below the skyline. The silvertip walked into view, climbing. He halted when he reached the summit, and peered down at us. Sam had spotted him instantly. I gave the bear six hundred pounds, which is about tops in these mountains. His handsome pelt winnowed when he moved. He was slab-sided and slope-backed. His long spring claws rattled on the rocks. Well, Sam had now turned in the saddle and brought up his .300 Weatherby Magnum. Maybe he didn't hear me tell him to dismount. The guy had a classic case of grizzly fever. I'll bet he had imagined this moment, with exciting variations, a thousand times. Before I could tell him again to hit the ground, he fired. Hair flew from the grizzly's forehead. The big animal grunted, then fell over and came tumbling.

But Sam had bought himself trouble. His mount, a high-headed bay pinto named Salty, tried to stampede. Sam reined him in hard and reached for the Weatherby's bolt handle. At this instant the grizzly landed on the sandbar between us. I saw that he had been bullet-gouged above the left eye. He at once popped his jaws and lurched up. I watched him over my sights. Salty, naturally, couldn't take all this. He let out a beller. He began pitching.

Well, Sam could ride a little. He stayed with the pinto, straight up, three jumps. The fourth jump stood him on his head in a willow bush. But he hung onto the rifle. He sat up and chambered a shell as the grizzly made a stumbling bound at him. He fired. The bear went down, finished. Sam spit out a mouthful of sand. His nose was bleeding. He was going to have a pair of black eyes. But he wore a wide grin.

"The big sonofagun cooperated," he said delightedly. "He was really coming for me, mister."

Sportsmen keep the *horribilis* legend alive. They admire grizzly temperament. They enjoy the danger and drama that hardcase grizzlies supply, and give the animals a slew of fan publicity. They often ask if it's true that grizzlies will make unprovoked attacks. The answer, of course, is yes, and the record is fairly gaudy. Take a hair-raising experience my Denna Indian associate Chilligan Redshirt had over on Slate Creek, in the western Talkeetnas.

"He was a no-good grizzly. A bad one," Chilligan said. "He's got no reason to be sore at me. I ain't done nothing to him. But he kills my dog, and then he tries to kill me. It happens at Lupine Flat, in June. I am heading for town with a pack of beaver skins, and have stopped here to make coffee and eat lunch. I've got this black three-month-old Susitna malamute pup with me. Named Teeko—Wolf. While I'm rustling some squaw wood, Teeko wanders two hundred feet up the grassy hillside and begins digging into a *hai-hai* marmot's den. A couple of minutes later I get the feeling I'm being watched. It sure ain't Teeko. He has now dug himself into the den. Only his tail is sticking out. But I feel eyes on me. I take a careful look at an alder thicket thirty feet above Teeko. I see a shadow move there. Then a grizzly steps into the open.

"He stares down at me. He is a copper-colored bear—maybe 420 pounds. High-humped and shaggy. Ornery looking. I ain't never seen him before. My .30-06 Remington is twenty feet behind me, lying across the pack of skins. I take a backward step. The bear don't like that. He shows his teeth. He rolls his heavy shoulders. I tell myself he must be an *anekdah doloon,* a man-hating grizzly. Anyway, he's asking for more trouble than he can handle. We watch each other. Then a hardluck thing happens. Teeko backs out of the marmot's den and the bear spots him. The pup is plastered with red dirt. He shakes himself, then looks down at me. He don't check the hillside above him. He's too busy letting me know how much he hates me. I now see the grizzly's mane lift, and yell to warn Teeko. But the pup don't catch on. He is still looking at me and wagging his tail when the bear starts his rush.

"I make a running dive for the Remington. But I know it's too late to save Teeko. When I turn with the rifle in my hands I see the bear coming fast down the slope at me. Teeko is lying below the marmot's den with his guts spilled out. It looks like the grizzly killed him with one wallop as he went past. I think, okay, tough bear, now it's your turn to die. Well, he makes a poor target on the hillside. He is traveling in long bounds over rough ground. But I cut down on his hump and shoot. I hit him, all right, but not where I want to. He keeps coming. By the time I get another shell chambered, he is on the flat. I think he knows he ain't gonna get to me. Because he raises his head and lets out a roar. I lay the gold bead square on his mouth and shoot again. I see teeth fly. The softnose bullet busts his head open."

"My friend, if I had an experience like that," Hank said, his eyes a-shine with grizzly fever, "I would spend the rest of my life telling folks about it."

Grizzly performance varies. Some grizzlies never get a chance to show fight. They stop an expertly placed slug and that's it. Others are too smart to fight. They know there's a heap more future in running. But the percentage of valiant hard-to-stop specimens is high. It is so high that even veteran woodsmen come down with grizzly fever. My sourdough partner Baldy Thomas, for example, had a swell case of it. Take the climax of a fall grizzly hunt he made on Spruce Creek, in the Talkeetnas, with young Dave Barry. "We're plumb lucky," Baldy told me. "We sight four grizzlies the first morning. They are eight hundred yards upwind, fishing silver salmon on that skinny riffle below the falls. We look them over with our 16X glasses. There's a blond sow, two blond yearlings, and a big mahogany-colored roachback male. The roachback looks trophy grade.

"It's a cinch stalk. There's good cover. The noisy fallen leaves are no problem because the creek is making a lot of racket. We work upstream through alder thickets to the riffle, and hunker down on a flat-topped boulder. The bears are now sixty yards above us. We get out our glasses again for a critical look at the roachback. He assays okay. His new autumn pelt is thick and clean. The yellow roach-mane reaches back nearly to his hips. He has a wide, blunt-snouted head. Dave says he wants him, and brings up his .375 Winchester Magnum. But I tell him to wait. Let the bear come ashore. A creek riffle is no place for a job of skinning. So Dave relaxes and we watch the roachback fish. He isn't doing so well. Dozens of bright silvers are trying to spawn on the riffle and the other three bears have scored. But the roachback keeps ending up with empty jaws.

"He tries again as a pair of husky silvers come splashing up the riffle. He crouches low. The salmon zigzag even with him. The water is so shallow that their backs are exposed. He now makes a fast bound, and grabs. He has done it exactly right, and deserves to win. But the salmon streak away from him. Well, he has a tantrum. He roars. He pounds the water. He pops his jaws. Then he takes off downstream after the silvers. They are long gone, of course, but as he comes abreast of us he meets another pair. He makes a pass at them and gets one by the tail. But he's sprinting so fast that he trips and goes over in a somersault. The silver flops free. It's funny. But the bear doesn't think so. He bounds up, raging—and spots us.

He stares. Then he charges out of the creek at us, bawling. Dave's .375 blasts. Blood and brains splatter. The bear drops.

"I congratulate Dave," Baldy said, "and the kid replies that he sure is thrilled. Also that he's dry-mouthed and sort of shaky inside, like butterflies. Shucks, I tell him that describes me too. And I'm proud of it."

Sportsmen expect a lot from grizzlies. And the animals produce. They have everything it takes. For example, consider a spring hunt I made as backpacker for Frank Lee and a hunter named Jim Harris. I was then eighteen, an apprentice learning my trade. The second morning we sighted two grizzlies from camp. They were seven hundred yards upvalley, on a wind-whacked fireweed flat, courting. We sized them up with our glasses. The male bear was a trophy yellowtip. I gave him 450 pounds. His winter-prime pelt was so long it rippled in the wind. He had a narrow head with standout ears and a ruff. He looked good. But as a Romeo he rated zero. He was letting the female tease him silly. A taffy-colored 350-pounder, she was an expert at dodging. He kept lumbering hopefully after her.

We began our stalk. It got complicated. We followed a game trail to the flat. The bears were still out of range. So our best bet was to work around the brushy rim of the flat. And we'd have to hurry, because the bears were moving away from us. Jim was wearing an expensive foofaraw buckskin jacket. He took it off and hung it on a limb, and told Frank he was ready. We jog-trotted through a half-mile of brush and blowdown to the upper limit of the flat. The bears were now four hundred yards crosswind. A reasonable chance. But Jim was panting. So we sat down and waited. The agile blond female bear was still playing hard to get. You see a lot of teaser sow grizzlies. So maybe the technique is necessary. Maybe male grizzlies need extra stimulation. Jim's breathing slowed. He knelt and lined his .30-06 Winchester.

The two bears stood quartering away from us. The female was now putting on a surrender act. Jim fired. But I guess he misjudged the wind. Anyway, he missed. I saw the slug hit two feet behind the target yellowtip. Both bears fled straight downwind. Jim fired again, and clipped hair off the trophy bear's neck. His neck shot was better. It knocked the bear down. But the animal bounced up and loped on. I thought he was hit behind the right shoulder. The two went into the timber where the game trail began. We trotted after them. Frank was in the lead. He halted at the timber's edge, and motioned for caution. Jim's foofaraw jacket lay there on the moss, ripped to tatters. Then we heard wheezing sounds. The wounded bear stood propped on his front legs behind some birch brush. Jim finished him with a head shot.

"Well, the wonderful brute made a token attack," Jim said. "I give him credit. He couldn't get at me, so he took my jacket apart."

The grizzly legend increases. Sportsmen add to it. New facts about the animals are discovered. For example, take the climax of a September hunt I made on the northern Kenai with Jack Benton. We sighted Jack's grizzly early the third morning. He was 350 yards upwind on a grassy timberline slope above Snider Creek, rubbing himself against a gnarled spruce "message tree." We looked him over with our 16X glasses. He was a tobacco-colored baldface. I gave him 460 pounds. He had a small hump. His back didn't slope. His face was triangular, with a thin muzzle and round blond ears. In some of the old natural history books this type of grizzly is listed noncommittally as the Kenai Bear. He now bit a mouthful of bark and wood off the message tree's trunk, and began chewing it. Jack raised his .300 Weatherby Magnum.

I kept my glasses on the bear. I was interested in what he was doing because I knew this message tree. I had found it four years ago. It was mysterious. Generations of grizzlies had visited the tree. They had worn its bark smooth. But what fascinated me was that they had apparently made a ritual approach to the tree. An ancient grizzly trail slanted up from the creek. The last sixty feet of it was pretty special. It consisted of a single line of paw prints worn down through five or six inches of redtop turf to mineral soil. I mean for some reason the many grizzly visitors to the tree had all stepped exactly in the same places. It was weird. I wish some savvy gent would explain it. The baldface was still chewing his mouthful of bark and wood. Jack's .300 hammered. The bear spun and bit at his shoulder. Then he made two bounds toward the sound of the shot, and fell over dead.

Grizzlies are also master bluffers. They'll make a sportsman look at his hole card. For example, there was an experience Bill Baker and I had one fall on Knik River. We were heading for my grizzly camp at the glacier, lining a sixteen-foot stampede boat. Late the fourth day a hard wind fouled us up. We were only a mile from the glacier front when the first wild gusts hit. I couldn't control the plunging boat, no matter how I rigged its bridle. So we brought her ashore. As we were making camp we sighted a grizzly crossing an open bar six hundred yards downwind. We put our glasses on him. I recognized the bear. He was a trophy-grade buckskin. A 440-pounder. He had a brown mane and saddle. His head was wide, with a short tan snout. He walked with a swagger. I saw him get our scent. He flinched, and half-reared to double-check the wind. Then he lit out at a gallop for cover.

Well, the bear lived hereabouts. So I figured we'd see him again. And we sure did. The wind quit two hours after sunset. We turned in. Some time later I got up to make sure the boat was safe. The pearl glow of moonrise showed above the peaks. As I stepped clear of the timber, rifle in hand, I heard movement ahead of me. Stones rattled. There was a splash. I knelt. There were no further sounds, but I waited. I had as much time as the prowler. Then the breeze eddied, and I smelled grizzly. I felt my neck hair lift. I tried to silhouette the bear against the river. No luck. I decided he was behind the boat. In the cargo was a crate of hams and bacon slabs for my camp. The bear probably figured this plunder was already his. Anyway, he was standing pat. It was my move. So I returned to camp. In about five minutes the full moon would rise. Then the odds would change considerably.

I woke Bill and briefed him. He dressed. He examined his .30-06 Remington. The moon rose and we eased down toward the boat. The craft was plainly visible now. But the bear had gone. We stopped and stood still, looking and listening. On our left was a solid bank of tree shadows. All of a sudden I knew the bear was there. I slapped the stock of my rifle. That did it. The bear roared. He was maybe sixty feet distant. He roared again. But he didn't show himself. He was running a big bluff. He wanted us to leave so he could loot the boat, but he was too smart to take any risks. The moon called his bluff. As it climbed it dissolved the tree shadows. In a moment we saw the bear. It was the buckskin. He had turned away, leaving. Bill now had shooting light. He fired. The bear staggered off balance, then recovered himself and charged. Bill fired again. The bear fell.

Back to the beginning. I skinned Sam Lowry's big silvertip. Then I folded the hide, hair side in, and lashed it and the skull behind my saddle. Ace flattened his ears and bared his teeth at me. I asked him who the hell he thought he was kidding. We rode to camp. I made a pot of coffee. The sun was now warm on the spring grass. We stretched out and lit our pipes. We watched the mountain morning grow. We were in one of the North's finest grizzly ranges, and we'd had it all to ourselves. Not another party within fifty miles. It was like the old days. Elbow room. It made a man feel grateful. Sam reached out and patted his silvertip skin.

"I'm a happy grizzly hunter," he said.

Adventures with Dall Sheep

An eagle's war cry ended the morning's peace.
The great Dall reared to meet his feathered challenge—
the bird flared. The ram was ours now.
Patiently we stalked....

"Listen, I vote we climb for that screwball ram," my client, Pete Waring, said urgently without lowering his 12X glasses. "What if some snow does clobber us? That's one hell of a Dall head, mister."

"All right," I said. "Let's climb."

This was on Wolf Creek, in Alaska's Tonzona Valley on a cold late-September morning, with snowfall imminent. When we sighted the trophy ram, he was showing off for three younger rams. We had gone out to locate our packhorses. I glanced up and saw the sheep—ivory-colored shapes grouped at the break of a snow-dusted hanging basin. We put our glasses on them. The ram seemed to be a lively performer. He had whirled, head lowered belligerently. The object of his phony hostility was a sheep-size boulder. He glared at it. He shuffled and faked. Then the rambunctious ham charged full-tilt. At the speed he was traveling he probably would have broken his neck if he had connected with the boulder. But he wasn't that reckless. He managed a close miss. Skidding to a halt, he faced our way. That gave us a good look at his horns. They surprised me.

I estimated the head would go 15x40 inches. It was typical of the Tonzona. The amber horns were wide and high. They were clean. No "brooming." Their tips had a stylish Asiatic outward flare. I counted nine growth rings. You don't see many better heads. Well, Pete said he was eager and snowfall didn't scare him any. Naturally. So I plotted a stalk. We backtracked three hundred yards to a canyon mouth. Above us now was a long talus pitch topped by a hundred-foot cliff. A ledge slanted up the cliff's face. It looked easy. But already a few snow-flakes were sifting down, and as we climbed the wind picked up. Then the edge of a snow squall hit us. The stuff was thick.

I could no longer see the valley floor. But we went on to the cliff. I found our ledge. The ledge wasn't dangerous. It averaged four feet wide, and the footing was good. We were doing okay despite the snow. But suddenly unexpected trouble struck.

Rocks rattled down. To mountain climbers that's a most discouraging sound. It got worse. A slab the size of a pack pannier landed on the ledge and burst like a bomb. Smaller rocks followed and then another big one.

Plenty spooked, we beat it on up the ledge. I now had the matter figured out. Our sheep were somewhere straight above us, fooling around on loose shale. We climbed a fifteen-foot rim. We muscled ourselves up to a patch of icy blueberry turf—and sighted the sheep. They were out in the middle of a slide-rock area, half-hidden by blowing snow, sixty yards crosswind. The trophy ram was sparring with one of his associates. Their hoofs of course dislodged rocks, which in turn dislodged other rocks. Pete checked his .270 Winchester, and I noted that he was panting. Presently the younger ram gave up. He stood statue-still as the trophy ram tapped his neck with a front hoof. I had seen this tapping bit before. It is, I believe, a grave Dall in-sult. Pete held his hand out and looked at it. Apparently sat-isfied that it was steady, he raised his .270. He fired. The tro-phy ram dropped.

"Every Dall-sheep hunt is an adventure," Pete declared when we had gone over to the kill. "You always get action. You can always count on suspense and thrills."

I said he was dead right, and got busy with tape and knife. (The horns averaged 14x41 inches.) His remark had nudged my memory. I was recalling a Dall hunt I had made with Bill Baker in the Mt. Deborah country. Killer coyotes figured in that one. We were eighty packtrain miles east of the railroad. While scouting a nameless creek one morning, we sighted twenty-six sheep on a lofty slope upstream. There was one patriarch ram. The others were ewes and their young. I sized up the ram with 16X glasses. He was unique. His horns would go around 15x42 inches. They were dark and scarred. Both were broomed. But I counted fourteen growth rings on the left horn. That made the ram at least sixteen years old. Close to a longevity record. Bill was fascinated. So I worked out a stalk. Thirty minutes later we topped a ridge four hundred yards crosswind from the ram. He had climbed. He was now well above the ewes, at the edge of a boulder field. He seemed nervous.

Bill stretched out. He said he needed to catch his breath. I now saw that the ewes had stopped feeding. As I watched, they began drifting downwind. Then we heard coyotes behind them. A shrill yip-yapping chorus. The ewes and their youngsters at once stampeded. In a moment we spotted the coyotes. There were three of them. They streaked out of some alders and cut in on the flank of the band. They were lean and long-legged, and they killed expertly. Within half a minute they had pulled down two lambs and were trying for others. Bill adjusted the scope sight of his .30-06 Remington. Our ancient trophy ram hadn't moved. The ewes started up to him, but changed their minds. Ahead of them was a wide mudslide scar. Smooth and cement-like, it dropped five hundred feet to the creek. A sheep trail crossed the slide. The ewes made for it. They were smart. It was a deadly place.

I figured Bill would take the ram first. But he chose the coyotes. And the lamb killers cooperated. I guess they didn't savvy mudslides. Anyway, they followed the sheep out onto this one. The trail was some eight inches wide. There were no other footholds. Not even for sheep. Bill fired. The lead coyote was a yellow brute with gray legs. I saw the 150-grain slug hit him. He tumbled off the trail and pinwheeled, squalling, down the long slope. The other two coyotes halted. They started to turn back. Bill fired again. One of the pair wailed and jumped aside—into emptiness. The remaining bravo raced for friendlier ground. He didn't quite make it. Bill dropped him at the rim of the slide. Swell. The assassins had deserved their fate. I turned to see how the ewes, lambs, and yearlings were making out. They were now off the slide, climbing a sandstone buttress. Plumb safe.

But the trophy ram had disappeared. We searched the mountainside for ten minutes with our glasses. No ram. Then I saw movement between two shattered pillars, 450 yards distant. The old-timer stepped into view. He was gazing down at us. Bill rested his Remington over a ledge. The gun blasted. I heard the slug hit. The venerable ram made a bound forward and came rolling.

"Pure adventure," Bill said. "A great sheep-hunting experience." (The horns averaged 14¾x41 inches.)

Sheep-hunting styles change. When I was a kid roaming the Chugaches we backpacked in for the big Dall heads. Later our customers switched to expedition-type hunts. Today it's come full circle—backpack hunts are popular again. Well, you get action. The guy toting his grub and gear on a packboard can go where the fancy heads are. For example, take a backpack hunt I made with Sam Weston high against the Chugach ice field. We went in from the Matanuska side. Late the fourth day we sighted seven good rams. But a cloud mass frustrated us. We had climbed to a shale summit overlooking Metal Creek glacier. The rams were a mile north of us, bedded down alongside the ice. I studied them with the 16X glasses. One had a splendid head. The horns were massive and close-curled, slung low in the impressive Chugach formation. I saw that much. Then the cloud mass bulged toward us, concealing the sheep.

We angled down to the glacier. We made a backpackers' camp on the ice. I had some moose jerky in my pack. I fetched water from a creek that spilled off the shale ridge. We ate and drank, then turned in. After a while the cloud flowed over us and stayed. At daybreak a scraping sound woke me. It came from above the ice. It seemed familiar. Then my memory hooked up. Somewhere yonder, close, a ram was brooming one of his horns. I put a hand over Sam's mouth and shook him. I whispered that we were in business. We pulled on our boots and waited. A dawn wind was now moving the cloud. Sunrise-tinted sky showed. Then we saw the seven rams, fifty yards distant. Our trophy ram was working on his right horn tip, grinding it against a boulder. I suppose the horn interfered with his vision. The other rams stood watching him. I touched Sam's arm and nodded.

There wasn't time for a check with the glasses. It didn't matter. I could see both horns. They would go about 15x40 inches. Sam brought up his .250-3000 Savage. I saw that he was shivering.

I don't know what warned the trophy ram. One instant he was busy trying to broom his horn. The next, he whirled with a snort. He took one look at us standing there in waist-deep cloud drift and went bounding up the slope. The other rams followed without spotting us. They were all headed into the bright sunrise glare. Sam fired and missed. I heard the howl of a ricochet. He levered another shell into the Savage's chamber and tried again. This time he scored. The trophy ram shied, then rolled back down the slope. A layer of cloud was concentrated at the glacier's edge. The ram plunged into it. I heard his horns clatter on solid ice. Watching our footing, we hastened over there. The ram had fallen into a crevasse. But it was a narrow ice crack, and his horns had wedged. I used our packboard lash-ropes to salvage the carcass.

"Most fun I ever had in my whole life," Sam said. (The horns averaged 14½x42 inches.)

When I was seventeen, backpacking for the Watana Kid, The Kid had booked a sheep hunter named Dan Summers. He took him into the western Talkeetnas. The fifth day we sighted a likely ram high on the divide between Montana Creek and Sheep River and climbed for him.

We toiled up to a lupine terrace, six hundred yards downwind from the ram. He was walking toward us. We put our glasses on him. His horns would go maybe 13x40 inches. They were clean and unbroomed. I observed that they were set low, like the Chugach horns, with no marked V-gap between them. Dan rested his scope-sighted .270 Winchester over a boulder and waited. The ram came on. He looked plumb lazy. But presently a parka squirrel whistled above him. The ram jerked his head up. Another parka squirrel whistled. Then whistles sounded all over the mountainside. I'll bet one hundred squirrels had joined in the chorus. The ram ran fifty yards. Then he halted, trying to look in all directions at the same time. I glanced at the Watana Kid. He wore an odd expression. The Kid was part Indian and superstitious. I had a good idea as to what he was thinking.

"I don't like this, gents," he muttered. "Any ram that parka squirrels will whistle at is best let alone. So maybe we better look around more."

Dan slipped the .270's safety latch. If he heard the Kid's remark, he paid no attention to it. He had a shot to make. The range was now 430 yards. There was no crosswind. The ram was again walking toward us. But the front view of a sheep doesn't give you much usable target. So Dan didn't hurry. When at last he fired, the ram stumbled and went down. An efficient kill. The parka squirrels stopped whistling. As we stood up, I saw something move in a wash forty yards ahead of the downed sheep. Then three grizzlies loped into sight—a big sow and two husky cubs. The Kid, sounding mighty relieved, said he'd be doggone because the mystery was solved. The parka squirrels, of course, had been whistling at the grizzlies, not the ram. Their reputation was intact. (The head averaged 13½x41 inches.)

Dall sheep hunters tend to be colorful, dedicated types. Fun to hunt with. For example, take a Dall hunt I made with Hank Peters over in the Yanert Basin. We went in from Broad Pass and made our base camp at the mouth of Edgar Creek. Next morning during breakfast I sighted a fine trophy ram. He was on a broken summit upstream, sham-battling a golden eagle. We got busy with our glasses. The eagle was circling. It screamed. Then it winged over and pitched down at the ram in a vertical dive. The ram reared to meet it. But at the last instant the eagle opened its wings. Pulling out of the dive, it began circling again. The ram curvetted. They seemed to be having a big time. Then a hard gust of wind hit the range shed. The eagle banked, letting the gust carry him upvalley. We now took a careful look at the ram's head. Hank was excited.

He had reason to be. It was a grand head. It would go perhaps 14½x42 inches. The horns were unblemished. Their spread was unusual even for Alaska Range sheep—at least thirty-three inches. I counted ten growth rings. The striking surfaces of the horns were deeply ridged and almost black. There was a considerable V-gap between the horns. Both horn tips were curved sharply outward. Well, the ram had spotted us. He appeared to be gazing straight into my glasses. He was a square-built specimen with some fat on him. I estimated he would weigh 160 pounds. His back and rump were stained rust-red by mineral soil he had rolled in. Wind gusts were belting him now, rippling his coat and blowing his ears flat. Clearly he enjoyed this. He stretched his neck out, mouth open. Then he made some frisky buck-jumps and swapped ends. Feeling good.

"That's my Dall ram," Hank said. "I like everything about him."

There are easy stalks and tough stalks. This one was an S.O.B. We climbed the backside of the mountain. Acres of wet cloud mist streamed past. Eighty feet below the summit we had to slant up a crumbling rock spine. It was dangerous. We were hanging on with both hands when I looked up and saw the ram. He was one hundred feet to our left, peering down at us. After a moment, he took off. Hank looked at me and grinned. We went on to the summit. The ram wasn't in sight. I hadn't expected he would be. Hank slipped on some ice and fell against a shale column. When he straightened, his nose was bleeding copiously. He said it would stop sooner or later. At this point the golden eagle coasted over us. The great bird skidded toward a ledge sixty yards distant. Then our ram materialized atop the ledge. He was watching the eagle. Hank's .30-06 Winchester banged. The ram fell.

As I said, Dall fans are fun to hunt with. They have what it takes. (The horns averaged 15x41 inches, with a thirty-three inch spread.)

Dall sheep always did rate tops on this frontier and not just because they are prime meat-critters. The trophy bug bit us early. We were horns-conscious. Every roughneck mountain man I knew as a kid kept his eyes peeled for big Dall heads. It was a hobby and a sport. Also, of course, it was business. Most of us knew the location of a few wonder-horned rams that we aimed to cash in on as soon as we found the right cheechako sportsmen. For example, there was a special ram I discovered north of the Kashwitna. He was shy. He stayed back toward the glaciers. I had got only glimpses of him with the 16X glasses, but he was something. His horns were the heaviest I had seen. Two years went by. Then I got a good look at him. It was late autumn, and six inches of snow had fallen. I was dog-sledding a trapping outfit upriver. I halted for a smoke and saw the ram.

He was seven hundred yards above me, on a wind-cleaned graywacke ridge. I got out my glasses. He had a ewe with him. She was biting icicles off his neck. I rested the glasses against a spruce. The powerful lenses brought the animals so close I could see black hairs in the ram's tail. Taking my time. I estimated his horns would go 16x39 inches—a great trophy head. Well, I now knew how to hunt him. Dall sheep have

routines and are punctual. It was almost a cinch that next year at this time I would find him up there on that same ridge. So all I lacked was a sportsman who didn't mind hunting sheep in snow and cold. The ram turned and saw me. I waved to him. He stamped the snow with a front hoof and lit out up the ridge.

I returned exactly a year later. I had booked young Tom Logan for the hunt. It was snowing. We camped a mile below the ridge. Next morning the sky cleared, and we spotted the ram and a ewe on a snowslide swath close beyond the ridge. The ram was courting, shoving the ewe around and nipping at her flanks. We hurried up through the timber and began our stalk. It brought us out on a rimrock 250 yards downwind from the sheep. The ram was still courting. Tom checked the muzzle of his .270 Winchester. As he knelt to shoot, the ewe saw us. She stared. Then she tried to dodge past the ram. When he blocked her, she struck at his muzzle with both front hoofs. She was doing her doggonedest to warn him. But he was rut-happy. He didn't catch on. The ewe feinted one way and ran the other, but he was faster. He crowded her against a boulder. Then Tom fired. The ram half-reared and fell over.

Bitten by the trophy bug, I had waited three years to put a tape on this ram's horns. They averaged 16-1/8x38 inches. I was as pleased as Tom.

As I dressed out Pete Waring's ram, I told him about a Dall hunt that got plumb bogged down in action and suspense. It happened in the Wood River country, in September. Jack Benton was my client. Scouting up Grizzly Creek the second morning, we sighted a group of twelve rams. They were high above us on a scarlet cloudberry slope. Just loafing. Enjoying the sun's warmth. I looked them over with my glasses. There were four trophy heads. I couldn't, at this distance, tell which was the best. Tying our horses, we began climbing. Forty minutes later we crawled over a dizzy cliff-brink three hundred yards downwind from the sheep. Two of the rams were now facing each other in warlike attitudes. As we watched, they demonstrated a bit, and then charged together.

It was some impact. You could have heard it down in the valley. Both rams went to their knees but got up fighting. They battered and slugged. Neither took a backward step. They weren't fighting over a female. There was no female present. Besides, the rut hadn't even started. I think they

were fighting simply to find out which was the most formidable. A matter of social status. You often see slam-bang
fights when boss Dall rams meet. I was hurriedly trying to
appraise their heads. The wind had begun to shift, and I figured
we didn't have much time left. But the rams were moving
around so fast I couldn't keep my glasses on a horn. I mean
we had action and suspense, all right—an oversupply of both.
Then we got some more. The other two trophy rams had been
swapping dirty looks. They now snorted and stamped. They
shook their horns, and they were fighting, too.

A plenty exciting show. I had never before seen two ram fights
going on at the same time. But it didn't last long. The wind kept
hauling around. I felt it on my right cheek. Then there was a
brief lull. Then a puff hit the back of my neck. That did it. Five
seconds later all twelve rams were in full flight. I told Jack to
take the nearest ex-combatant ram. He knelt. His .30-06 Remington crashed. The ram wheeled over, heart shot. Well, the head
averaged 15x38 inches, and Jack was delighted with it.

"Every Dall-sheep hunt is an adventure," Pete Waring
declared again, chuckling.

I buy that, friends.

Grand Stalks for Smart Billies

Stalking mountain goats is pure drama—
plus work, sweat, aches,
pains, and mighty groans!

"**H**ey, what the hell? All of a sudden those goats are adrift in space. The mountain isn't there anymore," Jim Blake, my hunter, said in a spooked voice, staring, through his 12X glasses. "Take a look, man."

"I'm looking," I said. "It's a snow mirage."

This was in Alaska's Kashwitna Basin. An overcast late-September morning. Six inches of new snow. A frosty wind combing the timberline parks. We had sighted the goats from camp. It was a mixed social group—two adult females, two yearlings, a kid, and a whopper billy. They rounded a snowy talus pile eight hundred yards east of us and halted, gazing down into the basin. I checked the billy with 16X glasses. He was heavy and patriarchal. High-humped. Square-quartered. His silky autumn coat looked cream-yellow against the snow. Using his head as a yardstick, I gave his horns nine inches. They were perfectly matched and jet black. They tapered to clean back-curved dagger points. Well, it was a cinch he had spotted us. So we fooled him by taking off northward into a line of riverbank spruces, which we followed upstream to a gulch mouth before we began our climb.

It was mean going. There had been an earlier snowfall above brushline, and it had crusted. The buried crust was slippery. Worse, it kept breaking noisily under our weight. We climbed

213

twenty minutes, then topped the ridge we had used for cover. The goats were now four hundred yards upwind. A fair chance—but Jim was panting. So we waited. The trophy billy stood apart from the other goats, on a flange of bare rock. He was biting at snow that had balled up on his front hoofs. He looked huge. I thought he might be one of the storied three-hundred-pounders. He bit off another chunk of snow and chewed it, wrinkling his nose. At this moment the mirage began. The eerie deception is common in these peaks. First a luminous blue wash flowed across the slope. Then the snow became misty. Cloud-like. You could no longer see its surface. The billy jerked his head up. I heard him snort.

Jim muttered that he'd better shoot, ready or not. He rose to a kneeling position and brought up his .270 Winchester. The billy half-turned to face us. Jim fired and missed. I saw the slug hit rock at eight o'clock. The billy fled, with the other goats breaking trail. Jim fired again—another miss. The mirage was now complete. Sky and snow were the same blue tint. There was no horizon. No shadows. No slopes. The cliffs hung unsupported in blue space. Jim fired again, but the billy kept going. I had often wondered if the mirage deceived goats' eyes. I now saw that it did. The five trail-breaking goats abruptly disappeared. A moment later they came back into view, climbing over one another. They apparently had tumbled ignominiously into an unseen gully. Jim tried again. This time I heard the slug hit meat. The billy bucked and fell over, finished.

"Pure drama—that's goat stalking," Jim stated when we had picked our way over to the kill. "And boy, they sure make you work."

I said it was a fact. The mirage was fading out. I got busy with my steel tape and belt knife. Jim's remark had brought memories to mind, and as I took off the cape I told him about a goat stalk Jack Benton and I had made above a glacier east of Lake George, in the Chugaches. We'd had a weather handicap. For three days the peaks had been cloud-hung. But early this particular morning the sky cleared and we sighted the goats. There were thirty-five of them, scattered across the pitches of a small hanging valley alongside Pass Glacier, two miles distant. It was a seasonal gathering. The snow is late going off this valley. As a result, its grass and browse have springtime succulence along in the middle of autumn. Goats assemble to feast on it. The stuff seems to act as a physic. I guess it helps prepare the goats for winter.

We headed up the glacier. A median line of shale dumps provided fair cover. But there were many crevasses and pot-holes. I mean it was a tricky two-mile approach. At the valley mouth we spent a half-hour looking the billies over. The like-liest candidate was a trouble-beset ancient. I estimated him at five hundred yards crosswind. He stood at bay in a little clump of ground-hugging aromatic vine willow. Goats are especially fond of vine willow, so naturally he had competition. A non-trophy billy and two fat three-year-olds were trying to evict him. Tentatively. He wasn't much for looks. His coat was patchy and stained. He had a sway belly. But he carried a fine set of horns. I gave them ten inches. As we watched, the three claim-jumpers closed in again. He attacked them instantly. He went in fast, hooking for their paunches—a magnificent battler. They retreated. But not far.

Jack rested his .30-06 Remington over an ice shelf. He sighted, then shook his head. With a crosswind it was too far. So we resumed our stalk. We toiled on up the glacier a quar-ter-mile, then left it via a moraine bridge. Our trophy billy still had problems—the claim-jumpers were moving in again. I wished them bad luck. We climbed to brushline, then followed a long bench to its upwind end. I figured we were now within fifty yards of the billy. Ahead of us was a forty-foot-wide snow stringer. Steep and risky. Beyond it rose a broken red shale spine. We went across the hard-packed snow at a run—the safest way. As we made a landing, rocks clattered above us. Then goats stam-peded around the upper end of the spine. It was the three claim-jumpers, with our trophy billy in dire pursuit. Sixty feet dis-tant. Jack's Remington crashed. The venerable billy dropped.

"Never worked so hard for a trophy," Jack said. "Or had so much fun."

There are no easy goat stalks. The goat has too much going for him. He lives in savagely hostile terrain. His icebound peaks are storm centers. He is smart—a clever tactician. He can out-climb anything. He seldom panics. His eyes are about equal to six-power glasses. He has sharp ears and a good nose. Thus you earn your goat trophy. You work and maybe risk your neck. And this delights today's adventurous goat fans. They like tough stalks. Brag about them. For example, take a stalk I made with

Hank Peters at the head of Granite Creek, in the Talkeetnas. Early the second morning we sighted a billy and a female. They were on a crest nine hundred yards up the valley. Watching us. I got out my 16X glasses. The billy was a promising beast. His new autumn coat looked plumb white against the sky. I couldn't make a close estimate of his horns because he was facing me, but I had a hunch about them.

His gaze centered on my glasses. Or seemed to. He stood in a lazy hip-shot pose. His long face with its hairy nose, dark eyes, and pin ears was trophy-handsome. He had summer fat on his ribs. I thought he would weigh 180 pounds. The female had crowded against him and was licking at a blueberry stain on his right hip. I got the impression she was about to open the rut season unilaterally. He swung his head at her. She bounded aside, watching him over her shoulder. I now got my first real look at his horns. They would go ten inches. Maybe better. Which made him a prize. So I began laying out a stalk. I could tell we were going to have weather trouble. A slaty cloud hung over the valley head. The air was still down here, but there was a stiff wind aloft. The goats were leaning against it. The temperature had dropped. I would have bet that some snow was going to fly.

There is only one sure way to stalk a goat. Put the mountain between you and him. We did that. But of course we climbed into blaring wind. And then snow pelted us. We inched up an ice-paved chute to the summit. You couldn't see one hundred feet. But my pro hunter's sixth sense was working. I knew the goats were still here—close. We waited in the lee of a shale column. Twenty minutes went by. Then something moved on a dead-ended shelf fifty feet below us. It was the female goat. She bounded into view, looking over her shoulder. And held the attitude. A shaggy coquette. I tossed a rock beyond her. She gave me a wild look, and fled past us in the blowing snow. Then the billy appeared. He was splendid. He stood figuring his chances. Then he came up off the shelf with a rush. Hank's .30-06 Winchester blasted. The billy crumpled, dead. Hank went over and stroked his mane. He was mighty elated.

"Thanks for a great stalk," he said above the gusty snow-wind.

When I was a kid we were all goat fans. There were no large moose populations in the Chugach and Talkeetna ranges then—forest fires hadn't yet cleared the way for browse crops. So we depended on the goats for meat. Also for cash money, since they attracted blue-chip cheechako sportsmen every fall. We respected and admired the critters. We liked everything about them. The rugged stalks we made for them became campfire sagas.

None of us goat-country roughnecks were trained climbers. We had no rock technique. Shucks, we didn't even know there was such a thing. But when it became necessary, we could get the job done. Take an experience Dale Evarts and I had in the Blue Hole, across Knik Glacier. We got a break the second morning. Three goats appeared on a wiregrass slope seven hundred yards downwind from camp. Two sizable billies and a female. The rut had begun here and the billies were plenty sex-wacky. These two stood twenty feet apart, heads lowered. They had been fighting—their elegant new coats were bloodsmeared. But the female didn't seem interested. She was busy scratching an ear with a hind hoof—sitting down to do it. One of the billies had trophy-class horns. I gave them nine and one-half inches which was good, since the trophy average was eight inches. The two sexy hardcases now charged together.

Their set-to was brief and bloody. Typical of goat fights. They went straight in and reared against each other, stabbing both horns. The trophy billy was heavier than his opponent. He forced him off balance and raked him twice across the face, then hooked him through the cheek and tossed him. The rival rolled ten yards down the slope. He lay there a moment. Then he got up and climbed back to his original position. The two stood glaring belligerently as before. I noted that the female was again scratching her ear. We now began our stalk. The goats hadn't seen us—some alders gave us good cover. We headed downwind one thousand yards, and turned into a side canyon. The canyon's west wall was next on the agenda. I knew it was going to be bad. It was brown sandstone and the stuff scares me. It crumbles. It has no clean edges. You can't trust it.

Well, there were two cliffs. The first was bad and took fifteen minutes. The second was a heap worse and took thirty minutes. We muscled ourselves up a chimney. We eased across a slide-rock gut. Then we came to a place where we had to jump five feet to a ledge. I made the jump and turned to watch Dale. He did all right. He landed in a crouch, balanced—but the rotten brown sandstone gave way under him. A two-foot slab of it. He was scrambling for a handhold when I grabbed his wrist. We rested a bit. Then we went up a dry falls to the top. Our goats were now 250 yards down the slope. The billies were again threatening each other. Then the female spotted us, and stamped. The three at once fled over the canyon rim. They raced across the grim upper cliff-face in a few easy bounds, onto a cloudberry terrace. Dale's .30-06 Weatherby banged. The trophy billy knelt, and died.

"I'm amazed I'm here," Dale said with feeling.

Goats are action critters. But also they are crafty. They make you think. A stalk for them can become as complicated as chess. Take an experience Baldy Thomas and Hal Baker had above Isaac Creek, in the Talkeetnas. "We hunt four days and don't see nothing but females and young stuff," Baldy told me. "Then around noon the fifth day we get lucky. We sight two trophy billies. They are on that long summit east of the forks. We check them with spotting scopes. They're gaunt old-timers, standing shoulder-to-shoulder. They haven't shedded out good. Their coats are ragged and iron-stained. But they carry first-class horns. There ain't much choice between them. Both heads will go over ten inches—which is great. Then I take another look and decide one set of horns is maybe a bit heavier than the other. Hal says hooray—but he'll be mighty proud to take either head.

"The old-timers have seen us. So I play it safe. Or try to. We climb the back side of the mountain, and top out at the downwind end of the summit. Takes us two hours. And our billies ain't in sight. But after a little scouting, we spot them on a cliff one hundred feet down the other side. They see us at the same instant and we trade stares. Their heads assay even better at this close range. But we're hogtied. All we can do is look. The narrow ledge they are on overhangs five hundred feet of space. Shoot a goat off there, and the fall would smash his carcass to smithereens. So the billies win this round. When they've sized us up, they head upwind across the cliff. Taking their time. Staying together. I figure they're buddies because their breeding days are over and other goats won't associate with them. We watch the pair, plenty disappointed, until they go out of sight. A man can get awfully discouraged at a time like this.

"But we ain't licked yet. This is a swaybacked mountain, and the cliff peters out yonder. I figure we can catch up with the goats. We work 150 yards along the summit to the beginning of its sag—just in time to see our goats angle down amongst some big crestline boulders. We get only one glimpse of them. They are smart. They've got perfect cover now, and know it. We wait a half-hour. The goats stay put. Then a golden eagle comes coasting along the crest. It banks, and circles above a lichen-covered boulder. That's good enough for me. I am certain-sure the eagle has located our goats for us. So we Injun down to said boulder—and a flock of rock ptarmigan roars up in our faces. They were the eagle bait. I cuss myself. But just then there's a pounding of hoofs. The two ragged old billies lope out from behind another boulder. Hal's .270 Weatherby hammers. The heavy horned billy falls.

"A 'pair of operators,' Hal says respectfully."

Back to the beginning. The snow mirage had flickered out. We dragged Jim's billy off the mountain. I finished dressing the carcass. I packed the meat and the trophy to camp. We loafed a while, smoking. Then I brought our eight horses in and spent a couple of hours tightening their shoes. Afternoon shadows now filled the valley. It was getting cold. I built a good fire of spruce logs in front of the tent. When the fire had burned down some, I raked out a bed of coals for cooking. I wired a rack of ribs to a willow pole and propped them over the coals. I made coffee. I heated a kettle of navy beans. The ribs were fat and I let the firm tallow scorch a little. When the meat looked about done, I made a thick slab of Dutch oven cornbread. Jim brought pack panniers for seats. We ate. The stars had come out. An orange aurora fan backlit the snowy goat peaks. Jim sighed luxuriously.

"May there always be mountain goats," he said.

Don't Turn Your Back on a Black Bear

Plunder makes a black bear do crazy things.
One time they'll run scared
and the next they'll be trailing you
for their next meal.

"That would-be camp thief chickened out," my hunter Pat Jarvis declared, laughing, as we reined in at a pattern of black bear tracks forty yards crosswind from our two tents. "He took a wistful look, and decided the project was too dangerous."

"No, he didn't," I said. "Get set for action, boy."

This was at the head of Yanert River, in the Alaska Range, on a windy September morning. We were bringing my eight pack cayuses to camp for a ration of salt. They had now picked up the bear's scent, and a snorty bay wanted to stampede. I could hear Tom Talkeetna, the Denna Indian wrangler, talking to him. The camp had at first looked all right. A pleasant high-country bivouac. But then I spotted something. Wind was bellying the 10x12-foot cook tent and when a hard gust whipped the entrance flaps apart I saw the shadow of a black bear on the rear wall. He was a sizable brute. He had his head cocked, listening. We had surprised him. He hadn't had time for any looting. I saw his mouth open in a soundless snarl. Pat couldn't see the telltale shadow—he was too far to my right. But he nodded, and slid his .30-06 Winchester out of its boot.

The bear stepped into view. He stalled at the tent corner maybe ten seconds, figuring his chances. He was a first-class trophy black. I gave him two hundred pounds. His thick autumn coat shone in the sunlight. He had some cinnamon-brown on his snout and a small off-white blaze on his chest. As for his chances, they weren't good. The only safe cover within three hundred yards was behind us—a tangle of alder brush and storm-thrown spruce timber. To reach it he'd have to make an almost suicidal run between us and a rimrocked bank. I doubted that he had the guts for it. But the handsome character fooled me. He took off in an all-out sprint as Pat brought up the Winchester. The black's course for several bounds was straight at us, and I guess the horses thought we were being attacked. Anyway, they panicked. Pat shot, but he didn't have a prayer.

His roan gelding was two feet in the air, swapping ends. The 220-grain softnose wailed off a rock behind the running bear. By now we had nothing but horse trouble. The bell mare I was leading gave a bawl and tried to yank free. At the same time Pat's roan reared and came down across the taut lead rope. The bell mare bit him. I felt my sorrel stud, Red, fight for balance, so I let the dallies smoke off the horn. The bear slammed past us thirty feet distant. He was grunting. He was so fat that his sides joggled. He didn't even glance at us. He was concentrating on reaching that cover. Well, Pat was no bronc-stomper. He didn't pretend to be. He now simply kicked his feet out of the stirrups and unloaded, fast, on the Injun side. He then lined the Winchester and fired. The bear fell skidding, fifteen feet from the alders.

"Mister, I owe this bear's ghost an apology," Pat said a bit later, kneeling at the carcass. "He was one reckless, gambling sonofagun."

I said sure. Black bears are unique. They are the only four-footed habitual camp thieves I know about that have a high popularity rating. Folks cuss them and praise them with equal enthusiasm. The larcenous animals are baffling because their raids seldom are motivated by hunger. I mean they risk their lives to loot camps when tons of berries and salmon are available. Moreover, they steal inedible items. There used to be a black bear on Knik River that stole my hip boots every chance he got. And for a classic example, one night during the Nelchina gold rush two black bears made off with a mule harness. I have lived many years amongst large black bear populations and done a heap of thinking about the animals. My conclusion regarding their thievery is that it must be, at least partly, a kind of screwball bruin sport.

Plunder excites them. They lose their normal caution and savvy. Consider a hunt I made with Tom Logan at my Toonakloot homestead. This was in September. There had been a frost and then some warm days, thus the blueberries were fermenting. The countryside smelled like a winery. Early the first morning we sighted two black bears feeding on a blueberry ridge six hundred yards east of the cabin, and checked them with 16X glasses. One bear was trophy grade. I thought he'd weigh 180 pounds. His coat was clean and silky. The other was an ornery looking specimen with unshed hair clinging to his ribs. As we were making our stalk, six spruce grouse pitched down a few yards from the bears. Our trophy black glared at them. Then he uttered a roar, charged the birds, tripped over something, and fell. I realized he was drunk.

So was his companion, it turned out. Also the grouse. The birds got up with extravagant wing-thunder and then circled back to the same spot. Big wine-filled berries hung in clusters there. But the birds didn't get to enjoy them. Both bears charged the flock this time—tangle-footed, *whowf-whowfing*. Meanwhile we had cut the range to 250 yards. Tom was ready to shoot when the grouse banked toward us. Their wings were set for a landing, and then they saw us and flared noisily. Well, the bears may have been barrelhouse plastered, but they sure understood what had happened, and they got on the ball instantly. They fled, stumbling and grunting, hellbent, into a willow thicket. It was too fast for Tom.

Clever bears. We hunted hard the next four days without scoring. But the fourth night three blacks outsmarted themselves. They made a raid on my meathouse. It was the second raid this fall, and was typical. The racket they created woke us. Tom grabbed his .300 Weatherby Magnum and I eased the front door open. The meathouse stood 150 feet distant. There was a bright hunter's moon. The bears ripped the screen door off the meathouse and two yearling blacks were on top of it fighting over a moose quarter. The third bear had rolled a five-gallon keg of salted salmon caviar into the yard and was trying to break it open. I recognized him. He was our hotshot trophy grouse chaser. He now spotted us, but didn't spook. He was excited, loot-happy and stupidly defiant. Tom stepped past me and fired. The bear fell over, dead.

"Friend bear, you were amazing," Tom said as we went out to the kill. "Thank you for a grand hunt."

Black bear raiders are sometimes dangerous. For example, there was a hair-raising experience my colleague Billy No-Dogs had on upper Goose Creek, in the Talkeetnas. This was at the end of May. "The bear acted nuts. If I hadn't been lucky, he maybe would have killed me," Billy told me afterward. "I'm heading into the peaks to pick up a grubstake. You know that tumbledown cabin on Lynx Flat? Well, out behind it last fall I find two mossy sluice boxes. They look fifty years old, and some mining crew has put a lot of gravel through them. I figure it's a cinch a few ounces of gold dust was pounded into the soft spruce planks and riffles. So I am going back there now to burn the boxes and pan the ashes. I'm backpacking— bucking snowdrifts. And it's late afternoon and I'm a half-mile from the Flat when I spot this whopper black bear up ahead.

"Oh, boy. I'm glad to see him. There just ain't no better eating than the meat of an early spring black bear. Not to an Injun's taste, anyway. I shed my pack and put my glasses on him. He's three hundred yards upwind on a caribou moss slope, heading toward the Flat. He'll weigh close to 250 pounds. The glassy snow crust had hacked his paws up—he's limping badly. I tell myself he must be in a plenty lousy mood. Well, I cut down on him with my .30-06 Remington. I hang the silver bead on the top of his shoulders and squeeze. The shot feels all right. It should have dropped the bear but he gets a break. He steps into a wash just as the rifle bangs. It's a clean miss. Before I can chamber another shell, he lopes out of sight down the wash. Man, am I disgusted. I pick up my pack and go on. Twenty minutes later I reach the Flat.

"I camp beside the old cabin. A herd of moose has been yarded on the Flat. Close-by I see two winterkilled carcasses sticking out of a snowbank. Well, I need firewood. So I take the ax and head over to some spruce timber on the creek bank. I find a pitchy windfall and start dragging it to camp. I'm feeling better. But as I round the cabin, I get a bad surprise. A black bear snarls. I take one more step and spot him—thirty feet distant, with his front paws on my pack. I figure it's the same bear I shot at. He snarls again. All that moose meat handy, and he

wants my few pounds of Injun grub. Or thinks he does. Well, he's between me and my rifle. So I use the ax. I drop the windfall and make an underhand throw. The ax turns over once and its blade chunks through his right eye into his skull. He jumps at me, then goes down.

"Man, you've got to admire a bear that game," Billy concluded, "even if he is a damned camp thief."

Gameness and orneriness are black bear characteristics. The wonderful brutes will even carry out grudge raids. Take the main event of a June hunt I made with Jim Baker. This was on Isaac Creek, in the Kashwitna Basin. The hunt opened well—we sighted a promising bear the first morning. He was on a snowslide swath five hundred yards crosswind when we looked him over with 12X glasses. He assayed good. I estimated he would weigh 190 pounds. His new coat was thick and glossy. So we made a stalk for him. He was preoccupied—he had found a patch of mountain celery sprouts and was stuffing himself. It was fun watching him. He would bite off a foot-long sprout and chew it blissfully, with his eyes shut. A real bruin gourmet. I now got a front view of him and saw that his forehead was deeply scarred. The scar looked like an old bullet wound.

We cut the range to four hundred yards. Jim now sat down and readied the scope sight of his .270 Winchester. I had my glasses on the bear when suddenly he opened his eyes and stopped chewing. He jerked to attention. Maybe a freak eddy of wind had alerted him. Or maybe it was animal sixth sense. Anyway, he spooked. With the partly eaten celery sprout hanging out of his mouth, he fled headlong into a pussy-willow jungle. Jim hadn't had a chance. Well, we spent five hours trying to locate the bear. The next day we tried again. Still no luck. The animal was a master tactician. That afternoon we climbed a wild-rose knoll to make a last search with the glasses. We both happened to glance toward camp and stared. Our trophy-beautiful, elusive, scarfaced bear was raiding us. In a sort of frenzy, we lit out for camp at top speed.

We had the wind with us, and moss was underfoot. But when we catfooted onto the scene, the bear wasn't in sight. Still, I knew he was here. Shucks, I could smell him. I could feel his presence. We stood looking and listening. He had totally wrecked the camp, and it had to be spite work. I noted that he had even torn our slickers to tatters. Apparently somebody had wounded him, and this was part of his revenge on humans. Well, alongside the ruined cook tent was a waist-high boulder that we had used for a table. That maybe was the spot. I pointed, and Jim began moving in. My hunch was good. Jim had taken four steps when presumably the bear heard him. With a startled *whuf-whuf*, the animal streaked from behind the boulder. He dropped my beaded sealhide rifle case as he passed us. Jim fired. The scarfaced bandit fell, stone dead.

Black bears are difficult neighbors, sure enough. But they put on some of the best dramas in the wilds. There was a special one I witnessed during a spring hunt on Knik River. I was a youngster then, backpacking for the Watana Kid and a hunter named Tim Dolan. We sighted two bears the second afternoon; a mated pair. We were heading across a mile-wide sandbar to our riverbank camp. Suddenly the Kid halted. The two bears had just walked out of some willows one hundred yards downwind from our camp and boat—but seven hundred yards crosswind from us. We put our glasses on them. The male bear was a trophy-grade 230-pounder. He had wintered well. His ribs were padded. His coat had a nice shine to it. The female was about half his size. They were both snuffing the wind. They had scented the camp and of course knew we weren't there.

Well, it was humiliating. We had to watch the bears raid our outfit while we made a stalk for them. They were cautious at first. They lingered in the final bit of cover. They circled the camp twice, working their noses. Then they rushed in. It was a lean-to camp. Our grub was under a tarp inside the shelter. The male bear went straight to it. I had my glasses on them again. He clawed the tarp aside and took a can of condensed milk between his jaws. He bit the can, then dropped it and lapped the milk that leaked out. So he was a can-biter. Not many blacks learn that trick, praise be. The female crowded alongside him. Obviously, to her can-biting was a fascinating new stunt. She poked the male bear with her snout. I saw her drool. Then she boldly grabbed the can. He took a swipe at her, missed, and picked up another can.

We shortened the range to 350 yards. Tim knelt now, and raised his .250-3000 Savage. But he was panting a little. Mostly from excitement, I thought. Anyway, he shook his head. The Kid advised him to wait. I put my glasses back on the bears. The male was now working on a can of peaches. As I watched, the female tried to snatch the can. The male bared his teeth at her and she backed away. She then gave him the sexy come-on treatment. Frisking. Inviting him to play. He fell for it. The spring rut clearly was more important to him than canned peaches. Pigeon-toeing, shuffling, he headed for her. And she dodged past him and grabbed the can and ran toward us. He galloped in pursuit, but she was fast. She stayed ahead of him. Well, Tim laughed and brought up the Savage again. He waited until the bears had covered fifty yards, then fired. Our can-biter went down and stayed down.

"Top drama," Tim said. "A great show."

Black bears go wacky over red meat. Take an experience I had one fall on Toonakloot Creek. I had shot a fine mulligan bull moose a mile above the homestead cabin. It was a gray snow-threatening afternoon. I toted a pack of meat home. When I returned an hour later for another load, I found that a black bear had laid claim to the carcass. I was right at the meat pile before I saw his work. I stood statue-still sizing up the scene. I knew I had trouble. I had made the kill in a little opening walled by birch brush. With no tree handy to hang the meat in, I had stacked it on shale slabs and covered it with the hide. The bear had rearranged things. He had tipped the pile over and buried it under a litter of moss and dead grass. Then he had deposited a mound of blueberry dung beside it as proof of ownership. I whistled—and a bear snorted ahead of me and to my right.

He snorted again. Then he walked into sight fifty feet distant. We regarded each other. He was heavy-shouldered and sum-mer-fat. I gave him 210 pounds. His jet coat practically glowed against the yellow birch leaves. I wanted him—he had outlawed himself, and he was swell smokehouse material. But the odds were against me. I saw instantly that I couldn't score. The bear was in a narrow gap between two thickets. At my first move he would flee. And one bound would put him into thick cover. I had my .375 Winchester Magnum in my right hand. The gun was chamber loaded, and I used iron sights. I was fairly fast with it. But the moves totaled too many. Bring the rifle up. Thumb the safety latch. Make a quarter-turn to the right. Point and fire. It would all take less than a second, but longer than the bear needed. However, I tried it—and the bear bounded into cover before I could fire.

He had good reflexes. He was savvy. I heard him a moment loping over crisp frosted leaves, then he was gone. Well, I cleaned up the meat and stacked it. I lashed a shoulder on my packboard. I covered the rest of the meat with the hide to keep birds off it. A red squirrel was now sounding off eighty yards downwind. I listened carefully. He was watching something, all right. The bear, I figured, had angled that way so he could keep track of me by scent. I shrugged into the pack-straps and started homeward. To make it easy for the bear, I lit my pipe. I plowed noisily through the brush. But after ten minutes I shed the pack and headed back. I took my time. No noise now. No smoking. I sighted the bear at forty yards. He was at the meat pile again. He had just picked up a rack of ribs. I spoke to him. He dropped the meat and raged at me. I shot him through the head.

The fat thief hadn't been hungry. I found his belly was crammed with blueberries and black currants. But the big pile of moose meat had made him daffy. He couldn't resist trying to steal it.

Back to the beginning. I skinned out Pat's bear and dressed the carcass. We hung the meat from a spruce limb. It was now a pretty morning, with cloud shadows moving across the tall Yanert peaks. I rustled some aromatic red willow wood and built a fire. I started a pot of coffee. I spitted the bear's liver and loin meat on green birch sticks and propped them over coals to broil. Tom Talkeetna, the wrangler, had given the horses their salt—upwind from camp so the bear scent wouldn't disturb them. Habit kept me watching the timberline parks. Our lunch meat was about ready when I spotted a black bear eight hundred yards downvalley. We got out our glasses. He looked trophy class. He was in a cloudberry patch but was leaving it, headed our way. We watched him until he went out of sight in a thicket. Then we got busy eating. I figured we'd see him again.

"You know something? Black bears have everything," Pat said, slicing off a chunk of sizzling hot tenderloin. "They are our sportingest and most admirable thieves. Bless them."

Jake and the
Willow Ptarmigan

My lab Jake was a ptarmigan specialist.
When he got the huge flock's scent
he halted, with his tail rigid.
Then a thousand ptarmigan took off.

"**M**an, I can't spot that mob of ptarmigan," my hunter Sam
Bowers declared as, squint-eyed and bemused, he scanned the
snowy hill-rimmed park close ahead. "You sure your dog Jake
isn't kidding? Hell, I'm supposed to have 20-20 vision."

"Jake doesn't kid," I said. "Look at those two owls."

This was at timberline in Alaska's Kashwitna Basin
on a gray November morning. There were twelve inches
of dry snow, and Sam was making his first hunt on webs.
He had fallen a few times, but he could take it. He stayed
cheerful. We had found the big flock of willow ptarmigan a mile above camp. I was watching Jake, my four-
year-old black Labrador. Jake rated as a hotshot ptarmigan expert—a specialist. He looked excited, and I started
to ask him how come. But suddenly things happened. First
I sighted two horned owls sitting in a spruce snag eighty
yards ahead. Then Jake spun, staring crosswind. His frost-
scarred ears lifted. He wagged his tail. I figured he had
heard some ptarmigan talking. Or else a freak eddy of
wind had brought him good news. Anyway, I snowshoed
alongside him—and saw a vast network of ptarmigan tracks.
Acres of them.

Jake now edged into the wind. I saw him tense when he got the huge flock's scent. He halted, tail rigid. I knew that his nose was aimed at a bird, but all I could see was empty snow. So I reached for my 8X glasses. In a moment I located Jake's target. It was a handsome willow cock, crouched motionless. His feathers were snugged tight, and he had his head tucked between his shoulders. Boy, he wasn't even blinking his eyes. Well, Sam still hadn't sighted a ptarmigan, but he seemed to be having a heap of fun. The birds' white camouflage fascinated him. I suppose it was a challenge. I asked him if he was ready to put the flock up. Before he could reply Jake snarled. I half-turned and saw one of the owls coasting in. The horned assassin passed us and winged over in a shallow dive. Sam, cursing, brought up his Parker 12-gauge double.

He let go a barrel. The owl crumpled. Then the ptarmigan hosts lofted. There were at least one thousand of the birds, and they took off in a cloud of frost crystals. Except for glimpses of black tail feathers I saw only hurtling white ptarmigan ghost shapes. Sam fired and missed, which was nothing to be ashamed of. Well, willow ptarmigan have a swell habit—they often come back over you for a second look. Sam reloaded, and the great flock swung around and angled in behind us. Now there is a way to make a 180-degree turn on webs in four easy moves. Sam had practiced it. This time, though, he flubbed the maneuver and landed flat on his back. But he wasn't out of action. The birds swept over us at 150 feet, and their camouflage was no good up there. Sam fired twice. Two birds fell. Jake fetched them.

"Okay, I'm a convert," the guy said, his webs untangled at last, laughing as he put an arm around Jake's neck. "Ptarmigan hunting is grand sport—and this friendly Jake is a grand dog."

I said he was right, and congratulations. Ptarmigan hunting with a dog is our newest popular shotgun sport. It's an action sport that attracts adventurous gunners. It's so new there isn't even a recognized ptarmigan dog. Jake was special. I had rescued him from the Anchorage dog pound when he was about eighteen months old. His free board time was up—they were getting ready to gas him. I shipped him home and put him to work packing—and in a sled team. Then I began taking him ptarmigan hunting and found he was a natural. I am aware that Labradors aren't expected to operate in pointer fashion. But after some coaching Jake did all right. He had bird sense and a good cold-weather nose. He was smart, strong, and willing. He could buck snow all day long like a wolf.

Jake aimed to please. For example, take a September hunt I made with Colonel "Muktuk" Marston. This was above Three Cottonwoods Lake in the Talkeetnas. We were backpacking, with Jake carrying fifteen pounds. We sighted ptarmigan the second day. I saw the flash of white wings four hundred yards up the mountain and got out my 12X glasses. The birds were on an open windy slope at snow-line, feeding. About sixty of them. Mighty elegant in their harlequin fall plumage. We began a stalk for them. My idea was to shed our packs when we got reasonably close. But another flock surprised me. These birds were down in the alders. Jake winded them and lumbered ahead. He halted fifty feet distant with his nose pointed at a thicket. Paws spread to balance his pack, he was confident. A gravelly voiced boss cock now began the alarm. Colonel Muktuk grinned delightedly and closed in.

The birds let him move abreast of Jake. But the worried cock kept squawking. It sounded like, "Cut out, cut out." Colonel Muktuk took another step, and the flock burst up. It was a family flock of nine birds. They flew directly away from us, wings battering. You could tell they were fat and heavy. Colonel Muktuk's Browning Auto 12 blasted, and the flock's high bird dropped. Jake got going before it hit the ground. He sorted the bird out of a windy alder clump and came galloping back with it. Well, he had put on a show. I'll bet that nobody had ever before seen a gundog point birds and then retrieve one while carrying a pack. Colonel Muktuk took the bird and said, "I thank you." It was the cock. We admired him. I gave him a pound and a half. His colors were buff, brown, black, and white. Jake *whoofed*—a contented dog wanting more work.

He soon got it. The other flock now flushed. The birds flew seven hundred yards north along the snow-line, and alighted near a canyon rim. We headed for them. When we were close I cached our packs. Jake then loped ahead, and pinpointed the birds in a strip of blueberry brush. Well, our medicine was a mite bad. Colonel Muktuk walked the birds up and scored. But a wind gust caught his kill and whirled it over the canyon rim. We watched the bird tumble past 250 feet of ledges and steep alder tangles and land on a talus dump. Dismaying, but Jake didn't hesitate. He knew where the bird was and went after it. Colonel Muktuk tried to accompany him, and was stopped at once by alder. I saw Jake pick up the bird. Ten minutes later he clawed his way back over the canyon rim with it. Colonel Muktuk knelt and solemnly shook his paw.

Alaska has a variety of ptarmigan. Five species that I know about. The three most important to sportsmen are the white-tailed, rock and willow ptarmigan. The willow tribe easily takes first place. They have everything. They are the largest of our snow grouse, they are beautiful, they have a wide distribution, and they are abundant. They are fast and hard to hit—scatter-gun deadeyes respect them. Usually they hold well for a dog. On snow they sometimes seem stupidly unafraid, probably because they place too much trust in their camouflage. But that's only sometimes. When you find them on bare ground they hunt cover. If there's no cover close they won't hold. But it's the early winter flocks of young birds that make a dog work. They are erratic, and their wacky performances can cause an honest dog to plumb wear himself out.

That happened to Jake several times. But he won anyway. There was an October hunt I made with Tom Logan at my Toon-akloot Creek homestead. I got up at sunrise this particular morning. I built a fire in the kitchen stove, and then it was time to let Jake out. I was worried about him. He'd had three brutally hard days and was beat. He now snorted, wagged his tail "Good morning," and hobbled outside, gimpy on all four legs. I told myself he'd had it for this hunt. Well, I started a pot of coffee. I woke Tom. Then I happened to glance out the window. There in a snowbank, thirty feet distant, stood Jake—on point.

I sprinted to the rear window. The willow brush was full of ptarmigan. A hundred or so of them. They were feeding on frozen buds and twig ends. I had a good view of them against dead leaves they had knocked down. Jake didn't seem to disturb them. He had sensibly halted eighty feet distant—they knew he couldn't get to them. A trim cock fluttered up at the thicket's edge and grabbed a tall willow sprout with his feather-webbed feet. It bent under him. He rode it to the snow—and two other cocks came running to share his bounty. Squawking, he attacked them. The three fought a brief battle royal, then dispersed. They left blood on the snow. I was sure this was a flock we had hunted yesterday. We had followed the birds three hours. Jake must have scouted fifteen miles, wallowing through chest-high drifts. He deserved some good luck.

Tom now joined me at the window. The gang of birds out there gave him a mild case of shakes. Well, I eased the front door open. We stepped into the hitches of our webs and rounded the cabin. When the ptarmigan saw us they ran out into the clearing. Their feather webs were 100 percent efficient on the powder snow, but their camouflage sure wasn't. Not this time. The sun had climbed treetop high and the birds were casting shadows; sharp-cut blue shadows, ten feet long. They didn't seem to know this. They held, standing tall, obviously believing they were safe. Tom put them up. They had to rise against a dark spruce background. He let go with his Remington Pump-Action 16 and a bird fell. The flock came back past us at maximum range, and he dropped another.

"A perfect ending to my hunt," Tom asserted. And lucky Jake, beat but triumphant said, "*Whoof.*"

Our frontier dogs were workers. They had to be. A dog that didn't earn his keep didn't last long. In the early days we had no canine specialists. If a dog possessed hunting talent he was used to hunt all small game. But when I picked Jake up, I broke away from that. I decided he was going to be a ptarmigan specialist, the first one. Training him was easy. But it's a fact I made a bad mistake with him. I was sledding supplies to the homestead on the first snow. Some ptarmigan sounded off in the timber, and I took Jake out of harness to locate them. He pointed the flock, and I shot a bird. A half-hour later a husky snowshoe rabbit hopped across the trail. Well, I needed the animal. So I hauled out the Winchester 12 double again and shot him. Naturally Jake thought he should be helping me. He fought his harness, barking. I saw trouble ahead.

It came a week later. We were at my trapline cabin on upper Goose Creek. It was a cold September afternoon and there were six inches of snow. I was sawing wood when I spotted a flicker of wings across the creek. It was a flock of ptarmigan alighting in a highbrush cranberry patch. I put my 8X glasses on them. There were eleven of the birds, still in mottled plumage. They looked plump, and I figured a couple of them, fried, would go mighty good with beans and cornbread for supper. Jake was behind me, curled up on my parka. I spoke to him. Then I got the Winchester 12, and we went out through the willows. A long-eared snowshoe rabbit fled ahead of us. It was a peak rabbit year up here, but of course Jake was supposed to ignore rabbits. He didn't ignore this one though. He jerked his head up. He let out an excited beller and charged hellbent in pursuit.

The birds stopped feeding. They stalled a moment as Jake headed straight at them. Then they took off upstream and kept going. The rabbit now circled back, and I intercepted Jake. I grabbed his collar. I plucked a handy sheaf of dead grass and clobbered him with it. It was a token punishment that wouldn't have hurt an unweaned pup. But Jake shuddered, grinding his teeth. His feelings were injured. Well, I cussed myself because it was all my fault. I mean if you don't want your dog to chase rabbits you shouldn't shoot rabbits in his presence. Besides, I now suspected that Jake hadn't known the birds were over there. Most likely, I thought, he was asleep when they came in and didn't wake up until I spoke to him. So probably he had honestly figured the rabbit was my target. A sorry situation. But we got a break.

It was dramatic. In early October, I brought Hank Peters up the creek for a ptarmigan hunt. Conditions were the same—cold sunlight and ankle-deep dry snow. Jake found birds around noon the first day, on a blueberry ridge west of camp. I checked them with my glasses. It was a flock of maybe twenty birds. They were in snow-white plumage, but you could see them against the bare knee-high blueberry brush. Jake moved in expertly. The birds held okay, but then I saw movement just ahead of Jake. It was a pair of snowshoe rabbits. They hopped out of a brush clump, spooked suddenly—and raced amongst the ptarmigan. Well, the flock roared up in some confusion. Hank fired both barrels of his Ithaca 12 double and got one bird. Jake fetched it. He was outraged. He was slit-eyed and *whuffing*. But he stayed put. Clearly rabbits were taboo.

"Thanks, pal," I said. "That made you a certified ptarmigan specialist."

Willow ptarmigan are nomadic. They are hatched above timberline in June and spend the summer up there. Their summer colors are buff and brown with white wings. In August they start switching to white body plumage and feed toward the lowlands. Owls, eagles, lynx, and foxes prey on them. They seem to distrust trees. At least, I have yet to see one of them alight in a tree. They roost on rocks or in snowbanks. Beginning in September, family flocks join up to form large traveling flocks. The birds wander all winter, but usually stay within 150 miles of their nesting grounds. The hunting season runs from early August through April. But snow depth seldom permits the use of a dog after mid-November.

Jake liked ptarmigan hunters. He shared their fortunes. Happy when they were scoring, sad and sympathetic when they weren't. A good companion. Consider the climax of a hunt I made with young Bill Adams. This was out of my cabin on Deshkah River, in late October. We had winter conditions— twenty-five degrees above zero and ten inches of loose snow. Two sundogs flanked the pale sun. Jake found birds the first afternoon. I saw him get their scent, and I reached for my glasses. We were in a tundra-rimmed dry river channel. I picked up a maze of tracks with the glasses. Then I spotted the birds. They were on the bare slope of a red clay cutbank, eighty yards distant. I estimated around thirty of the phantom-white birds. Their actions puzzled me. They were milling about on the barren clay as though they expected to find something edible.

Jake froze. The birds were getting nervous. They had halted their strange activity and were watching us, heads bobbing. Then a cock squawked, "Cut out, cut out" and they rocketed up. Their camouflage was good now—they had the snowy Talkeetnas for a backdrop. I swung an imaginary shotgun on them. Just as I pulled, the kid blasted twice with his Winchester Auto 12. He didn't score. Jake sighed, his tail drooping. Bill said he was sorry. Well, the birds swung back past us—high and with the sun behind them. Bill didn't shoot. I wouldn't have, either. We now headed for the cabin and a surprise adventure. A recent hard wind had scoured the cabin's dirt roof clean of snow. The exposed gravel should have told me something.

I felt sorry for Jake. He was really low. Well, we ate supper and turned in early. I pounded my ear until sunup. Then a pattering sound on the roof woke me. I listened and thought it must be hail. But Jake allowed otherwise. He wagged "Good morning" as usual, then rolled his eyes at the roof. He grinned. He frisked in a happy Labrador war dance. And at last I caught

on. I now understood the outback scene. I knew what was happen-
on the roof. The clue was gravel. Ptarmigan need gravel for
their gizzards. And no doubt it is hard to find in winter. But
there was plenty on our roof. Bill was awake now, and I briefed
him quietly. We dressed. Bill checked his Winchester. Then I
yanked the door open and the kid bounded outside. The startled
flock of thirty-plus ptarmigan erupted from the roof. Bill shot
two. Jake loped after them.

"Most fun I ever had," Bill told me. "Sporty grouse and a
personality dog."

Back to the beginning. Sam was an eager-beaver. We hunted
on, and by late afternoon he had taken five more birds. We then
returned to my Injun-type camp—a birchbark lean-to and a cache.
I built a good fire of spruce logs in front of the lean-to. The
sun went down. A wind aloft was tearing snow-plumes off
the peaks. Theatrical. I fed Jake a couple of sun-dried king
salmon bellies and a half-pound of beef tallow. Then I dressed
four of Sam's ptarmigan. I stuffed the birds with winey frozen
blueberries and chunks of buttered bannock bread. I packed them,
topped with bacon strips, into a Dutch oven to roast. We now
sat on spruce boughs, smoking our pipes and enjoying the fire's
warmth. Jake stretched out between us. Sam stroked the dog's
head. After a while I made coffee, biscuits, and gravy. We ate
as colored aurora lights flared over the ragged summits.

"Today we helped pioneer a rewarding new shotgun sport,"
Sam said. "It makes me grateful, man."

The Grizzly Is
One Big Surprise

The big blond grizzly was busily guarding the
carcass of a bull caribou. Suddenly he jerked
his head up and growled; 30 yards downwind
another grizzly appeared, ready to fight.

"**M**ister, those grizzlies are going to fight," young Cal
Howard said, his glasses rested on a jack-spruce snag. "The
handsome one that just showed up is a bandit. Look at him.
He's about to . . ."

"Let's get down there," I said.

This was in Alaska's Mt. Deborah country, six packtrain
days east of the railroad, on a frosty bright September noon.
We had been checking the bars of a pretty grayling creek. There
was considerable grizzly sign, most of it fresh, so we climbed
a creek bluff and got out our 16X glasses. A bald eagle presently
befriended us. It circled a bunchgrass opening six hundred
yards crosswind and screamed. In a moment we saw what
interested the bird. It was a blond Toklat-type grizzly, a fat
three-hundred-pounder. He was busily guarding the carcass
of a bull caribou. His chest and head were blood-smeared.
I saw that he had torn the bull's throat out and broken his
neck, also that he had eaten part of a shoulder. He was now
clawing grass and blueberry turf over the rest of the carcass.
As I watched him, he jerked his head up and snarled. Thirty
yards downwind from him another grizzly appeared.

239

This one was a silvertip. I gave him 350 pounds. He was built, with a striking trophy pelt. He came out from behind a clump and reared up, visibly sampling the wind. Then he swaggered toward the blond bear and the caribou carcass. I suppose he was meat-starved. Most mountain grizzlies are. It seems to be a chronic state with them. But he had hard luck. I mean the blond bear sure wasn't hospitable. He at once bogged his head and attacked. We were partway down the slope when this happened. Halting, we used our glasses again. The two bears came together and rolled, biting and striking, raking with their claws. They lunged up and circled. The silvertip was limping, and I could see blood on the blond bear's belly. Well, they closed again, each trying for the other's throat—and then suddenly the silvertip quit. Whirling, he loped back into the close-packed spruces.

We resumed our stalk. Cal, plenty excited, said he wished he had gotten a chance at the silvertip. The bear's beautiful thick pelt, he said, had fascinated him. Well, we worked through a belt of alders and blowdown, then followed a game trail until it petered out. The opening was now two hundred yards distant. I figured we would sight the blond bear at any moment. But the unexpected happened. Something moved fifty yards ahead. It was in deep shadow, but I made out what it was—the silvertip. He was likewise making a stalk—heading for the opening again. I guess he had thought it over and decided he could take the blond bear, after all. He ghosted through the timber, blending with it. It was spooky to watch him. I saw that Cal was ready, so I spoke to the bear. He spun with a roar, and showed us his fighting teeth. Cal's .30-06 Winchester blasted. The bear went down, finished.

"I wish I understood grizzlies," Cal said, sounding awed.

A lot of guys wished that, I told him as we went over to the kill. In fact, I had once asked three veteran grizzly hunters to please explain the grizzly's status as a great game animal. Their "for example" replies all stressed surprise behavior. My sourdough partner Baldy Thomas was first on my list. Baldy had lived in grizzly pastures going on fifty years. "Grizzlies are great because they are plumb dangerous, and you can't outguess them," he said. "They'll attack and they'll run. They are fearless and shy. They'll charge into gunfire, and they'll take off at one whiff of man scent. Sportsmen have been partial to grizzlies for 150 years, mainly because the animals are ninety percent unpredictable. For example, take a baldface that Jim Bates and I tangled with at the falls of Montana Creek, in the western Talkeetnas. We backpacked in from the railroad, a two-day trip, and found Jim's bear the first morning.

"We spotted him at five hundred yards. We're following a birch ridge above the creek. When we come in sight of the falls, we get busy with our glasses. The wide foam-patched pool there is the end of the line for four salmon runs, so naturally it's a grizzly hangout. Right now the wind is blowing rainbowed mist across the pool, but I spot a dark sow grizzly and two blond cubs. They are at the water's edge waiting for a salmon to come past. I've had my glasses on them only a few seconds when the sow turns, staring through the mist. Then the wind eases, and I spot our baldface. He must have just arrived, because his coat ain't wet. He's a whopping 450-pounder. I guess you've noticed that you find the biggest grizzlies on salmon streams. This one's pelt is coffee-colored, and he has a tan face. Well, a female silver salmon now begins jumping in the pool's outlet, trying to break her egg skeins loose. The bears make a run at her.

"The baldface is fast. He would have got there first, but the sow fouls him. She crowds him off balance. Then she sprints ahead and tries for the salmon. But, man, she's got no technique. She just jumps off the bank with her mouth open, grabbing. And, of course, misses. She goes plumb under and comes up spouting creek water. She's sore now. She tops the bank with a rush and bats a cub out of the way. Then she makes a jump at the baldface, like it's all his fault. He is long-suffering. He dodges her and wades into the outlet. Well, Jim rests his scope-sighted .300 Weatherby Magnum over a boulder, but I can see it's no use. Mist is blowing again, and a piece of rainbow covers the baldface. The big animal is only a colored shadow. Jim looks at me and shakes his head, so we begin a stalk. We're nearly off the ridge when the sow gets really tricky. She wades out to the baldface.

"She's shoulder-to-shoulder with him. And then he catches a salmon. I've got my glasses on them. As he starts ashore, the sow tries to snatch the fish away from him. But all she gets is trouble. He belts her clean off her paws. He then climbs the bank and lopes into some alders. Well, it's a small thicket, so he's practically ours. But still I don't like the setup. I guess I have a hunch or something. Anyway, we close in. Spray whirls over us. The wind is blowing in crazy gusts. All I can hear is the thunder of the falls. Then here comes the baldface. We don't have any warning. He simply busts out of the misty alders straight at us. I believe he figures the sow has followed him. But he keeps coming. Well, Jim has switched to iron sights. He brings up the Weatherby and fires. The baldface drops, skidding. Dead.

"Jim has a mild case of shakes. He reaches for a smoke, and says, 'Now I know what frontier folks mean when they say the grizzly is unpredictable,'" Baldy concluded.

I next asked the Watana Kid why the grizzly was great. The Kid had a heap of grizzly savvy. He was a pro's pro. We all took our hats off to him. "The grizzly is great because he's full of surprises, and because he makes a hunter proud," he said. "Your sportsman knows the bear's reputation. He knows that a mistake can maybe get him mauled or killed. So when he scores he feels he's a pretty good man. For example, take the time young Dan Clark and I ran afoul of a killer yellowtip. This is on the Susitna, in September. We're floating downriver in a fourteen-foot poling boat—a good way to hunt grizzlies. It's a frosty afternoon, and we've just passed Cottonwood Island. A quarter-mile ahead is the cabin of old Tom Owl, an Indian wolfer. Well, I spot something in the cabin dooryard and get out my glasses. If it's old Tom, I aim to holler hello. But I see it ain't him. It's a fine husky grizzly.

"He's a yellowtip. I give him 320 pounds. The wind is rippling his pelt, and the underfur shows dark gray. Only the long guard hairs are tipped with yellow. He has a wide head, with a mutton-chop ruff. Well, it's a mighty curious scene. The bear is standing there gazing up at old Tom's tall siwash cache, like he owns the place. I take a careful look at the cabin. The door is shut, but the moose-gut window is open, and no smoke is coming out of the stovepipe. It sure don't look right. Something is wrong. I pick up the pole and head for shore. The stiff current carries us down three hundred yards. Then we beach the boat in an eddy and begin a stalk. There's a game trail along the bank. We have followed it a hundred yards when we find old Tom. He's lying facedown across the trail, with his rifle under him. I figure he's been dead a couple of days.

"It's plain how it happened. Old Tom was toting a pack of moose meat home. I find his packboard in a willow thicket. Near it are some cleaned moose bones. I also find grizzly claw marks in the trail. They show that the bear attacked from behind. One bite through the back of his neck did for old Tom. I pick yellowtip hairs off his caribou hide jacket. Well, we go on to the clearing. Our killer bear isn't in sight, but I figure he hasn't gone far. We park on a saw log at the edge of the timber and wait. Four or five moose birds are scouting the cache, a sure sign there's fresh meat hung in it. All at once I get the feeling we're being watched. I turn, and the yellowtip steps out of the spruces fifty feet distant. I nudge Dan. The grizzly then surprises me. He chomps his jaws and starts running toward the cache. Dan whips up his .30-06 Remington and drops the bear.

"'End of a man-killer, and that was a score I'm proud of,' he says, looking inches taller."

I thanked the Kid. And I was now remembering a spring grizzly hunt in the Wood River country. I was just a lad then, working as assistant to Tanana Stewart. Our sportsman was a gent named Al Stone. We went in from the railroad by packtrain, a four-day trip. The third morning of the hunt we located Al's trophy bear. A cold wind was whining out of the peaks. Snowfall was imminent. We had climbed a grassy slope behind camp and were using our 16X glasses. I spotted the bear. He was on a cottonwood-rimmed river flat 650 yards upwind, with a sow and a yearling. The color of his coat fooled me at first. It exactly matched a silt-dusted snowdrift behind him. Until he moved I thought he was part of the drift. He would weigh four hundred pounds.

Al was delighted, with reason. There are plenty of blond grizzlies around, but mighty few off-white ones. We hurried down the slope. We worked through a mean tangle of fallen timber and went into the windy cottonwoods. It was snowing good now. In a moment we sighted our bears, three hundred yards distant. Al rested his .375 Winchester Magnum over a limb, but he was panting and didn't shoot. I put my glasses on the bears. The sow was digging Hedysarum roots. She and the yearling were plain ordinary grizzlies, with coats the color of well-used burlap. The elegant male stood watching the sow. He was restless. He rolled his slab shoulders and moved closer to her. The rut period was in full swing here, and I guess he figured that digging roots was a dumb waste of time. Anyway, he put a foreleg on her neck—and instantly the yearling bounded in and took a bite at his flank.

It was dramatic. I suppose the tough youngster thought he was protecting mamma. Anyway, he sure set his teeth in a tender spot. But he had more courage than good sense. The trophy bear spun, slugging. I heard him bawl. He landed two glancing haymakers, and then the yearling got his paws back under him and fled—toward us. The trophy bear tore after him through the blowing snow and the sow followed. Al bent over his .375, but before he could shoot, the three bears went into some red willows. Only the yearling came out. He shook his tan coat, looking back. Well, we waited a half-minute then headed for the thicket. The snowy forest floor was noiseless underfoot. The yearling saw us and took off. I expected we would soon come upon a mating scene. Instead, the sow galloped into view, *whuffing,* her back hair bristled, with the trophy bear chasing her. Al downed him at forty feet.

"Man, they were loaded with surprises," Al said when we had admired the fancy off-white pelt.

I next asked old Tex Cobb to tell me why the grizzly was great. Tex rated as the dean of Alaska woodsmen. He had hunted grizzlies from the Endicotts to the Stikine country. We gave him credit for being a grizzly specialist. "That's an easy question," he said. "The grizzly is great because he's a challenge. He has a reputation. His record as a man-killer goes back to the first mountain men. Crowd him, and he'll come for you. And when he starts, he's hard to stop. So of course most sportsmen are hot to tackle him. They want to find out if they have the stuff to go up against old *horribilis* and win. If he was a scaredy kind of bear, they wouldn't give a doggone about him except for his pelt. Take an example, a fall grizzly hunt I made with Bill Teller in the Chugaches. We're up at the head of King River, backpacking. We spot Bill's grizzly one morning while we're eating breakfast.

"He's on the mountain above camp, seven-hundred yards distant, in a steep lupine meadow. We forget about breakfast and get out our glasses. One look and I see the bear is a real prize. His pelt is copper-colored, shading to yellow on his shoulders. I give him 380 pounds. He's hunting parka squirrels. He has dug around the rim of a big shale slab, and is now trying to upend it. He seems certain-sure there's a squirrel under the slab. But he's having trouble—he can't get a good hold on the slab with his paws. You can see he's sore. Finally he shoves both his snout and his paws under the slab and hoists. The slab tilts up and rolls crashing down into the alders. But there ain't no parka squirrel. It has somehow made a getaway. The bear is so disappointed he hauls off and pounds the air. Then he starts digging under another shale slab. We begin our stalk.

"We're lucky. There's some bad alders between us and the grizzly, but we find a dry creek bed leading up through them. The wind favors us except for a few freak williwaw gusts. We make a fast climb to brushline. Here we get news from our bear. A boulder rumbles down the slope, and we hear the bear roar. It sounds like he's lost another parka squirrel. We go on to the meadow's edge. Thirty yards directly above us is a sandstone ledge, and the bear's rump is sticking out from behind it. He is digging again. Bill checks his .30-06 Remington, and I open my mouth to holler at the bear. But just then a williwaw wind eddy whirls past. I guess the bear gets our scent. Anyway, he pulls a surprise. He lets out a snort and heads hellbent for cover in the alders. Then he sees us. Well, we're in his way, and the handsome cuss is already sore, so he attacks. Bill fires and the bear, head shot, rolls past us into the brush.

"'Oh boy. I always wondered if I could do that,' Bill says as we go down to the kill. I tell him nobody could have done better," Tex finished.

I thanked Tex. He and the others had given me savvy answers. But I figure there's another reason why the grizzly is great—he's a symbol of tough independence. Our so-called progress hasn't affected him. He is still the world's most unafraid and unsophisticated bear. Except for rifle-toting humans, he is still the boss of his ranges. For example, take a short-fused grizzly I met over on Yanert River. I was a kid then, wrangling ten horses for Frank Lee and a sportsman named Sam Hart. It was a fall hunt. We went in from Cantwell, a four-day trip, and located Sam's bear the second morning. I had gone out to bring in the horses. I found them bunched on a pea-vine flat, and mounted my sorrel gelding bareback. I got the string headed campward along a creekbank game trail. Then suddenly the animals spooked. I saw movement upwind, across the creek. It was a blond grizzly.

Well, I unloaded and reached for my glasses. I had a solid hold on the sorrel's halter, but the other horses were stampeding. The bear looked good. His pelt was wheat-colored. He had a deep chest and massive shoulders. I gave him 340 pounds. He was what the old-timers called a "Swede" bear. He stood under a resin-streaked grizzly "message spruce" that generations of the bears had bitten and clawed. He was behaving peculiarly. He kept shaking his head and pawing at it. He presently reared up and rubbed his head against the scarred tree trunk. I now saw what was bothering him. Three or four porcupine quills were stuck in his left ear. I suppose they were annoying. Anyway, he pawed at them again, and then had himself a tantrum. He bit the tree and struck at it. Then he turned toward me, roaring. He must have heard the horses.

But he didn't have the wind. He glared and bristled, then began biting chunks out of the message tree. I swarmed aboard the sorrel and highballed to camp. Frank and Sam were waiting. I told them about the Swede bear, and within seconds we were headed down the creek. But the bear had moved. We approached the beat-up spruce carefully. We stood looking and listening. No bear. But shucks, I could feel the animal's presence. I knew doggoned well he was close. I guess Frank knew it too. Anyway, he motioned Sam to stay plenty alert. Then, in a thicket sixty feet distant, a willow tip bent against the wind. A moment later our Swede bear walked into view. Unafraid, showing his teeth, he looked us over. Gents, I was proud of him. He was some independent grizzly. Then Sam's .30-06 Winchester banged. Our bear, chest shot, started for us and fell against the message tree, stone dead.

"He was wonderful," Sam said, so thrilled he had turned pale.

Back to the beginning. I skinned Cal Howard's silvertip, and lashed the pelt and skull on my packboard. Cal wanted to try some grizzly steaks for supper, so I cut out both backstraps and added them to the pack. We then sat down and lit our pipes. The sun was well above the peaks now, and the autumn-killed grass was warm. I felt good. Some geese were towering over a lake north of us. I could see white sheep and caribou on a watershed to the eastward. The bright wind smelled of frosted leaves and spruce resin. Grizzlies always pick the best country. They are experts in that respect—and it makes them easier to hunt. You know you'll find them where the meat, fish, and berries are—and where road-builders aren't. The splendid animals were plentiful here. I had once seen eight of them on the blueberry ridge behind us. I felt beholden for being alive in such a fine reach of country.

"Hooray for grizzlies," Cal said, stroking the silvertip pelt. "They are the greatest."

I said I would second that.

Grand Stalks for Giant Moose

*A huge warrior bull moose is an awesome creature
that provides the ultimate in hunting adventure.*

" **W**owee! man, what a trophy bull," Hank Peters said ecstatically as he tried to improve the focus of his 12X glasses. "He's wonderful. Magnificent. But I wish the hard-case so-and-so would hurry and cross that ford."

"Here he comes," I said.

This was in Alaska's Tonzona Valley, five packtrain days west of civilization. On a bright mid-autumn morning, we had been scouting through a stand of frost-painted timberline cottonwoods. We had found fresh sign but no moose. Then a couple of ravens began bonk-bonking across the river. Glancing that way, I saw the mirror flash of an antler blade. It was some six hundred yards upwind. We hastily reached for our glasses. A busy moose drama was taking place over there. Three moose were involved—a bull, a cow, and a yearling. The bull was a deep-shouldered fifteen-hundred-pounder. His antlers were wide, but I couldn't make out any details. He was moving around too fast. It appeared that he wanted to ford the river, and his cow opposed the idea. So he was antler-whapping her. The yearling, I gathered, was a chance spectator.

We eased out to the river. The moose were now only one-hundred yards distant. I asked Hank to be patient. It was a mean ford, and I sure hoped the bull would cross it under his own power. But the cow was being mighty stubborn. Gigas cows are geniuses at fouling up your stalks. They are wary and suspicious. They seem to have a highly developed sixth sense for danger, and they don't relax. The bull now hazed this one to the water's edge again. He was pretty rough with her, and suddenly she turned on him. Rearing, she struck at his muzzle. Her action stopped him. He stood glaring boggle-eyed at her, and I at last got a look at his antlers. They would go seventy inches. The palms were shallow and flat, with thirty-five points. The brow guards would go fifty inches. Well, our bull pawed the gravel. Then he lowered his head and jumped at the cow.

She was smart. Whirling, she plunged into the ford. The bull was right behind her. They were on a brisket-deep riffle, with rocks thirty yards below them. The cow came across okay. But the bull had hard luck. He was in some midstream thank-you-ma'ms when the yearling decided to cross over, and I suppose he heard it. Anyway, the bull turned his head to look back—and his upstream antler dug into the water. He didn't have a prayer. The current spun him. He rolled off the riffle and hit a rock. He floundered. Finally he got his hoofs on bottom and lunged ashore. The cow was scanning the timber. I am sure she sensed our presence. But the bull was a reckless Romeo. After coughing up some river water, he limped over to her. He bit her neck. He put a foreleg over her withers. Then Hank's .30-06 Winchester crashed. The bull dropped, stone dead.

"Plenty dramatic, mister," Hank declared.

I said that described it. The Gigas moose has everything. He is the most popular big-game animal on this frontier. His trophy antlers are symbols of sport and adventure. His meat is prime quality. His hide and sinew have many uses. Me, I grew up in a moose economy. Our fall moose hunt was a vastly important project. With a meat bull down, you knew you'd at least eat well during the winter. Guys who for some reason didn't score, consumed a lot of skinny snowshoe rabbits. You tried your doggonedest to time the hunt right. You needed cold weather so the meat would keep. But if you waited too long, the cow-chasing bulls would lose their fat. You hoped for a noisy wind to aid your stalk, and when you made your kill, you thanked the bull. You remembered the spot where he fell, because it was a lucky place.

The huge critters are colorful. They rampage and perform. They put on some of the most exciting rut-season dramas in nature. For example, I once witnessed a moose battle royal. This was at timberline on the Kashwitna. A rain-threatening, early fall morning. I was just a kid then, backpacking for Tanana Stewart and a hunter named Jim Ross. We sighted Jim's trophy bull ten minutes from camp. We were on a lupine ridge, working our glasses. The bull walked into a spruce park five hundred yards upwind. He was a husky fourteen-hundred-pounder, with well-padded ribs. Tanana said his antlers would go sixty-eight inches. I counted thirty-two clean points. The brow antlers were massive. Well, Jim wanted the bull, so we plotted a stalk. But when we were partway down the hillside, the bull went out of view into a strip of spruces. Then, crosswind, a cow wailed.

She sounded desperate. Usually a rut-smitten cow will wail once or twice, then will shut up and wait for action. But this one kept wailing. And she had great vocal equipment. Every bull hereabouts must have been getting her message. We presently spotted her. She was in a pea vine opening three hundred yards distant, and I had guessed wrong about her. I had pictured her as a plump moose debutante. Instead she was swaybacked and keg-bellied. Her hip joints stuck out. I mean she was ancient. But she got big results. As we resumed our blind stalk, two mulligan bulls appeared from nowhere. They trotted into the opening and stopped, bristling, when they saw each other. Neither would weigh better than eleven hundred pounds. Their antlers were narrow and skimpy. But they were rugged characters. They didn't show off at all. They just took aim and slammed together.

The collision was awesome, but it didn't faze them. They hammered and slashed, backed off and attacked again. The cow was quiet now. I guess she figured she had it made. We halted. We had a good view of the opening, and it was a cinch Jim's bull would show up there. Jim checked his .30-06 Remington. Then I spotted the trophy bull, coming through the timber at a gallop. He was great. He tore into the opening and watched a moment. Then he charged at the mulligan bulls. They were too busy to disengage at once. He belted one of them in the ribs, and turned to clobber the other. But at this point they both attacked him. It became a bloody mixed-up fray. Each bull was battling the others. Then Jim fired, and the trophy bull went down. The mulligan bulls fled, with the cow following them. She was running like a three-year-old.

"What a thrill," Jim said, so excited he had turned pale.

The splendid brutes are fascinating. They have everything going for them and can be tricky to hunt. Your best bet always is to head for high ground if there is any and use your glasses, and it'll help if you learn to check wind direction automatically. I personally like a straight upwind stalk. You are less likely to be embarrassed by wind shifts. Regarding clothes for moose stalking, a medium-weight forest-green wool cruiser outfit is hard to beat. As for footgear, most pro-hunters up here wear rubber-bottomed shoepacs, but I admit I like tennis shoes. It's a good idea to carry your glasses, without the case, inside your shirt. A case knocks against things. It's noisy. Of course, every moose stalk is different. A man probably could make a thousand of them and still learn.

Gigas bulls are always dangerous. For example, take an experience Baldy Thomas had one aurora-lit night at his cabin on Montana Creek. "This bull is something special," Baldy told me. "First he tries to stomp my malamute pup, Chook. Then the noble S.O.B. takes me on. The way it happens, I have been gone from the cabin a month. When I come home, four inches of early snow have fallen—and I ain't shot my winter's meat yet. But the prospects sure look good. There's fresh moose sign right in the dooryard. I have stacked some empty salt salmon kegs under the cache, and a salt-hungry bull has discovered them. He has smashed the brine-mixing keg and chewed up part of an oak stave. I tell myself that the bull don't know it yet but we have a date. Not this evening, though. It's late. The sun is going behind a peak.

"Well, I build a fire in the Yukon stove. I rustle some grub for Chook and me. Then I turn in early. But I don't get much sleep. I've pounded my ear maybe two hours when Chook wakes me. He wants out. So I get up and open the door for him. And the cuss has fooled me. He dashes outside yip-yapping like a wolf pup. Then I hear a moose snort and the pound of hoofs. Oh, boy, that's my winter's meat, forty yards behind the cabin. I start dressing. Sure, I know. I could have sprinted out there in my red underwear, barefoot. But I ain't asking for more rheumatiz than I've already got. The sound of hoofs is now coming this way, and I hear Chook yelp. Then he hits the door. Well,

I grab my .375 Winchester Magnum and let the pup in. I see the moose disappearing into the timber. It's a big bull. But I don't get a shot at him.

"I finish dressing. Then I tell Chook to relax, and I step outside. There's a lot of colored aurora fire overhead. I look and listen. I figure the bull ain't gone far. He's ornery and salt-hungry, and he wasn't spooked much. Besides, it looks like he's made himself to home here. Five minutes pass. Then I hear him grunting. He's behind the cache, in a clump of second-growth spruces. Eighty yards distant. Well, I make a stalk for him. The wind is in my favor and I cut the distance in half. Then the bull stops grunting. I stand still. After a bit I hear antlers rattle in some little spruces sixty feet ahead. It seems the doggoned bull is now stalking me. I wait. A green aurora fan drifts overhead. It gives fair light. So I slap the Magnum's stock. The bull crashes into sight, attacking. I shoot and he goes down, finished.

"He was a grand warrior bull," Baldy said. "I go over and talk to him a while, Injun fashion. He has fat on his ribs. Later I measure his antlers. They go sixty-seven inches."

Weather can be a moose hunter's best friend. In the timberline parks fair weather is good hunting weather. That's because you make your stalks over noiseless grass and moss. But down in the big birch forests, rain and wind are apt to be your allies. Down here crisp, fallen leaves are a major handicap. Often they are so noisy that you can't hunt over them. So you hunt along stream bars, game trails and tundra rims. It's standard practice and will get you a moose. But a hunt in stormy weather is easier and a heap more fun. Rain is an aid and a hard wind is wonderful. Wind gives you sound cover. It confuses the moose's ears. With a wind roaring through the birches and the air full of bright leaves, you can make beautiful close stalks. It's fun. It's basic sport. Which is what moose hunting is all about.

Luck comes in handy, too. Luck saves bollixed stalks. For example, take the climax of a moose hunt I made with Walt Evarts on upper Goose Creek. This was in mid-autumn. A frosty mountain noon. We were scouting up the creek when some magpies began squawking crosswind. They sounded hysterical. So we climbed a rimrock and got out our 16X glasses. The birds were two hundred yards distant, circling a point of gaudy wolf willows. I couldn't get even a glimpse of their target. But

I spotted something else—a trophy bull moose and two cows, in a wide burn six hundred yards crosswind. The bull was polishing his antlers on a lone jack-spruce snag. He was a rangy 1,450-pounder. His antlers would go sixty-nine inches. Both palms were dished and deeply cleft. I counted forty points. The brow guards were heavy, with two long matched tines protecting his forehead. The antlers were dark, stained by birch sap.

Walt said he sure wanted the bull. But he didn't like the range. So we made a stalk. We backtracked. We angled up a bluff. We headed in through close-set scrub spruces. We were doing fine, and then suddenly the cover ended. There was nothing left between us and the moose but a couple of snags. The magpies were still squawking, nearer now, and Walt's bull was still grooming his antlers. Tatters of velvet hung from the beams, and the wind kept blowing them across his eyes. He was trying to grind the stuff off. The cows were gazing downwind, toward the magpies. They seemed worried. I guess their danger sense was prodding them. One of them now pawed the ground. The other tossed her head and stamped. The bull ignored them. Well, I tried again to spot the magpies' target, and this time did better. I made out a shadow in the painted brush. It moved. It became a crouching grizzly bear.

I asked Walt if he wanted a grizzly. He said no, he had taken one. He was lining his .300 Weatherby Magnum on the bull at 450 yards, but didn't shoot. He now told me he had to get closer. I bought that. A man knows his ability. But our stalk was stalled. I pointed out the grizzly. The animal was a dark-coated 350-pounder. He looked gaunt and ornery. I suppose he needed to fatten up in a hurry for hibernation. At any rate, he was stalking the moose. And he'd soon spook them. I mean we had a situation. But luck saved us. The bull leaned too hard on his snag, and it fell over. This griped him. He had an antler-swinging tantrum. Then he trotted toward us, the cows following. He halted at the first snag. Grunting, he butted it experimentally. The range was two hundred yards. Walt fired. The bull flinched and went down.

"Hunter's luck," Walt said as the grizzly, the cows, and the magpies took off. "The best moose medicine there is."

Moose calling is useful. I learned the calls and tricks as a kid, and became fairly expert. At least the moose responded. Most bulls would bristle when they heard me and swagger over to make a check. I got a kick out of it. It was a swell act to put on for visiting sportsmen. But I had my fingers crossed. I couldn't believe the moose were really fooled. Shucks, they have the sharpest ears in the wilds. I finally decided they were just plain belligerent and curious. But anyway, I know I have flimflammed one bull for sure. This was at my Toonakloot homestead, in January. A slick-headed bull was feeding from one of the slash piles. I grunted at him, but he went right on feeding. I then had an idea. I grunted into the empty rain barrel. Boy, that sound did it. He whirled, ears laid back. I cherish the triumph.

Back to the beginning. I took the head and cape off Hank's bull. I dressed and quartered the carcass. Then we brought the horses and took the meat to camp. We hung the quarters from a hangman's cottonwood limb. They had the good sage-like smell of an herb the Tonzona moose eat. I now built a fire and made coffee. The day had come in crystal clear. We smoked our pipes and drank coffee. This was one of the North's great big-game hunting valleys and we had it all to ourselves. Toward evening I spitted the bull's inside backstraps on green sticks and propped them over cottonwood bark coals to broil. I heated a kettle of black-eyed peas. I sliced and broiled two firm half-pound Boletus mushrooms. I made marrow gravy and baked dutch-oven biscuits. For dessert there were sugared blueberries. We ate in the tall flare of sunset.

"Man, this is the way to live," Hank said.

Stalks of the Alaska Ranges

For top adventure and suspense, try hunting
Dall sheep in Alaska's high country.

"**O**kay, that's your trophy Dall ram up there," I said to Jack Bowers in the early magic of this frost-glittering mid-September morning. "He's toting a head to cheer about. But you're going to earn him."

"Let's go, man," Jack said, bright-eyed eager.

We were on Metal Creek, in Alaska's Chugach Range, four backpack days from the highway. At daybreak we had climbed to a glaciered hanging valley above camp. Our medicine was good. Rounding some moraine boulders, we sighted eight sheep on a lofty upwind terrace. They hadn't seen us. So we stepped back into cover and got out our 16X glasses. The band consisted of five rams, two yearlings, and a ewe. They were preoccupied. They had found a clump of gone-to-seed wild celery, and the boss ram was monopolizing it. He was a heavy-horned veteran. Big and rangy. The greedy so-and-so stood there chewing a mouthful of celery seeds, his eyes half-shut in gourmet delight, while the other sheep watched. I kept my glasses on him. I now wanted a front view of his head. In a moment, reaching for more seeds, he faced me.

He assayed great. I estimated his horns would average 15x39 inches. Like most Chugach horns, they were massive, with thick striking surfaces. The tips were clean. I had counted ten growth rings. By this time Jack was ecstatic about the head, so we started climbing. And almost at once things began going sour. First the wind hauled around. I felt it on my cheek, and knew we had trouble. Then a lookout silver marmot spotted us and gave a shrill alarm whistle. Next we ran out of cover. We were now at the rim of a steep slide-rock gut. The sheep were only 450 yards distant, and by a miracle the marmot hadn't spooked them. But still it looked like we were stopped. The scree slope ahead offered no cover at all. I told myself it had been a haywire stalk, but fun. I could see that Jack was fascinated.

Then we got a break. But it didn't seem like one. Our trophy ram lost his seed monopoly. One moment he was doing fine. The next he was being hoorawed. The lone ewe started it. Rebelling, she trotted past him into the celery patch, and the other sheep followed. Our ram wheeled and bogged his head to attack—and the wind shifted just enough. The sheep froze as they got our scent. Then they stampeded up the mountain. They had to cross the slide-rock. And, boy, I knew what was going to happen. Sure enough, they dislodged shale chunks. Then the whole slide flowed. We got down behind a boulder. When the thunderous uproar ceased, we saw the sheep posed on a ledge high above us. I guess they thought they were plumb safe. Anyway, they let us cut the range to three hundred yards. Jack then raised his .270 Winchester and fired. Our ram toppled off the ledge.

"Excitement and drama," Jack said when we had gone up to the carcass. "That's why Dall sheep hunting is great." (The horns went 15½x38 inches.)

I congratulated Jack. I told him he was typical. Dall sheep hunting attracts rugged, hard-hunting guys. The tougher a stalk gets, the more they seem to enjoy it. For example, take a weather-complicated stalk I made with Jim Devers. This was on Sheep Creek, in the Talkeetnas, three backpack days east of the railroad. We sighted Jim's ram the first morning. He was in a high lupine meadow showing off for two ewes. We grabbed our glasses. I couldn't tell much about his head at first—he was moving around too fast. The sun had just topped a peak, and he was sham-battling his shadow. He leaped and pounced. He stood on his hind legs, pawing. Shucks, it was a Dall war dance. But the ewes weren't impressed. One of them was scratching her rump on a boulder. The other seemed to be gazing up at a mass of storm cloud that had drifted against the mountain.

The ram now quit performing. He faced upwind, working his black nose. He apparently had got a whiff of something he didn't like. I figured it was weather. The high-piled cloud bulged with action of some kind. Well, his head was first class. I thought the horns would average 14x38 inches. They were pale amber and unscarred. The tips flared outward in fine argali fashion. This ram was a handsome beast. His new coat had come in thick and snowy. He was deep-chested. He carried his head high, with style. Proud of himself. Jim said he sure wanted him, and was so intense his voice cracked. I took another look at the cloud. It was slate-gray. I saw lightning flicker in it. If we made the stalk we would certainly climb into a storm. But Jim was mighty eager. I hated to disappoint him. So I said okay, let's climb. We'd been in storms before.

We took the shortest route. It was bad—alders, rimrocks, and cliffs. But at last we topped out in a cluster of huge granite boulders. And just in time. The sheep were five hundred yards upwind. Close beyond them towered the cloud. It was plumb black now and full of lightning. I saw our ram stamp the shale. Then, before we'd had time to catch our breath, he and the ewes trotted toward us. I suppose they hoped to find shelter amongst the boulders. But they had started a mite late. A williwaw wind gust now hit the slope. Then hailstones pounded down. They were marble-size and struck so hard they bounced. The sheep broke into a run. Jim was laughing—the hail had knocked his hat off. He waited until the weather-smart ram was fifty yards distant. Then his .30-06 crashed. The ram stumbled and went down.

"Wonderful," Jim declared, beaming, as hail ricocheted off his bald spot. "A 100-percent perfect stalk, mister." (The horns averaged 13½x39 inches.)

Folks ask where they should go for a fine Dall sheep hunt. And I tell them it depends. These splendid sheep are plenty widespread—from the Kenai to the Brooks Range. So it depends on what kind of Dall hunt you want to make. If you're a backpack guy, the western Chugaches should suit you. They are adventure peaks. High and glacier-studded. A hundred-mile spread of dramatic hunting country. And the rams here grow amazing heads. The Boone and Crockett Club lists forty-four great Dall heads from the Chugaches. Much of the area is ideal for gents who favor the packboard and the siwash camp.

You simply choose a creek and pack in from the highway. You'll probably find your sheep hanging around glacier ice—they like the forage and the temperature up there. Take time to shop for a grand head. It's a happy way to hunt.

Dall sheep hunters are apt to be dedicated types. Also single-minded. But they have a terrific lot of fun. Consider a hunt Frank Lee made with Pete Burns at the head of Healy River, in the Alaska Range. "It was an exciting hunt," Frank told me. "In fact, we have to take Pete's trophy ram away from four meat-hungry grizzlies. . . . We go in by packtrain from the railroad, a two-day trip, and pitch camp in the last willows. The next day we locate our target ram. We're eating lunch. I glance up and see some white dots in the Wood River Pass. A couple of minutes ago they weren't there. So they ain't snow patches or white quartz rocks. We reach for our 12X glasses. Well, it's a band of six rams. They are right at grassline. One of them is grinding his left horn tip against a boulder. I steady the glasses. He looks good.

"He's an ornery critter. He knocks some lichens off the boulder and they fall onto his back. He crow-hops to get rid of them. Then the sonofagun stomps them. But his head is a winner. I estimate the horns will average 14x41 inches, and I give the spread thirty inches. I suppose the left horn tip blocks his side vision. Anyway, he's doing his best to grind it off. Well, Pete allows it's a marvelous head, so I plot a stalk. I check two routes. One is up a snowslide cut crosswind from the sheep. It looks all right. But then a flock of rock ptarmigan flies out of it. They boom straight up—scared. This is interesting. I try to spot what flushed them. A minute passes. I'm watching a shadow under a grassy point. It moves. Then, holy smoke, a parade of grizzlies files into view. A fat brown sow and three husky blond yearlings.

"Well, the sheep haven't spooked—the grizzlies are two hundred yards below them. So we're still in business. We head up the right side of the pass. The wind stays in our favor. When we're three hundred yards from the band, I put my glasses on our ram again. The character really aims to shorten that horn. He isn't grinding the tip anymore, he's hammering it against the boulder. I can hear the *whack-whack* sound clear over here. And I guess the grizzlies hear it too. Because suddenly the four of them come busting up out of the snowslide cut. They are now above the sheep. The sow rears, peering down the slope. Then she starts a rush at the sheep just as Pete brings up his .250-3000 Savage. Pete fires, and the trophy ram drops. The bears take off.

"'Some surprise,' I say when we've gone over to the carcass and I'm using my steel tape. Of course I'm referring to the grizzlies, but Pete is a single-minded Dall sheep fan. 'Yeah,' he says with a big grin. 'They average 15x41 inches.'"

For sport, adventure, and fine trophy Dall heads, the Alaska Range is hard to beat. It is vast and beautiful. It is unspoiled. Nearly every valley shed on the north slope has a Dall sheep population. And some of these spots have never been hunted. But it's all packtrain country. A man afoot just couldn't operate here. The distances are too great, and the stream fords too swift and deep. You need horses. With them you've got the country licked. The best departure point is Healy Station on the Alaska Railroad. If you head eastward from there, you ride into the fabulous Wood River, Yanert River and Mt. Deborah, all Dall sheep ranges. If you line out westward, you first pass through Mt. McKinley National Park. Then cross a divide, and the trophy-rich Kuskokwim Dall ranges are ahead of you. East or west, you've got it made.

Dall Sheep are mighty wary. And they climb high. But you don't have to be under forty to hunt them. Or an athlete. For example, take a hunt Tanana Stewart made with white-haired old Tom Waring. "The ram we harvest is on a mean mountain," Tanana told me. "It's risky. But old Tom is a champ. We are over in the Tonzona Basin, five packtrain days west of Healy Station. We locate our ram early the second day of the hunt. He's on a cloudberry slope high above Wolf Creek with another ram and seven ewes. We haul out our 16X glasses. His horns are clean and close-curled. I figure they'll average 15x39 inches. There is a deep V-gap between them, and I count nine growth rings. He's all right. An elegant trophy specimen. The other ram is a gaunt old-timer with heavy but badly splintered horns.

"Tom likes the trophy head. So we begin a stalk. We go out through some jack-spruce timber to the mouth of Wolf Creek. From there on it'll be straight climbing. But first we check the sheep—and it looks like something has happened up there. Our target ram is now glaring at old Busted Horns. The seven ewes have gathered in a huddle. It seems to be a plain case of boss ram orneriness. Anyway, our ram presently trots over to Busted Horns. He taps him twice on the neck with a front hoof, and waits. Oh, man. I've seen this before. I explain it to Tom. Busted Horns has been challenged. He's now got to fight or back down. Well, he backs down. The poor old cuss. Humbling himself plenty, he touches his nose to one of the trophy ram's horns. Then he stands there with his head down. I hear Tom growl as we start climbing.

"We angle up a broken red sandstone point. It gets tricky. Just below the top we come to a water-cut chute. It's steep, and there's new ice in it. But we tackle the place. Tom hasn't said a word for thirty minutes. He looks sore. I gather he is thinking about that poor old ram. Well, partway up the chute Tom has trouble. A foothold crumbles. I turn and see him hanging by his fingertips. It ages me some. But then he finds another foothold and climbs on to the top—grinning. A rugged old gent, for sure. The sheep are now 250 yards upwind, on a talus pitch. Our ram is facing us. I guess he has a sixth-sense warning. Because he suddenly whirls and gallops up toward a cliff. Old Busted Horns is in his way. He butts him aside and puts on speed. Then Tom's .270 bangs. Our ram drops, rolling.

"'We old-timers gotta stick together,' Tom says, laughing, his white hair blowing in the wind, as we hurry over to the carcass. 'Thanks for a heap of fun.'" (The head goes 14x39 inches.)

A Dall trophy cape requires savvy care. It is delicate, and strange things can happen to it. A cape, of course, is the skin of any big-game animal's head, neck and shoulder points. You should avoid shooting holes in a cape. Your taxidermist probably would charge you plenty for repairing the damage. And try to keep it from getting bloody. Dall sheep have hollow hair, and if the pelt soaks up blood it can't be washed out. The best way to preserve a raw cape in the field is to dry-salt it. But remember that horses are crazy about salt. Give the packstring a chance, and they'll eat your cape. So will porcupines. It's usually a good idea to roll a salted cape up and secure it with twine. But be sure to use only clean white twine for the purpose. Colored twine may leave indelible stains.

Dall sheep aren't clever tacticians. About all they know is to climb. But they make you work and scheme. And they produce some wonderful surprises. For instance, there was the climax of a late-September Dall hunt Tex Cobb made with Bill Chase in the Talkeetnas. "This ram sure startles me," Tex told me. I figure we've lost him. I'm cussing myself. Then, holy suffering, I hear something right behind me. This happens on a summit above Sheep River, thirty-five miles east of the railroad. We have backpacked in, and our luck ain't been good. For two days we see only young stuff. Then, around noon today, things change. We spot Bill's trophy ram. He's on a fog-patched caribou-moss slope upwind from camp, with three four-year-old rams. We check him with 12X glasses. He is a prize. I give his horns 16x40 inches.

"Well, we make our stalk, and I try to hurry it up. I'm worried about that fog. Finally we come out, panting, on a saw-toothed rim five hundred yards downwind from the sheep. And here we stop. There ain't no cover ahead—unless we can use fog for cover. A bank of the pearly gray stuff is now moving toward the sheep. I put my glasses on our ram again. He looks even better this time. His horns make him seem plumb top-heavy. They look too big for him to be carrying around. But he handles them all right. A golden eagle is circling the slope, and he keeps threatening it. He prances and shakes his head. He chases the bird when it coasts past. It's fun watching him. But I am considering that fog patch. It has been moving right along. It's tall and getting taller and will reach the sheep any minute. I figure we can maybe use it.

"But I cross my fingers. The fog blanks the sheep and then rolls over us. Well, we can see fifty feet, so we continue our stalk. When we have covered three hundred yards, we wait for the fog to lift. But it don't. I soon realize that this ain't no fog patch, it's a doggoned mountain cloud. And I know what the sheep will do—they'll climb up out of it. So we had better do likewise. It's our only chance to score. I convince Bill, and we start climbing. It's creepy but not dangerous. Well, we top a buttress into open sunlight. But our ram ain't in sight. The four-year-old rams are bunched on a crest close ahead. The eagle circles us. I am now sure the stalk is a bust. But just then, surprise, shale tinkles behind us. We turn—and our ram climbs out of the pea soup cloud thirty yards distant. Bill's .30-06 blasts. The ram falls over dead.

"'I thank you,' Bill says, saluting the carcass. 'That was a solid thrill.'" (The head goes 16x41½ inches.)

A Dall sheep hunter needs luck. For instance, take an experience I had when the government farm colonists came to Matanuska Valley. These gents were eager sportsmen. I put on three Dall hunts with them in thirty-five days. A record, maybe. The last hunt was with young Tim Wallace. We backpacked to the head of Wolverine Creek in the Chugaches. Well, this was late autumn. Snow falling when we arrived here, and by morning six inches had come down. Rough. But the sky now cleared, as we located Tim's ram. He was on a rimrocked slope above camp, courting a knobby-horned old ewe. We looked him over with our glasses. I thought his horns would average 13x41 inches. They were dark and heavily ridged. I gave the spread twenty-eight inches.

We made our climb. And it wasn't so bad. We had alders to hang onto. But a wind was making, and I didn't like that. We detoured once to check on our ram. He was still courting the old ewe, and getting nowhere. She kept running from him. Well, we toiled up a chockstone chimney and came out at the ram's level. He was now 450 yards upwind. Tim might have scored at this range. The kid could shoot. But while he was catching his breath, the wind suddenly roared—and blizzard-type snow hid the slope. We took cover behind a boulder. A quarter-hour went by. Then luck favored us. The wind flawed, and we spotted the ewe. She was 150 yards distant, running again. But I guess she had second thoughts. Anyway, she halted, looking back. Then our ram showed up. Panting. Tim's .30-06 banged. The ram half-turned and fell.

"Pure adventure, mister," Tim said as we headed for the kill. "An exciting stalk." (The horns went 13½x40 inches.)

Back to the beginning. I took the head and cape off Jack Bowers' ram and dressed the carcass. Jack had brought his packboard. He wanted to help. So I made up two heavy packs, and we toted them down to camp. I buried the brisket in a summer snowbank. I hung the quarters from alder poles laid across two boulders. This was a siwash camp. I made coffee over a fire of rabbit-killed twigs and served it in half-pint tin cups. The sun was high now. We lit our pipes and stretched out on springy caribou moss, loafing. After a while I started a brisket stew, using dried vegetables. Five rams had appeared on a mountain across the creek. We watched them until they went out of sight. I felt good. It was a swell day. We ate as purple afternoon shadows filled the canyons. Stew, bannock bread, and sugared blueberries. Jack looked at me across the twig fire and raised his coffee cup, smiling.

"Here's to Dall sheep," he said. "May they flourish forever."

Adventures with Giant Moose

Our Alaskan moose are superstars
with more surprises than almost
any hunter bargains for.

"He's a grand bull moose. I sure want him," Pete Waring said, sounding fascinated. "But hell, we've run out of cover. The wind is changing. That heifer over there is gonna spot us. And . . ."

"Take it easy," I said.

This was at Swan Lake, on the northern Kenai. A crystal late-August morning. We were only five minutes out of camp. We saw sunlight glance off polished antlers and reached for our 16X glasses. The bull was in a willow-dotted burn above the lake's outlet; he was about seven hundred yards crosswind. He was walking toward us, head down, trailing something. He looked good. His antlers would go sixty-seven inches. The palms were wide and had thirty-nine points. He would weigh fourteen-hundred pounds. Well, he now lost the scent trail he was following. He cast ahead for it, quartering. No luck. So, he backtracked and soon picked up the trail. But the delay had infuriated him. He tossed his head. He jumped at a willow bush and antler-whacked it. Then he came on in a hard-boiled swagger. Some bull. Well, I scanned the burn and presently located his target—a long-legged moose debutante.

She was nervous. She stood half-hidden in a patch of bright wolf willows, 250 yards crosswind. She was watching the oncoming Romeo bull, but her big black-rimmed ears kept swiveling. We were bellied down behind a quartz boulder. I checked the wind. It was still changing. If it shifted another five degrees, both moose would get our scent. Well, the bull now lost the heifer's trail again. He circled and missed finding it and had a tantrum. He pawed the ground. He buck-jumped. He swapped ends and antler-scythed another willow bush. I put my glasses on the heifer. She was fidgeting. This was her first rut season, and I guess she didn't aim to spend it stooging around. Anyway, she suddenly craned her neck and uttered a ululating alto wail. It was loud and eerie, and it had a magical effect on the bull. He stared, waggling his ears. Then he headed for her at a dead run. Pete let him come all the way. Then his .300 Weatherby Magnum blasted. The bull went down.

"I salute all gigas moose," Pete said.

I told him I would second that. Our giant Alaska moose are superstars. They have something for everybody. They are plenty sporting. They carry the world's widest and heaviest antlers. Only the ancient Irish elk beat them, with heads that went ninety inches and better. They yield a lot of fine meat. Many backwoods folks rely on it. A man waits for the first hard frost to make his hunt. He shoots himself a mulligan bull—a fat four-year-old, if possible. With the meat hung in his cache, he has it made. He can now face the big snows with confidence. Shucks, the Susitna-Denna Indians even expect to hunt these moose in the hereafter. It's great moose country up there, the shamans allow. High and open. The bulls are always fat. They don't say anything about trophy heads, but it's a happy prospect anyway. I buy it.

The huge critters are dramatic. Take the windup of a September packtrain hunt I made with Tom Logan on the Dog Fork of the Kuskokwim. It was the second morning of the hunt. Chill and misty. We were on a lookout bluff at timberline, above a gaudy dwarf cottonwood flat. Two moose were in sight—a bull and a cow, five hundred yards crosswind. The bull was polishing his antlers on a snag. The cow stood behind him snipping browse. He was an ancient character. Swaybacked. Skinny. But he had been a husky; he had the bones. I gave him a thousand pounds. His antlers were narrow and warped, with a scatter of crooked tines. They would go only forty-eight inches. Well, I resumed searching the flat with my glasses. The mist was lifting now, raveling through the cottonwoods. After a bit I sighted another bull. This one was a rangy thirteen-hundred-pounder. I steadied my glasses. He had a lowdown project going.

Bristled, he was stalking the old bull and the cow. He would trot a few yards, then halt and listen. He had about three hundred yards to go. I couldn't see his left antler—too much brush. But I had a hunch he was trophy class and then some. We decided to try for him. We hastened off the bluff. We sprinted a hundred yards across a mist-hung swale and crawled through fifty yards of wet redtop grass. I was heading for the cow. She was our bait. In a moment we spotted her again. She was busy. The old bull had stopped grooming his antlers, and now had romance on his mind. I wanted to get closer. I was afraid the drifting mist would give us trouble. So we took a chance with skimpy cover—and the cow saw us. She snorted, but the bull didn't believe her. Or else he didn't give a doggone. We crawled to better cover behind some alders. And now our target bull arrived on the scene.

He was a real hard case. He didn't waste any time with show-off preliminaries. He just stepped around a pile of windfalls and charged. I heard the cow snort again, and this time the bull believed her. He had maybe five seconds' grace. But he did all right. He managed to pivot and brace himself. It was a battering-ram collision. Both bulls went to their knees. They lurched up, grunting, and I now got a fair look at the target bull's head. It would go sixty-nine inches. The palms assayed okay. There was a fancy lot of ivory-tipped points. So I gave Tom the signal, and he arose to a kneeling position. That was too much for the sentinel cow. She gave a final snort of alarm, and fled into the misty cottonwoods. Tom's .30-06 Winchester crashed as the two bulls slammed together again. The target bull fell, heart shot. The old-timer bounded clear of him, clever-footed, and trotted after his cow.

"Most exciting hunt I ever made," Tom said.

Gigas moose please conservationists. They have something special going for them. Something that hasn't been explained. Fifty years ago they were scarce in most parts. You had to sweat to find one. I mean we ate a lot of sow bosom and snowshoe rabbit meat. Then in the 1930s the moose population began to increase. It was a real boom. Before it leveled off, the big animals spread down onto the Alaska Peninsula. They crossed Anaktuvuk Pass into the high Arctic. They became abundant on the Susitna and Kuskokwim watersheds. It was wonderful. A phenomenon to celebrate. Perhaps someday we'll find out what caused it.

Rutting bulls are erratic and dangerous. For example, there was a scary experience my sourdough colleague Kobuk Jones had one September night in the Talkeetnas. "This bull was a mean brute," Kobuk told me. "A killer. I'm lucky I had the drop on him. The way it happens, I'm packing a load of gear up to my headquarters trapline cabin. But I have got a late start, and nightfall catches me at timberline. So I eat some supper and bed down. I'm on a little bunchgrass bench between a beaver pond and a rimrock. Well, I slumber okay until an hour or so after moonrise. Then the wumpety-bump of trotting hoofs wakes me. I sit up. It's a moose heifer, and she tears right past me. Ears laid back. I'm wondering what has spooked her, when I hear more hoofs coming my way. This time it's a bull. A big sonofagun.

"He spots me at one hundred feet and halts. The moonlight sparkles on his antlers. His coat looks almost black. I hear him blow. Well, my .30-06 Remington is on the sleeping bag beside me. I pick it up easy-like and check the chamber load. The bull takes a step toward me. His ears are sticking straight up. I guess he can't figure out what I am. He's handicapped—the wind is against him, and I'm lying in a patch of shadow. So he tries a bluff. He rears high and comes down shaking his antlers. He jumps at his shadow. Boy, he's a spectacle in the moonlight. And I now realize what's bothering him. I'm between him and the runaway heifer. She crossed my bed-ground bench, so he aims to. He wants me to move out of the way. Well, I ain't about to. I was here first. I carefully line the Remington on him, but I sure hope he won't make me shoot. I want us to part peacefully.

"Because listen. It's three miles north along the timberline to my Slate Creek cabin. Most of it bad going. Alders and slide-rock. And this bull is a whopper. He'll weigh anyhow fifteen hundred pounds. It would take me a week to pack the meat home. And I'd be cussing myself plenty, on account of the cabin is in a moose pasture. Mulligan bulls use the clearing for a hangout. I ain't never had to pack meat more'n five hundred yards. Well, I can tell that this bull is about through bluffing. His neck hair has lifted. His eyes glitter in the moonlight. 'Be reasonable, moose,'

I say to him. 'Let's not have any trouble, huh? Please.' But it's no use. He just snorts at me and grits his teeth. So I decide to fire a shot past his head. But as I raise the Remington, he starts for me. And that's his hard luck. I drop him with a chest shot.

"So I spend a week packing and cussing," Kobuk sighed. "What a bull."

Timberline moose hunts are the best. For me, anyway. It's open country. Pretty country. High above the tundra bogs and brush jungles. It's smart to come in by saddle mount and packtrain. Mobile. With a cayuse under you, you can hunt a heap of terrain. And up here you can use your glasses to swell advantage. When I was hunting afoot with Indian friends and we shot a moose, we would move camp to the carcass. It beat toiling under those loads of meat. But with horses doing the work, I have transported a carcass fifty miles. It adds up to happy hunting. An ideal way to take your giant trophy moose.

These gigas moose are hard-case Romeos. They give their cows a rough time. But they protect them, too. Take an episode that occurred when I was wrangling horses for old Frank Lee. We were over in the Tonzona Basin with a hunter named Jim Curran. It was a bright late-autumn morning. Frost on the ground. We climbed a lupine ridge and got out our glasses. There was no shortage of moose. I counted eight in the timberline park below us. And as we were sizing up the heads, another candidate appeared. This bull and two cows came galloping toward us out of an aspen grove eight hundred yards upwind. They had a situation. Six wolves were hazing them. But I could see that the wolves weren't serious. They were just having fun. I suppose the frost had made them frisky. They began jumping at the bull's flanks. Yip-yapping. They hadn't hoorawed the cows since we sighted them, and now they lost their chance to.

The bull dropped back until the cows were well ahead. Then he spun, raking and striking.

He scored. The wolves were only long yearlings. They had a lot to learn about moose. With my 16X glasses steady on them, I watched them foul up. Three of them were bunched at the bull's left flank. They tried to fade aside, but didn't make it. They got in one another's way. The bull was upon them before they could separate. He caught a gray wolf in the belly with his left antler tip and tossed him. He then came full around and hit the same wolf with his right antler blade. The wolf was

slung fifteen feet, end over end. I heard him wail. He landed
on his back and scrambled into some willows. The bull now
swung an antler at a brown wolf and missed. But he followed
up and clobbered the wolf with a front hoof. For an animal
his size he was astonishingly fast. The brown wolf took off
on three legs, and the other wolves joined him. The bull shook
his antlers. He turned to check on the cows.

The cows were still heading our way. But they were in some
birch brush, and I guess the bull didn't spot them. Anyway, he started
off at a tangent. Then he halted, his temper flaring again. He bristled.
He uprooted a bush with his brow tines and savaged it. Well, we now
got a good look at him. I gave him fourteen hundred pounds. His
antlers would go sixty-six inches. Each palm was split into two mis-
matched parts. But they were heavy and had forty points. The brow
antlers were massive and would go forty-five inches. A unique trophy head. Well, the bull now spotted the cows. His mane flattened
and he came highballing across the park. Jim adjusted the scope sight
of his .375 Winchester Magnum. The bull caught up with the cows
250 yards from us. He sniffed them over, grunting. Then he began
antler-whipping them. They crowded against a cutbank and took it.
Then Jim fired. The bull flinched and fell over.

"He was great," Jim said.

These giant moose have adapted easily to civilization. Road
building hasn't made them abandon any of their important ranges.
Nor has hunting pressure. They just get smarter. For one thing,
they seem to know when they can trust people. In deep-snow
months, they often gather near backwoods camps and villages.
They become a major nuisance along the Alaska Railroad. They
invade cabin clearings. A sizable band of moose made permanent winter headquarters at my Toonakloot Creek homestead.
I enjoyed being host to them. They behaved like domestic animals.
They would stand around and watch me perform chores. They
never showed any fear of me. But their trust was strictly seasonal. At spring breakup they always took off.

The splendid brutes get tricky come autumn. Especially
the cows do. If a hunter alerts them, they'll generally cause
him to work and scheme. Take a mid-September packtrain
hunt I made with Bill Baker in the Wood River country. We
sighted a trophy bull the first morning. We had climbed a
timberline hillside and were searching with our glasses. I
saw the bull's antlers flash. He and a young cow were in a

scrub birch forest 650 yards upwind. The bull was a prize. I gave him fifteen hundred pounds. His neck was rut-swollen. He sported a "muff" instead of a "bell" at his throat. His antlers would go sixty-eight inches. The palms were flat and shallow, with forty-two points. The brow antlers spread thirty inches and were nicely balanced. He was late shedding his velvet—long ribbons of the stuff hung from both palms. At the moment he was battering his antlers against an alder bush, trying to clean them. Well, Bill said he wanted him. So we began a stalk.

We did all right for a hundred yards. Then the birch forest stopped us. Crisp fallen leaves lay ankle-deep under the gnarled trees. They were too noisy. So we scouted for a better route. Presently, we got another look at the bull. He was now scraping his antlers on a fire-charred snag. Charcoal had blackened his forehead and both ears. A grotesque sight. The cow stood facing us, head up. But she was just naturally suspicious. She couldn't prove anything. Well, we scouted on, and were lucky. We found a dry flood channel that led in the right direction. We followed it fifty yards and then our luck suddenly ended. A snowshoe rabbit was feeding on the bank ahead of us. It reared up and peered at us, then fled out across the noisy birch leaves. Seconds later a moose snorted. We caught one glimpse of the animals. They were headed crosswind at a fast trot. The cow was in the lead.

Well, I believe they circled and got our scent. Anyway, they were alerted. We spent two days trying to locate them. Wasted effort. I suspect they were hiding out in the birch forest. But on the third morning we got a break. A hard wind blew out of the peaks. We climbed a cloudberry point and searched with our glasses. After a while we sighted the cow. She was at the creek, drinking. The bull wasn't with her. But I knew she would show us where he was. All we had to do was watch her. She finished drinking and headed back into the windy timber. And the bull came trotting to meet her. He was sore. I figure he had been asleep and she had sneaked away. Anyway, he belted her with an antler blade. He bit her neck. Then he got romantic and put a foreleg over her shoulder. Well, we made our stalk. It was easy. The booming wind covered for us. We rounded a thicket two hundred feet from the pair. Bill's .30-06 Winchester hammered. The bull knelt and fell over.

"Pure suspense," Bill said. "A perfect hunt."

Our gigas moose helped pioneer this frontier. We were all their fans. We admired and respected the animals and were plenty indebted to them. In winter we had what amounted to a moose economy. We subsisted largely on moose meat. And we wore moosehide. Indian women tanned the hides and made jackets, moccasins, and gloves for us. A secret was involved. Inexplicably, the tanned hides came out a rich golden brown. I tried for years to discover how they were dyed. Finally, a boyhood friend, Billy No-Dogs, revealed the secret. The women used rotten spruce sapwood. Powdered it and rubbed it into the leather. Our snowshoe babiche, of course, was cut from moosehide. And there was a trick to preparing a hide. You pulled the hair off while the carcass was still warm. I mean we depended on these outsize moose. They rate a vote of thanks.

The long-geared critters are fun. There is no such thing as a dull hunt for them. Consider an experience my associate Baldy Thomas had at the head of Snider Creek, on the northern Kenai. "I'm shepherding young Mike Benson," Baldy told me. "It's a cold September morning, with snow clouds. We are on a blueberry hillside five hundred yards north of the creek and have just sighted four moose. Directly below us a lone cow is stuffing herself with red willow browse. Upstream four hundred yards two rut-ornery mulligan bulls are squaring away to fight. And down on the creek bank a fine big bull is stretched out asleep. I can't see his right antler—it's hidden in waist-high redtop grass. But the left antler is promising. It is eighteen inches deep and has twenty clean points. Well, Mike wants to try his luck at calling moose.

"Me, I don't do much moose calling. It ain't necessary in timberline country. But hunters get a kick out of fooling the animals, and in this case it can't do no harm. So I sit back and listen to Mike perform. He aims his horn at the sleeping bull and starts grunting. It sounds okay. That is, it ain't no phonier than most moose calling you hear, including my own. But it don't excite the bull any. His ears twitch. He half-raises his head. Then he flops down and goes to sleep again. He has probably been chasing cows and fighting for three weeks. Day and night, without stopping for more'n a few minutes sleep and some hurry-up browsing. I can see that he's gaunt. He needs some shut-eye. Mike gives out with a couple more grunts. This time the bull's ears don't move. He plain ain't interested.

"But the cow is. She has stopped feeding and is staring up the slope. I see her try the wind. The rut ain't wore her down none. She is plump. Her fall coat is thick and smooth. She moves like a yearling. Well, Mike grunts again and she answers him. She opens her mouth wide and gives a yodeling beller that you could hear a mile distant. She gets action. The two mulligan bulls stop threatening each other and face her. And the sleeping bull wakes up, listens and lets out a grunt. He surges to his hoofs. I now get a look at his right antler. He is trophy class, all right. His head will go seventy inches. The palms are matched and have thirty-eight points. Mike drops the birchbark horn and lines his .300 Weatherby Magnum. He fires and the shot is good. The bull drops.

"'Hooray for gigas moose,' Mike says, and I congratulate him."

Back to the beginning. I took the cape off Pete Waring's bull. I cleaned up the skull. Pete helped me skin, dress, and quarter the carcass. Then we scouted for our eight horses. We found them five hundred yards beyond camp, loafing on a bunch-grass flat. It took us an hour and a half to saddle up and bring the meat and the trophy to camp. We hung the quarters from a pole lashed between two spruces. The meat was fat. I built a fire and made coffee, which I served in half-pint China mugs. A rainbow had formed across the lake. We stretched out on sun-warmed caribou moss, drinking coffee and smoking our pipes. The horses stood watching us, sleepy-eyed. This was the Kenai high country, the beautiful area where sportsmen first began hunting gigas moose for their trophy heads. We used to call it Moose Heaven. Pete sighed luxuriously.

"Man, I hate to go home," he said.

How Tex Cobb Came Up
an Alaska Legend

*Tex was special. A roughneck master woodsman
and a natural showman, he may well
become a sourdough folk hero.*

"**W**hoa. Git back there, yuh slant-eyed knotheads. That grizzly'll massacree yuh," my sourdough partner, old Tex Cobb, hollered at our five siwash malamute pack dogs as they tried, clamoring, to crowd past him on the narrow trail. "Git back, damn hit."

The dogs were tough. They defied him.

This was in Alaska's ice-ribbed Knik River Valley, the autumn Tex turned eighty. We were heading for the main glacier front to repair a wind-damaged trapline cache. Using the dogs, let me state, was Tex's idea. Me, I was no pack-dog man. The ornery brutes fought. They were geniuses at getting into trouble. Besides, they couldn't pack much. I would a heap rather have left the string at Matanuska and wrastled a boat upriver. But Tex had outtalked me. He was set in his ways regarding dogs. So we packed the characters and took off. At midafternoon the next day we came to Jim Creek ford. Tex was in the lead, and I heard him speak sharply to the dogs. Then I saw the coastal baldface. He stood at the water's edge, fifty yards upwind, with a flopping silver salmon between his jaws. He was high-humped and slope-backed. He had a nice tobacco-colored pelt. I gave him six hundred pounds.

I guess he heard us. Anyway, he reared up, and the dogs spotted him.

I lined my .30-06 on him and waited. Cussing. I hoped we wouldn't have to shoot the animal, because he was a solid business asset. I knew gents who would pay $1,000 for the sport of harvesting him. But we had a risky situation. The dogs were carrying maximum loads—thirty pounds apiece. It made them slow and clumsy. If they tackled the bear, he would probably kill them all. Tex glanced at me, then stood his rifle against a birch and shed his pack. Our lead dog, an eighty-five-pound black quarter-wolf bravo named Kobuk, now snarled and lunged ahead. Tex belted him across the eyes with his hat. Then he grabbed him, collar and tail, and heaved him amongst the other dogs. It was quite a feat for a man his age. And I believe it saved the string. They at once began to fight, and the grizzly made up his mind. He tried to roar at us with the salmon in his mouth, but only spluttered. Then he fled hellbent downstream. We quelled the dog fight, and Tex gave me a comical look.

"Amazin'," he said, massaging his back. "I only slung ol' Kobuk about six feet. But I think hit put a crik in my spine, by gad. I *must* be gettin' old, huh?"

Tex was special. He was a roughneck master woodsman and a natural showman. People liked him. He did things that tickled them and said things they got a kick out of repeating. He talked, dressed, and acted the way they thought a top pro woodsman should. As a result, today—fourteen years after his death—admirers are building a legend around the guy. It could well be he'll wind up a sourdough folk hero. The unique new state needs one, and he seems to be its likeliest prospect.

He was a big man. Two hundred wolf-lean pounds. Six feet, two inches tall. Powerful and easy moving. With green eyes and graying black hair. He never owned a suit of clothes. He smelled of woodsmoke and seldom got a haircut. He ate with his belt knife. A sporting girl once asked me, smiling secretively, if he *ever* took his hat off. I joined him when I was fifteen, and learned my basic trade working with him. The whole bit. From trophy hunting to dog mushing. From diamond hitches to beaver sets. He did well by his hunters. He found high-grade trophies for them and sent them home happy and thrilled. I enjoyed his technique because he sure aimed to win. When he needed to, he came up with some novel and daring hunting stratagems.

Take a September Dall sheep hunt we made with a visiting sportsman named Walt Harris. This was up at the head of Carpenter Creek in the western Chugaches. We were backpacking. Early the third day we located two fine rams. They were on a high, rimrocked slope northeast of camp, sparring halfheartedly. Beyond the slope bulged some blue-black cloud masses. We sized the rams up with 16X glasses. One set of horns was terrific. Like most good Dall horns you find in the Chugaches, they were heavy and tightly curled. The butting surfaces showed scars, but the outward-flaring tips were undamaged. I could see that Tex was impressed. He cleaned his glasses and took another long look. The horns just might, he presently allowed, go 16x41 inches. Then he asked Walt if he was weather shy. Because those clouds, he said, had an ugly color to them. Walt, excited now, said the hell with weather, let's get up there, man.

"Why, shore," Tex said.

So we began our stalk. And before we had climbed five hundred feet, snow sifted down. Scattered wet flakes. Walt studied the sky. Clearly he was having second thoughts. But Tex took care of that—he complimented him on his climbing. He said he had good rock savvy and the balance of a steeple jack. Walt beamed. We toiled on and topped out in a water-cut cranny at grassline. Our rams were now four hundred yards upwind. They stood thirty feet apart, glaring at each other. They had been fighting. Bloody slobber dripped from the target ram's mouth. Both animals were panting. Walt sat down to rest until he was steady enough to shoot. As we watched the rams between snow flurries, they shuffled and feinted. They shook their heads. Then they suddenly charged together. It was a spectacular collision. The lesser ram went down, rolling. And before he could get up our target ram stepped in and butted him again, then again.

Tex told Walt he'd better shoot. He sounded urgent. Walt nodded, and carefully set the Lyman iron sight of his .270. Fussing over it. He should have attended to this earlier. Because as he raised the rifle to shoot, wind battered the slope, and the snowfall thickened. I could still make out the rams, but they were shadow shapes. Impossible targets at this range. Walt started to curse, then shut up. After all, lousy weather didn't disturb him any— he'd said so himself. I mentally saluted Tex. The old gent now stood up. He would, he said, show us a trick, he hoped. Motioning us to follow, he walked toward the rams. Of course they saw us, but they didn't spook. I suppose it was dumb curiosity on their part—Tex never offered an explanation. Anyway, they let us cover a hundred yards. Then Tex halted, and Walt rested the .270 over a ledge and fired. Our trophy ram dropped. The other ram fled.

"I thank you, mister," Walt said to Tex, fervently, when he had gone over to the carcass. "I've learned things this morning. Maybe more than you realize." Which were my sentiments exactly. (The horns averaged 16x39 inches.)

Tex was a great reader. Devoted to the adventure and sporting magazines. Men's magazines. Friends at Anchorage collected secondhand copies for him, and we dog-sledded them to our trapline camps. Tex would gloat over each new supply. I doubt that these publications ever had a more dedicated fan. He not only read the beat-up copies, he studied them. Even the advertisements. He knew the work of all the writers and illustrators. He knew the editors' names. Naturally I caught his enthusiasm. In the evenings, camp chores finished, we would talk about favorite authors and their plots and story characters. I still remember characters that Tex thought were great—Smoke Bellew, Shark Gotch, Typhoon Williams, the Major, and Khlit of the Curved Saber. Fascinated, I soon began writing myself, and the stories sold. I suspect I had the country's only trapline literary education. Thanks to old Tex.

Tex ignored his years. Or tried to. For example, there was a crazy bronc-taming ride he made when he was sixty-five. The legend makers apparently have missed this episode—I haven't heard any campfire yarns about it. We were over in the Wood River Basin with Dan Evans, for a grizzly and a caribou. We had eight desert-bred packhorses, fresh up from Yakima. With the burrs still in their tails. At sunrise the first morning we rode upvalley, scouting. Our medicine was good. Less than a mile from camp we sighted around a hundred barren ground caribou. The band was six hundred yards crosswind, loafing in some frosted wolf willows. We got out our glasses. Several of the bulls were trophy grade, and one of them was remarkable. He stood at the near edge of the band, quartering toward us. He had tall basket-type antlers and a beautiful snowy cape. Tex opined that the main antler beams might go fifty-two inches.

We tied our mounts and made an easy three-hundred-yard stalk. Our bull was now looking straight toward us. Head up. Alert. Dan cut down on him with his scope-sighted .30-06 and fired. The animal fell over. Tex congratulated Dan, then asked me to fetch our mounts and a packhorse. He was already reaching for his steel tape. So I lit out, trotting, and was back with the horses in thirty minutes. The packhorse I brought was a chunky red roan named Solo. He had worked fine on the trail. But when he saw the bull carcass and got a whiff of blood, he rolled his eyes and snorted. Tex talked to him and petted him, and I thought he had him cooled down. But the sonofagun fooled us. He let us load the trophy and the meat onto him, then he suddenly gave a bawl and came unglued. Well, he could pitch. He was fast and strong, and knew the moves. He threw the pack hell, west, and crooked, as they say.

"All right, hard case," Tex growled. "I'm next. We'll find out jest how tough you are, by gad."

He roped the roan. He stripped off the sawbuck saddle, and put his own on him. I wanted to object. Sure, I knew the cayuse had to be tamed. And now was the time. Or he'd probably be a spoiled horse the rest of his life. But I figured Tex was too old for the chore. He obviously didn't, though, so I kept quiet. He led Solo to open ground. He took hold of the bridle cheek, stuck his thumb in the cayuse's eye, and stepped aboard. Well, it was a busy contest. They were both good. Solo went up high and came down hard, grunting. I counted the jumps. He made fourteen, which is aplenty. And he was a tricky so-and-so. He would drop a shoulder, or turn his head one way and pitch another. But Tex stayed up there, riding pretty. Fanning with his hat. We cheered him. He had style. But he was taking a beating. When Solo at last quit, panting, Tex's nose was bleeding. He looked at us and managed a grin.

"A lotta fun. Ol' Solo is some cayuse, huh?" he said, leaning wearily on the pommel, blood dribbling off his chin. "But he'll tote that pack now, I reckon." (The bull's antler beams averaged fifty-one inches.)

Tex was mighty fond of food. He had picked up the word "gourmet" in his reading, and often told me that was what he was, by gad. But he was a miserable cook. I remember a certain dinner. We were trapping out of a cabin on upper Goose

Creek, in the Talkeetnas. Since it was Tex's day to cook, the menu was short—pinto beans boiled with a fat porcupine. Tex helped himself from the iron pot. He tasted the beans, and frowned. He gazed at the pot. Then, after hesitating twice, he added a smidgen of salt. Tasting again, he smiled. And this was no act. The old boy was plumb serious. We finished the meal, and he sighed happily. He had seldom, he said, eaten better trapline grub, by gad, even though he had cooked it. I figured he wanted praise, so I tried to oblige. I told him I had just decided to become a backwoods beanpot gourmet myself.

That broke him up.

I rated Tex a great moose hunter. He understood the animals. If there was a trophy bull around, he could find him. I actually believed he could think like a moose. Yeah, I know. I'm sounding like some of Tex's campfire biographers. But take the climax of a hunt we made with Mike Bowers. This was on the Kashwitna River burns, in September. We went in by packtrain. Moose were plentiful, and the weather favored us. But for three days we saw only cows and young stuff. The trophy bulls were roaming, looking for sex and trouble. We found scent holes they had pawed. We found battle sites—the ground torn up and tufts of bloody hair scattered around. And that was it. Then, on the fourth morning, we got a break. We were scouting a willow-dotted flat. Several whiskey jacks began squawking crosswind, and we headed that way. Then we heard the bull. He seemed to be having a full-scale tantrum.

He was uttering war grunts. We heard him antler-whack a bush and stomp the ground. I mean he was really sore. He had it bad. We moved in closer. There had been a rain, so the fallen leaves weren't noisy. In a moment we spotted him. He was in a little redtop opening, 150 yards distant, facing upwind. He was pawing. His mane was bristled. We got out our glasses, and Tex made *hmmm hmmmmm* sounds as he studied the bull. Well, he was a husky moose, probably a six-year-old. I gave him twelve hundred pounds. His head would go around sixty inches. Which is to say it was a fair trophy head, but not an exciting one. Nothing to *hmmm hmmmmm* about. I saw that he had been in a brawl. There was a raw gash on his left hip, and another on his withers. I concluded they were the main reasons for his hostile mood. Our Mike now asked Tex if he could shoot. Tex said to wait, please.

Maybe we could do better, he said. He had been thinking. The bull yonder had been in a fight, he said, most likely over a cow. And he had lost. That was why he was so sore. His antics showed that the other bull was somewhere upwind. Close. So it just might pay us, he said, to go take a look. Well, Mike bought it. We began a blind stalk. We had covered seventy-five yards when we spotted two moose. A bull and a cow. They were in an aspen clump 120 yards upwind. As we got busy with our glasses, action developed. The cow reached up to bite off a twig, and I guess the bull felt lucky. Anyway, he reared over her. But she was fast on her hooves. Squealing, she dodged away. He let out a grunt and bounded after her. His antlers were tremendous. When he turned, he seemed to be banking. Tex said to take him. Then Mike's .300 magnum banged, and the bull went down. I felt respect for Tex and his moose thinking. I remarked, as we headed for the carcass, that he certainly had figured those bulls.

"Aw, they weren't so smart," he said in the hearty voice he used when kidding. "Why, this one didn't even have brains enough to let his cow finish breakfast." (The antlers went 69½ inches.)

Tex got along fine with the Indians. Consider the way he acquired his Indian name. We were coming down the Susitna River on a raft, returning from a cabin-building project. It was a windy late-August noon. One thousand yards ahead was Montana Creek and the village of Chief Wasilla Stepan. We wanted to land there, but the wind was strong against us. Tex, however, shrugged and said don't worry, the Injuns would lend us a hand. He then fired a couple of shots to alert the village. But nothing happened. The place looked deserted. He fired more shots. I beat on a frying pan with my knife handle. We both hollered. This went on for five minutes. Then at last two canoes put out from the bank. Chief Wasilla was in one of them, laughing. I now caught on. They had heard us from the first.

Chief Wasilla shook hands with us, still chuckling. "You a good man," he said to Tex, "and you need an Injun name. So we give you one. It's Nis-Too-Ice-Ten. Means Sourdough-On-A-Raft." This was an honor and Tex knew it. Proud, he blushed like a kid.

It was a grand life. Folks have pointed out the advantages I missed, such as proper schooling and social polish. But I tell them I did all right. At the age of twenty-one, I could take a packtrain through five hundred miles of mountain wilderness and bring it back in good shape. Give me a few traps and snares, and I could make a fair living. I could build a cabin. I knew the passes and fords in three mountain ranges. I could speak the difficult Denna Indian language. Moreover—and maybe it's the most important item—I learned to enjoy simple things. We got pleasure from a mouth-organ solo. A plain moose-brisket stew was wonderful fare. Some blueberry wine in a tin cup couldn't be beat. I recall a winter morning in Rainy Pass. Tex had halted our dog team to watch the sunrise. It was purty, he

said. Real purty. But some people, he added, would argue that we were wasting good time watching it, the poor dopes.

Tex was a kindly roughneck. For an example, I offer a mid-May brown bear hunt we made with young Bill Sand. This was back at the head of Chinitna Bay, on the west side of Cook Inlet. The big bears were numerous here, and it was beautiful country. We met Bill's trophy specimen at daybreak the first morning. We had gone up the beach to dig some butter clams for our breakfast. Bill saw a clam's spurt, and ran toward it. And just then the bear, a whopper, stepped from behind a pile of drift logs, ninety feet distant. Both Bill and the bear froze. The bear was reddish-brown, with blond ears. I gave him eleven hundred pounds. Tex said, "Take him, boy, if you can." But Bill didn't move. He stood there staring at the bear, his .375 magnum in one hand, and a shovel in the other. I sympathized. The bear was simply too close to cover. He had all the odds.

Bill explained later. He said he thought that maybe, if he froze, the bear might come farther into the open. Then he'd have him dead to rights. But the animal was too crafty. He swung his head, sizing us up. I could see a scar on his muzzle. I saw some white-stocking gnats spiraling above him. The huge brute now showed us that he hated our guts. Baring his teeth, he gave a long snarl. Then he whirled and was gone—behind the drift pile and into the alders. Using our glasses, we presently got another look at him. He loped into a saw grass opening 450 yards up the beach. Facing our way, he reared high, and I thought I heard him roar. Then he took off again. Well, we put in the rest of the day hunting him. No luck. And when we returned to camp, Bill was so discouraged he looked sick. Tex tried to talk him out of it and failed. Bill said he should have blasted a shot, win or lose. He had let us down hard, he declared.

Tex liked the kid. So he made another attempt. He spun some big windy bear yarns. He told some bear jokes. And when we were ready to turn in, the camp was almost cheerful again.

Surf mounted during the night. Crashing in. Tex sat up, listening, and said surf like that would certainly fetch the beachcomber bears. At dawn we arose and hunted eastward along the drift-strewn beach. A mob of gulls were screaming ahead of us, and we checked them with our glasses. Oh, man. The birds had found a beluga whale carcass. I knew now that we had it made. Because the noisy birds and the whale were perfect bear bait. We got down behind a tide-mark boulder and waited. Twenty minutes went by. Then a fat sow bear with two cubs came off the hillside. They passed us, making for the dead whale. And five minutes later, Bill's bear arrived. He walked out of a gully mouth fifty yards upwind.

The bear passed our ambush. Then Bill stood up and said, "Hey!" The animal spun. He was still ornery. He bristled. He took three swaggering steps toward us, popping his jaws. Then Bill shot him through the head.

"Congratulations, boy. Yuh did that jest right," Tex asserted with a big smile. "You're a savvy hunter, an' we're proud of yuh." As I said, Tex was a kindly roughneck. I'll bet the kid will never forget that praise.

Back to Jim Creek. We looked the dogs over and found they were trailworthy. The fight was mostly noise. So we led them across the ford. Kobuk had been sulking, sorry for himself. But he now trotted up to Tex, wagging his tail. Tex knelt and put an arm around the dog's neck. He assured him he was a fine, valiant animal. Good-looking, too. Kobuk moaned with delight. We then lined out up the Knik sandbars. Tex took the lead, rifle slung on his left shoulder, hat tilted to one side. I watched him with special interest, because today we had been associates exactly thirty years. He still carried himself like a man in his prime. . . .

Tex reached ninety. He died at his Kalgin Island fishing camp, down Cook Inlet, on July 3, 1962. He once told me: "I was born in west Texas in 1872. I came to Alasky as a young man, an' I've had me a good time ever since, by gad."

The Greatest Grouse Dog

"Red was a happy dog.
He never showed temper and really
seemed to love a difficult hunt."

"**M**an, that beats me. Your hotshot spruce grouse dog is acting nuts," young Bill Baker said, squinting against the early sun
as we moved in behind Red, my veteran Irish setter. "Just lookit
him. He's gazing up at the sky."

"Like hell he is. Get set, son," I said. "Red's warning
you that—"

This was a mile south of my Goose Creek cabin, In Alaska's
game-rich Susitna Valley, on a grand mid-autumn morning.
We seemed to be loaded with luck. Twenty minutes ago, at
first shooting light, we had scouted upwind along a timber-
dotted blueberry ridge. Red must have had a solid hunch.
Anyway, he worked close, and I presently saw him hit grouse
scent. He quartered, checking. With the sun on his coppery
coat, he was a handsome cuss. I could tell he was excited—
he had flagged his tail. So I figured it was a big flock. I
knew the birds favored this ridge. I had found flocks of up
to twenty here. Glancing at young Bill, I saw that he had
caught on. He was watching Red bug-eyed. Well, by now I
was excited myself. I'm a spruce grouse fan. Always was.
Okay, we moved in, crowding Red a little. Then it happened.
We heard the wing-thunder up ahead in the sun-dazzle—beyond scattergun range.

Red looked back, his ears flattened. Apologetic. The kid sighed audibly. I advised them both to relax—shucks, we were still in business.

Well, it was a good flock, all right. Shading my eyes, I made out maybe twelve birds. They had got up ninety yards distant, stubby wings flashing. The racket they made told me they were fat and full-fed. Boy, several of them were practically lumbering through the air. But they weren't spooked. They had lifted straightaway, and none had banked for a look at us. Most likely, I thought, they had been feeding since sunup. Now, their crops stuffed with sugar-sweet berries, they probably were bound for a loafing place. And sure enough, in a moment they pitched into some spruces. Swell—I wanted them to stay there. So I gave out with a bald eagle's hunting scream. (Actually a whistle, the way I do it.) It may sound phony to the birds, but still it makes them cautious. They take cover. I now got out my 8X glasses. Red had loped ahead. I watched him catfoot into the timber. Then he pointed, in high style. Tail stiff. Right front paw picked up. Mighty pretty.

We hurried forward.

It was suspenseful. When at last we were in shot range, I felt myself grin. I was really enjoying this. Well, I now motioned the kid to walk them up. I made the luck sign. And just then Red broke point—in goofy fashion. Turning crosswind, he gazed upward. Like he was maybe watching a cloud. Gents, I'll bet my mouth hung open. The kid shrugged, and stepped ahead. And as he did so, Red moaned. Then, belatedly, I understood. Kneeling, I scanned the spruces in front of Red. Sure—some of our birds weren't on the ground. I now located five in the nearest tree. They were perched motionless, clearly scared an eagle would get them. Okay, I told the kid where the birds were, and he spotted them. Just in time. If he'd kept on, he'd have had grouse flushing around his ears. I was plenty proud of Red.

The kid nodded thanks and angled forward, and the flock roared up. His Savage 12 over-and-under boomed twice. Two birds fell. "Forgive me for misjudging you, friend," he said, hugging Red, "you are some operator."

The spruce grouse rate up here. Although they are found from Bristol Bay to Labrador, we regard them as *our* frontier grouse. But the method of hunting them sure has changed. When

I was a kid we took them with .22 trapline pistols, and there wasn't a trained spruce grouse dog in the land. I finally graduated to a shotgun. And I successively owned two dogs who were fair at hunting the birds. Then, sort of by accident, I acquired Red. It happened at Goose Creek. I had been up in the peaks. When I got back I found I'd had visitors. They had camped on the creek flat, but had left no clue as to who they were. Well, that night a sound at the cabin door woke me. I got up and lit a lamp. I opened the door. Standing there, eyes shining in the lamplight, was this Irish setter pup. He was about ten months old. He was skinny. And he had a raw gash across his forehead—a bullet wound, unmistakably. But he was polite. He wagged his tail. Well, I said "Howdy" and invited him in. And mighty soon I had canned milk heating on the stove, and the first-aid gear laid out.

He was a fine pup. I liked him at once. I doctored him and fed him, and let him know he had a friend. Then, when nobody showed up to claim him, I trained him to hunt spruce grouse—the way we frontier roughnecks thought the birds should be hunted. By the following August, he was an expert.

Visiting gunners praised Red. Bragged about him. But his tactics often baffled them. For example, take a late-autumn hunt we made with Dale Evarts. This was up at the forks, on a frost-jeweled afternoon. It had turned out to be a big grouse year. We'd had a mild spring, with no hard rains. Consequently, the chick survival rate was high. Now there were family flocks everywhere. Red found one bunch smack in the trail, feasting on wild-rose hips. I counted seven birds. They were all this year's grouse—full-grown but still unwary. I thought they would average a pound and a quarter. They apparently had lost their brood hen. At least I didn't see her. Well, they stared at Red. Then I'll be doggoned if one of them didn't jump up and grab another rose hip. They were the kind of grouse that some folks call fool hens—until they learn better.

Dale walked them up. As they rocketed clear of the rosebrush, his Remington 16 pump-action boomed. The lead grouse spun in.

Red trotted to the downed bird. But he didn't pick it up right then. Instead he stood listening, head cocked. This was a special trick I had taught him. A real grouse-getter. Our flock of six birds had headed upwind, flying low and fast, and

had vanished into a stand of spruces. For them today was ini-
tiation day. They'd been shot at. And from now on, boy, nobody
would ever call them fool hens. Well, I was listening too. Also
I was watching Red's ears. Dale didn't know what was going
on, but he kept quiet. Two minutes passed. Then I saw Red's
ears twitch. At the same instant, crosswind, I heard a faint
whap-whap of wings. Great. That was a signal for more action. Red now fetched the dead bird, bringing it smartly to
Dale, who beamed. I tossed Red a salute. The sonofagun hadn't
missed a cue. He was a 100 percent pro. He rolled his eyes
at me, and lit out crosswind.

This must have seemed pretty unusual to Dale, but he followed, looking fascinated.

Red took it easy. Our trick was reliable. I had borrowed
it from a piratical old black fox. You listen of course, for
the birds to land. Their wings make a considerable racket
whipping foliage. But there's a catch. The birds are shifty—
they twist and turn before they drop in. Thus you lose the
wind. Which is a major handicap because your dog now has
to start guessing. Well, I briefed Dale. Close ahead was a
scrub willow flat. I figured that was the place. So did Red.
He halted, and looked back at me. With his nose blanked,
he wanted some advice. Okay, I reached for the 8X glasses.
Resting them on a windfall, I soon located our birds. They
were sneaking through the painted brush. Scrooched low. Fur-
tively peering our way. Gun-wise veterans, all of a sudden.
I pointed, and Red moved in. The birds froze. Then they
lofted, and Dale took the high bird.

"Thrilling, mister," he said as Red retrieved for him.

Spruce grouse are forest birds. White spruce forests, that
is. In hard winters they subsist partly on white spruce needles.
You seldom find the birds above timberline or out on open tundra.
But they do like certain forest-edge places, such as blowdowns
and old burns. Because these areas produce a heap of summer and fall forage. Yellow-flowering pea vine. Salmonber-
ries and black currants. Wild raspberries. Grass-seed crops.
All of which are big items in the spruce grouse's diet. Brood
hens usually nest in forest-edge spots. And come autumn, family
flocks often assemble at favorite edge berry patches. Maybe
four or five families together, forming super-flocks. So naturally smart gunners work the edge. It's always a good way to

pick up a couple of birds for your supper. And if you're lucky, you may find yourself in the midst of a spruce grouse bonanza. Which is a fabulous experience.

The birds are tops. But you sure need a rugged and savvy dog. Which Red was. For example, consider an episode that took place one cold November afternoon up at the creek head. I'm backpacking some gear to my main trapline cabin. Snowshoeing. Red is plodding behind on the broken trail, and looks half-frozen. But when we come to the cabin clearing, he suddenly lunges ahead. He snuffles the icy wind and flags his tail. Oh boy, I get the message. Spruce grouse. At once I have a tantalizing vision. I see myself forking two fat grouse, browned and sizzling, out of a Dutch oven. Boy. I mean it's been a long day—I'm hungry. Okay, I get busy with the glasses. Straight upwind, just below the sod-roofed cabin, is a frozen one-lodge beaver pond. A half-acre deal. Its near bank is covered with snowy highbush cranberry thickets—and I now make out grouse trails amongst them. Then I spot a feeding grouse. Then another, and another.

Wonderful.

I kept a Browning Auto 12 at this cabin. So I get over there in a hurry. I shed my pack and check the gun and its loads. Then I take a final look with the glasses. I locate one of the grouse. It's under a waist-high cranberry bush one hundred yards distant, but the glasses bring it right up to me. It's beautiful. Its colors are brown, buff, black, and off-white. It is looking up at a cluster of frozen berries. As I watch, it squats and jumps, and yanks the cluster loose. Then it plants a foot on the berries and feeds greedily. And hooray for it, I think. Because cranberry-fed grouse is gourmet fare. Okay, I motion Red to get going, and he tries to look stylish as he moves in. But it's rough. Powder snow had drifted two feet deep here, and he hasn't got much hair on his belly and crotch. Just watching him makes me shiver. Well, at this point the lone grouse spots Red. It bobs its head nervously. Then it flushes—and eight other grouse rocket out of the snow-plastered brush with it.

They bank wide over the pond. Their idea, I guess, is to get a good look at Red and me. I swing the Browning on them, but I don't shoot.

I don't like the range. It's a mite too far—prime crippling range. Well, I've disappointed Red. His tail droops. I tell him I'm sorry, and we watch the grouse head for a bank-side spruce. The tree is completely snow-hooded, but they plow right into it. And their wings dislodge, I'll bet, a wagonload of snow. The powdery stuff eddies in a rainbowed cloud, hiding the tree. Which presumably spooks the birds. Anyway, they take off again. This time they angle closer, and I let go a shot. I try for the lead bird. It falters, then somersaults onto the pond. Red wallows after it—and just as he picks the bird up, the new ice breaks under his sixty-odd pounds. Scary. But the water isn't deep there. So I wade out, noisily busting ice, and convoy him ashore. He is shaking and snorting. I guess he figured he was a goner for sure. But he hangs onto that grouse, gents, until I take it from him.

"Pal, you're the best and the toughest," I tell him as we spring for the cabin's Yukon stove.

Red was a happy dog. The spruce grouse played some fancy tricks on him, but he never got temperamental. No sulks. No "setter blues." In fact, he seemed to especially enjoy a difficult hunt. For example, take an experience we had at the creek mouth. This was on a bright September morning, right after the first frost. A nice flock of grouse was resident down there, and I wanted a few of them. Shucks, my meat cache was empty. The last of the creek's four salmon runs had ended. And this morning I'd waked up thinking about cabin-fried grouse with sourdough biscuits and brown giblet gravy. Man. Well, I figured it was easy. But we went down to the mouth and carefully worked the timber's edge—and drew a total blank. So I took time out for a smoke. We were in this black currant patch. Its leaves had fallen. The shiny jet berries, fermented now, hung in big clusters. Wine-smelling. Red, beside me, started to lie down. Then he stiffened, looking crosswind. I turned—and here came our grouse. Wings set.

I grabbed the Browning.

There were six of the birds, and I remember thinking this was too easy. I supposed they hadn't seen us. When they did, I thought, they'd flare high and wide. They'd make perfect targets. And serve them right for being careless. So I didn't really hurry. I stood up and found good footing—about one second too late. The birds had fooled me. They were sideslipping in, eighty feet distant. Before I could swing the gun on them, they went below the brush tops. It was plumb astonishing. Because I now realized they had seen us all along. My gosh, they had to have. Spruce grouse have sharp vision. Well, Red looked as startled as I felt. He cut his eyes at me, and sort of tiptoed forward. When he had covered thirty feet he halted, and I closed in behind him. But nothing happened. I still hadn't seen a bird. Red shivered. This flock was sitting plenty tight for some reason. We waited half a minute. Then suddenly I caught on—and laughed.

The birds were drunk.

They had gorged themselves on fermented berries. I now recognized the signs. All northern berry-eating birds get high, I guess, at this time of year. But our spruce grouse are real topers—they get plastered. Okay, I gave Red the go-ahead signal. I was doubly eager now, because wine-flavored grouse is extra-special provender. I aimed to feast tonight. Well, Red took four or five steps, and I saw the birds run. They ran maybe 150 feet, changing directions. Red followed them. Then they flew several yards, but I didn't have time to shoot. Then they ran again. And this went on. Crazy. We crossed the creek flat. It was fun, but I was sorry for Red. The tipsy birds were making him look bad. They had cramped his style. So I let go a shot into the air. That did it. The birds got up in earnest, and I downed two of them. Red brought them, prancing. Despite everything, he had stayed even-tempered. As I said, he was a happy spruce grouse dog.

"Obliged, Champ," I said. "I sure wish your former boss could see you work, the miserable so-and-so."

Grand Stalk for Great Dalls

"Sure, I'm a Dall sheep fan.
I claim the critters are noble, and hunting
them is an especially great sport."

How the hell did I get myself here, I thought, clinging with both hands to a lofty backshelved cliff brink. I watched this patriarchal Dall ram stare bug-eyed—with his fancy-horned head held aristocratically high, and his grass-polished black hoofs braced on the shale—at the foot of a bizarrely beautiful rainbow, five hundred yards crosswind from me.

This was a spectacle. The Dall stood in the rainbow's glow. So close to the bright pot-o'-gold colors that his coat was orange-tinted. While his massive horn curls caught red-lavender lights. I had looked him over with 16X glasses and liked him. He was sleek and chunky built, with summer tallow on his ribs. An O.K. candidate for my trapline meat cache. His horns, I estimated, would go about 14x38 inches. He seemed fascinated, gazing fixedly at the arc of pure colors. A couple of minutes had passed since he last checked the slopes. Which encouraged me. Because my stalk was stalled. Everything had gone haywire. The ram had roamed. The weather had crossed me. And this cliff was a first-class S.O.B. It consisted of crumbling brown sandstone. Killer stuff. But, hopeful again, I now muscled myself up and got an elbow planted on the rim. I hung here a moment, sweating, with eighty feet of space under me. Then I hauled myself up and across to a safe spot. Just as—*cra-ash, boo-oom*—a sizable chunk of the rim broke off.

Fooled you, by gosh, I heard myself croak.

This is above Knik River. On a cloud-patched mid-September morning. I freeze, but the ram isn't alarmed. He only glances my way, then resumes contemplating the rainbow. No doubt he's heard a mort of rocks band down that cliffside. Hunks and slabs of the doggoned brown sandstone weathering off. I now sit up. I'm eager and excited. That old Dall-hunting magic—the wonderful mixture of suspense, beauty, danger, weather, plotting, dizzy heights, and toil—has hit me hard again. Praise be. I rest my iron-sighted .270 Winchester over an outcrop, and cut down on the ram. I need him. I've been on a fifty percent salmon diet since June. But nope. The gold bead blends with the golden rainbow light. Well, I have the remedy for that. I carefully black the bead with a match flame, an old snow-country trick, and try again. No trouble this time. The .270 crashes. I hear the 130-grain slug hit and see hair fly. The ram drops and comes rolling.

Sure, I'm a Dall sheep fan. All out. I claim the critters are noble, and that hunting them is an especially great sport. And, folks, I qualified as a pro some decades ago. Back when I was a kid, actually. Before I began shaving. I started out working for top guides, old Tex Cobb among them, as a backpacker. We hunted Dall rams through the Kenai Mountains, the Chugaches, the Talkeetnas, and the Alaska Range. Yeah, I was lucky. It was a grand apprenticeship, and I'm nostalgic regarding it. Which maybe is why I'm plenty enthusiastic about today's Dall sheep hunters. They are tough, adventurous guys, the ones I know. Savvy guys. They understand how to enjoy a Dall hunt. The whole experience. They get a kick out of sunrises and sunsets, a boss ram's tippy-toed gait, crestline views, the way a golden eagle rides the wind, frost-painted willows, a marmot's picket-pin stance, the curve of a ram's horn against his neck, spruce fragrance, starlight on a glacier, the long echoes of a rifle shot, and the smell of burned powder. They are like the buckskin old-timers—hard-butt sentimentalists.

Dall sheep meat is A-okay. Maybe the best in the peaks. Its flavor is great. It's seldom tough. It looks good and smells good. The fat is firm. A thick round steak broiled over willow coals is a gourmet treat. So is a brisket stew. And you sure can't beat a smoky-tasting barbecued shoulder. Or a couple of sizzling breakfast chops topped with bacon strips. But it's

hard-earned meat. I mean the work begins when you pull that trigger. Your best bet, usually, is to roll or drag your kill down to timber, and dress it there. And it'll pay you to do an extra-careful job of skinning. In a wind-sheltered place. Otherwise the doggoned brittle hair will give you trouble. It sticks to the meat and is difficult to see—until you find it floating in the stewpot. A meat saw would be welcome, but a man never has one, it seems. So you quarter the carcass frontier style, with your knife and the camp ax. And here I will advocate a heresy. A shocker. Use a file to sweeten the knife's edge. Sure, sure, I know. But try it anyway. The rough edge will please you.

The amber-horned animals are fun. They pull some rare surprises. For example, consider a hunt I made at the Knik headwaters. This was above my No. 3 cabin, on a weather-whacked mid-autumn morning. The first frosts had come. So, at last, meat would keep. And I sure needed a fat carcass. My diet lately had featured skinny rabbits. Okay, I got busy scouting with the glasses. I expected it would be easy to locate a meat ram. Shucks, the cabin was built on a sheep mountain. I called it Meat Market Peak. But my luck was shot. Or something. I scanned the usual ram hangouts for three days, my gosh, and drew a blank. It was mysterious. But then, early the third morning, I got a break. I hit the ram jackpot. They were on the mountain's west shoulder. Twelve of them. Silhouetted against an ornery-looking sky. I steadied the glasses. A Dall show-off was taking place. Two trophy types were sparring. They were good, too. Spring-legged and crafty. The others were watching. Well, I assayed the group. It was a slew of horns and meat to choose from. But I at once spotted my target ram.

He stood apart. Forty feet from the group. Bobbing his head. He was thick-chested and keg-bellied. He would quarter out good, and I wanted him. Well, the cuss had wrecked his horns. He was a tragedy in that respect. Many Dall rams deliberately damage their horns. It's a Dall trait. But this character had made a project of ruining his. They were broken and splintered. Broomed. Rock-scarred. At least one-third of each curl was missing. It was sad because, before he worked on them, the horns probably had been in the forty-odd-inch class. The sparring excited him. He bobbed his head and shuffled. He pranced. Then, suddenly, he declared himself. He made for the action.

A horn-swinging recruit. Oh boy. The sparring rams backed off and stared. Then they both attacked him, for serious. One hit him head-on. The other clobbered him in the ribs. As I said, they were good. Well, that did it. He retreated. He'd had aplenty. The two didn't follow, but they were through sparring. I now picked up the .270 and began climbing.

Another bad stalk, I thought.

I climb into wind. It's been threatening since dawn. Now, all at once, it roars across the slopes. A gusty half-gale. I find a rocky wash—graywacke—and use it for cover. As soon as possible, I check on the rams. I spot them seven hundred yards distant, on the summit. My ram is lagging 150 feet. He now turns and glances back, as though he feels my gaze. His ruined horns look dark and massy. I am tempted. I start to raise the .270. But nuts, it's too far. I duck into the wash and climb. Thirty minutes later I sight the bunch again. They are two hundred yards distant now. And—surprise—my ram isn't with them. Well, he's got to be close. I step ahead, scanning the formations. The wind booms. Bits of scree whip past. This is my favorite kind of stalk. The suspense is swell. And wind always did thrill me. Presently I locate him. He is standing under a broken ledge, one hundred feet distant, watching his backtrail. He spots me at the same instant. Whirling, he gallops along the open crest. I put the .270's sights on him and fire. He goes down skidding. Heart shot.

By noon I had the quarters hung up. They sure decorated the meat cache. I was proud of them. The current bag limit was two rams, plus as many as a man needed for meat if he was doing any prospecting. One was plenty for me. I now set to work fleshing the head. I aimed to spike it to the roof peak. The same idea I'd had at the No. 1 cabin. Not as a trophy head, but as a great hunting adventure symbol. Wayfaring Dall sheep hunters who saw it would catch on, I thought. And I hoped it would bring them memories, the good ones—of sheep trails, cliff faces, summit winds, the smell of frosted lupine, sunlight on a ram's coat, the feel of scree underfoot, scarlet cloudberry pitches, the thrill of sizing up a top head, and the sound of a bullet smashing home. When they spotted these displayed horns they'd know I was a solid Dall sheep fan, by gosh, advertising the fact.

Goats of the Skyline Rim

*"The goat is probably our toughest
big-game animal to take.
But he is worth it. He rates among the elite."*

Friend goat, that's a horrible summit you've picked. And you're on the worst part of it, I thought as, with 16X glasses, I assayed the whopper hermit billy I had just spotted atop yonder snow-striped mountain. *But you're a likely critter, sure enough. So here I come.*

This was at the headwaters of Knik River, in Alaska's Chugach Range, early on a frosty mid-September morning. I had located the goat from my trapline cabin. I was in the dooryard sawing some firewood and, I recall, daydreaming about goat chops. I mean I was meat hungry. But it was my own fault. There was plenty of game around. I had simply let myself be immobilized by a slew of autumn chores. Anyway, there he was, two thousand feet above me. I put the big glasses on him and recognized him. He hung out up there. He was a solitary, a recluse. Every goat range has a few of them, and usually they are first-class meat animals. This one looked great. He was wide-chested and fat. I gave him 260 pounds. His shaggy off-white coat was beautiful. His horns were trophy grade. Facing away from me, he now walked over to the rim and looked down. Then he pawed the shale and stamped.

The handsome sonofagun was hostile. I wished I could see what had griped him.

Well, I stalled maybe thirty seconds more. Then, goat-hunting magic hit me hard, and I said the devil with chores. They could wait. Collecting my .270 Winchester, I started climbing. It was chancy the first five-hundred feet, but fun. I was in a wide snow-slide swath, with almost no cover. Just scattered clumps of wild celery. The billy would have seen me if he had glanced my way. But he was preoccupied. He was peering down over the rim again, acting hard-boiled. He shook his horns. He buck-jumped. Well, by this time he had me all-out curious. But I reached grassline before the mystery solved itself. I saw movement on a ledge close below him. Then six plump young female goats filed into view. Clearly they were bound for the summit, and he didn't want them up there. Which made sense, I guess. The place seemed to be his private bachelor retreat.

But I had my own problems. I was now at a grim part of the mountain.

The green sandstone cliff above me was a killer. Wildly eroded and crumbling. Besides, I have a special distrust of green sandstone. The stuff always gives me trouble. But I found an ancient goat trail leading up the face and took it. Theoretically, a man should be able to climb as well as a goat. But in prac-tice he sure can't. Halfway up a handhold gave way, and I had to jump sideways and balance myself on a tiny shelf. It scared me. When I got squared away I was shaking. And that made me sore. But then I felt a grin start. Shucks, I enjoy a dra-matic climb—if it doesn't get too all-fired hair-raising. I toiled on, in bad going. And twenty minutes later I topped the sum-mit. It was narrow and snow-drifted. The hermit billy stood seventy yards distant, still demonstrating. Well, I suppose he sensed me. Anyway, he gave a startled grunt and whirled—and the six plump debutantes bounded up past him. I dropped him with a chest shot.

The goat is probably our toughest big-game animal to take. But he is worth it. He rates among the truly elite sporting spe-cies. Sure, I am a biased fan of his, with good reason. I grew up in Chugach goat country. I strung my first traplines here. As a result, I learned early to admire the mountain goat. We Chugach roughnecks depended on the goats for our winter meat. We slept in goatskin bedding. My notion of real security those days was a nearby band of the animals. Of course, it was al-ways hard-won meat. Goats, and don't ask me why, won't live on a pleasant mountain. They like crazily broken cliffs and potholed glacier ice. They like tangled alder jungles. They thrive in deep snows. We used to cuss them for all this, but we were chesty proud of being goat hunters. We bragged colorfully about how almighty smart and hard to get the Chugach goats were. It had become our trademark campfire topic.

But it was honest bragging. For example, take an experience my sourdough colleague "Kobuk" Jones had one windy September afternoon above his headquarters on Metal Creek. "This billy like to kilt me," Kobuk told me afterward. "But I can't complain none. Man, I was dumb enough to think he was easy. . . . I first sight the wonderful cuss from the roof of my meat cache. I am up there nailing on some birchbark shingles. By habit, I scan mountain slopes every few minutes. And toward noon I spot a white dot under a rimrock, fifteen hundred feet above me. It wasn't there the last time I checked. So I climb down fast and get the 12X glasses. Well, it's a sizable billy, stretched out asleep. I rest the glasses and look him over. He'll go around two hundred pounds. His pelt is clean. His horns would make any sportsman happy. Man, I tell myself I am plumb loaded with luck this morning.

"Because he's easy. He's directly above camp—he could roll into the clearing. Also the timing is right. Last night there was a good frost, and the moon had a ring around it. A carcass will keep now. And, mister, I can use some fresh meat. I have been eating salted humpback salmon and sow belly for a month. So I grab my .250-3000 Savage and climb. After a while I take another look with the glasses. And duck. My sleepy billy is now standing up. I see him try the wind. Well, that don't worry me too much—I am crosswind from him, scrooched behind a boulder. But he is suspicious. Maybe he had a bad dream. Anyway, he shakes himself and lies down again, this time keeping his head raised. So I change course. I slant up the face of a red shale cliff, using it for cover. It's risky. The rock is frost-slippery, and the wind is treacherous. But with that easy meat waiting up there, I figure I can afford a few risks.

"Well, I top out okay. Plumb eager. And get a surprise.

"The billy has moved. I guess he heard me on the cliff. Anyhow, he is now eighty yards up the mountain, hustling along a ledge. He sure ain't sleepy no more. But he's still easy, I tell myself. Well, I raise the Savage—and he sees the movement. He breaks into a run. I shoot and it's good. He tumbles into a steep wash straight above me, then comes pinwheeling. And I now see something awful. He has dislodged a bunch of rocks, and they are clattering down with him. Hallelujah. I sidestep the goat, all right. No sweat. But the rocks are something else. The air is suddenly full of them. One knocks my hat off. Another grazes my shoulder. Man, I am busy. Then a fist-sized rock clobbers me on the rump, and I go down, rolling. More rocks whiz past me. At last, plenty dazed, I grab holt of an outcrop and sit up. I see the goat carcass lying on a shale dump thirty yards below me. I hobble and stumble down to it.

"Okay, I'm sold," I mumble to the billy's ghost. "There ain't no easy goats, and never were."

You backpack in. That is, you do for an ace Chugach goat hunt. I have tried to use horses in these sky-busting peaks, with no luck. Horses just can't hack it. The trails are too steep. The alders are too thick. Good grass is scarce. Horses can't ford the battering white-water creeks. But today's visiting goat hunters are a hardy lot. Most of them are veteran backpack guys. They tote their own grub and gear, and favor siwash camps. Usually they hire only a guide. So they are admirably mobile. They get back into the isolated goat pastures along the Chugach glacier system, where the prime action is. Goats are still plentiful up there, and the bands haven't been combed over. There are grand trophy heads for the taking. Some game species do best at the northern limit of their ranges, and this seems to be true of our goats. I believe the next record goat head will be taken on a Chugach peak by a backpacker sportsman.

The goat's survival quotient is good. One of the best. The main reason is, he discourages predators. He is too fast and clever with his dirk-pointed horns for them. Too willing to fight. I mean any meat pirate dumb enough to attack him is a cinch to get hurt. Or killed. True, the coyotes take a few kids. They invade the high meadows and make hit-run raids. But if they had to depend on goat meat for a living, they would all starve. The wolves don't score at all. They respect the goat. Besides, they seldom climb. The grizzlies and black bears just don't try. I have several times seen bears and goat bands meet on the lofty cloud-country trails, and it was the bears that yielded right-of-way. The golden eagles now and then knock a kid or yearling off a cliff. But it can be dangerous hunting for them, too. I once saw an attacking eagle misjudge a gusty wind, and get speared clear through on the horns of a guardian billy. The point is there's easier meat available.

Terrain is the goat's No. 1 ally. And he is a genius at using it. He likes it upended. The more savagely scrambled a mountainside is, the better it seems to suit him. Sure, in spring he sometimes feeds down into the timber. You even see him crossing valleys and swimming rivers. One spring I met a goat out in the middle of the mile-wide Knik sandbars. I saluted him, and we went our respective ways. But in autumn it's a totally different deal. Then you usually find the goat high on a hostile brute of a mountain. I mean you can count on him for thrills. To get a fair shot, you often take bigger chances than you would stalking a man-killer game beast. Pro hunters generously praise the goat. They have been there. They know what it takes to outsmart a boss billy.

The goat is a great ego-builder. When you climb for him, you know you're bucking odds. So when you score, naturally you feel entitled to shove your chest out some. I'll always remember a certain late-fall meat harvest I made at the upper Knik. I had been away the whole autumn with some sportsmen, and it was now sunrise on my first morning home. Mighty happy to be here, I opened the cabin door to scan the near mountainside with my glasses. The first morning often is the best one. Because if your luck is good, the goats haven't yet discovered you're in the area. I was lucky, I thought. I sighted three goats on a scarlet pitch seven hundred yards up the mountain. A husky billy, a female, and a yearling. But as I sized up the billy, he whirled and stared exactly into my glasses. I saw him shuffle and paw. It was weird because he couldn't possibly see me. I concluded he had ESP or something like it. You encounter such animals.

But I was thrilled. I like to hunt goats alone. And I urgently needed meat. The cache contained only a few strips of last year's jerky, rock-hard and mildewed. Steadying the glasses, I took a careful look. The billy was a prize candidate. I gave him 175 pounds. His quarters were chunky. His pelt looked silky-prime. Well, he still hadn't switched his gaze, and he was now fidgeting nervously. I saw him snort. Some goat. But I was eager. I snatched up my .30-06 Winchester and began a climb. I now lost sight of the goats for twenty minutes while I battled up through the alders. Then, when I was able to check again—no billy. The spooky character had pulled out. But I figured he hadn't gone far. Squatting behind a quartz ledge, I took the slopes apart. I failed to sight the billy, but the other two goats told me where he was. They were looking up at a dry watercourse, three hundred yards distant.

That was hint enough. Knowing the mountain, I now knew where I would find my billy.

I stood up, and the pair took off. But they soon got curious and halted to watch me. I hurried over to the dry water channel. It was a walled chute, crooked and moderately steep. Slide-rock had collected in it a foot deep. Which made it a deadly place. But the billy had climbed it—I found his tracks in some scree. Eighty feet above me was a wide shelf. I had often scanned it with glasses, and knew it was a perfect hideout. The billy, I told myself, had to be there. So I took a chew of cigarette tobacco and began climbing. The chute was really booby-trapped. If the hair-triggered rock slid, it would sluice me out of here and bury me. So I plotted every step. I moved balanced slabs of shale that I couldn't bypass. I was sweating. It took me thirty long minutes to climb the eighty feet. But when I muscled myself onto the shelf, my ESP billy was standing only forty feet distant. I suppose he had believed I would never find him up here. He stared boggle-eyed, then turned to flee. I shot him through the neck.

I dragged and rolled my billy down to timber. I dressed the carcass. I packed the quarters and the head and hide to camp and hung them in the meat cache. It was a pretty mountain morning. And still early. The pointed spruce shadows reached plumb across the dooryard. I felt great. Humming a tune I had made up, I started a pot of trading-post coffee. Then I cut four extra-thick chops and put them in my sunken-keg cooler at the spring. They were for lunch. I could hardly wait. Next I got to work fleshing the hide. I never used a so-called graining block. Sitting with my back against the now sunny woodpile, I whittled the fat and stuff off with my belt knife. A family of pet whiskey jacks presently arrived. Five of them, panhandling in musical chorus. I tossed them a handful of fat. Then I smelled the coffee and went in and got some.

From habit, I checked the mountain. The six plump young female goats were grouped on the summit, watching me. I waved a greeting.

Black Bears
Were My Neighbors

*"Mostly black bears will respect humans.
But you can't count on it."*

"**W**elcome, bear neighbors. I'm delighted to see you," I quietly greeted the three handsome black bears I had just spotted on a fireweed creek bar five hundred yards crosswind from my Toonakloot homestead cabin. "Because it happens the doggoned meathouse is empty again."

This was at sunup on a perfect Alaska spring morning. I had stepped outside, bucket in hand, to fetch some fresh water for coffee. Sighting the bears, I sprinted right back for my glasses and rifle. I wasn't sure at first what the animals were up to over there, but I had an exciting hunch. They stood in a row at the creek's edge, watching a sun-gilded riffle. They were working their noses. They had their pin ears pricked forward. Two of the trio were plump adults—swell meathouse material. The third was a slab-sided yearling. As I put the glasses on him again, he eased into the water. His head was cocked as though he had heard something. Then I saw the lone male king salmon. He was battling up the steep riffle—a humped, hook-nosed fifty-pounder. Ocean-bright. Oh, man, the bountiful spring run had started.

The eager yearling now galloped out, splashing, to intercept the great fish.

I admired the youngster. He had get up and go. But he was overmatching himself. Taking a stand on good gravel footing, he half-crouched and waited. The other two bears had also waded out, but were above him. I held my glasses steady on the scene. The big king salmon came barreling straight up the middle of the shallow thirty-foot-wide riffle. He had turned on power, probably because this skimpy water scared him. His whole blue-gleaming back stuck out. He was tossing spray as high as my head. I had glimpses of his fixed, staring near eye. Well, the yearling waited till the king was abreast of him, then pounced. His timing was okay. He got his teeth set in the fish's dorsal fin. But then his luck ended. The king pinwheeled, yanking him off balance. He slammed him across the face with his huge square-cut tail. Then, as the adult bears closed in, he twisted free and rocketed back downstream.

I began a hurry-up stalk. When I was fifty yards from the creek, a seagull cruised in, treetop high. It banked over the brush-bordered riffle, screaming. Boy, I knew what that meant and broke into a run. I now heard splashing and wallowing sounds. A bear *whowf-whowfed*. In a moment I ducked under some creek-bank pussy willows, and beheld a spectacle. The sunrise-tinted riffle was crowded with king salmon. And the three bears were among them, grabbing with teeth and claws. The gray gull kept screaming. I saw the yearling scoop up a medium-sized king. Then one of the adult bears caught a beautiful forty-pound female and headed ashore with it, toward me. The fish's bright carnelian eggs were spurting. When the bear topped the bank, he saw me and gave a muffled snarl. I lined my .30-06 Winchester and shot him through the head.

"Bear friends, that was a great action show," I said, feeling springtime good as I got out my belt knife to dress the meat carcass and the king salmon. "Many thanks for everything."

Me, I am a solid black bear fan. I give the animals star rating. If there was any way to prove it, I would bet that they thrill more hunters per season than all our other bears do. Sure, I know, there are more black bears. But they have a heap going for them, too. We roughnecks on this frontier had unique opportunity to assay the black bear's sporting qualities. It was all black bear country. Blueberries, currants, and highbush cranberries were abundant. Four runs of salmon filled the creeks from June till September. With food so easy, the animals flourished.

At Toonakloot, for fifteen years, black bears were always resident on or near the homestead. And I was proud to have them as close neighbors. Of course, they occasionally gave me trouble—every black bear is a born bandit. But they supplied first-rate meat and skins and a grand lot of sport. Colorful action sport. Happy-type sport.

Black bear meat was a big treat in the spring. I would be down to the monotonous tail ends of my winter's grub. Beans and salt sow bosom. Or beans and jerky. Then the black bears would arrive. Boy, I blessed them. They are always fat when they emerge from hibernation. Their meat is tender. They smell

of cottonwood buds. Parts of a good spring carcass actually are white meat. I would feast royally. But of course the fresh meat wouldn't keep, so I would preserve most of it as bacon and ham. I would separate the large muscles and pickle them sixty hours in strong brine. Then I'd wipe the chunks dry and hang them in cool red-willow smoke till they were cured to my taste. Ten days or so. I would render out the fat and store it in stone crocks, saving the cracklings to mix into cornbread. I mean black bears are rewarding animals. Their meat and skins helped us pioneer the land.

Mostly, black bears respect humans. But you can't count on it. For example, consider what happened to my Denna Indian partner, Billy No-Dogs, one pretty spring morning. Billy was coming down the creek-bank trail with a pack of steel traps. "I spot fresh black bear tracks," he related afterward. "Then I round some blowdown and spot the bear—a husky 180-pounder. He's in a patch of wild celery sprouts beside the trail, sixty yards upwind. And he's sore about something. His mane is bristled. I have a hunch there's another bear close-by, and they've maybe tangled over the celery patch. But anyway, I decide we can use this one. He's an okay meat bear and his pelt looks good, and we won't have to tote him far. Well, my .270 Winchester is hung on the left horn of my packboard. I make a quick grab for it. But just then the bear chomps his jaws, snarls, and steps out of sight behind an alder clump.

"Well, I now do a dumb thing. Stupid dumb. And me, I'm supposed to understand black bears. Man, I'm a Black Bear Clan guy. The animals are sorta my brothers. But you'd never have guessed it, the way I foul up. I wanta stampede this meat bear back into the open. So I shed my pack and let out a black bear war beller—*wagh-h-h*! Then I sprint down the trail at that alder clump. Well, our meat bear stampedes, all right. I have surprised him plenty. He bounds out from behind the alders snorting and *whuffing*. But I don't get a chance to shoot. Because just then there's a loud *wagh-h-h*! in the brush behind me. Oh, boy—that other bear. I shoulda listened to my hunch. Well, I take a quick look and see that he's close and coming fast. And I realize that he's attacking because he thought I was running away from him. But there ain't no time to shoot. Sucker, I think, and make a wild jump down off the trail.

"It all happens in maybe ten seconds. My jump has landed me eight feet below the trail, in a mess of rocks and devil's clubs. Man, I'm stumbling, fighting for balance. And here comes the bear. I know I still don't have time to turn and put a slug into him. Not a prayer. It looks like he's got me, and it's all my fault.

"I get partway turned. Then he reaches me. He gives another beller and comes in low, at my legs. Well, there's no use trying to dodge. I just thumb the Winchester's safety and swing my shoulders and shove the muzzle at him. When I fell the barrel dig into him I lean on it and shoot. I hope I've got him in a good place. Then his weight slams against me and I tumble backward. He lands on top of me, and pops his jaws in my face, but I kick him with both feet and roll clear. He is now coughing and strangling. Well, we both get up, and I see that I have shot him through the chest. He is dying, but he roars as I chamber another shell and takes a staggering step toward me. Some bear. Then I finish him with a shot between the eyes.

"I say good-bye to him, using the old respectful Clan words," Billy No-Dogs told me.

September is a magic month for black bear hunting. The bears are sharp and lively then. They give you some memorable workouts. Busy putting on weight for their seven months winter sleep, they tend to gather sociably at favorite feeding spots. I once saw twenty black bears eating cloudberries on a five-hundred-acre mountainside. Of course, autumn pelts don't grade as high as spring pelts. The guard hairs are shorter, and the underfur isn't as thick. But shucks, only an expert can tell the difference. I always delayed my fall meat hunt as long as I dared, waiting for frosty meat-keeping weather. And this was apt to be plumb suspenseful—I've done some high-powered worrying. Because if I held off too long, the bears would vanish into their dens. But when I read the signs right and harvested my bear just as the frosty days began, it was a grand feeling.

Black bears are daring burglars. They usually ignored my cabin—I had it pretty well bear-proofed. But they sure gave the 8x10 screen-sided meathouse attention. Generations of them left their claw marks there. One crisp September afternoon I caught up with an especially greedy but hardluck thief. I was on a birch ridge eight hundred yards across the valley, gathering some caribou mushrooms for supper. Coming to the timber's edge, I checked the cabin bench with my glasses. A bear-inspired habit. What I saw made me curse and laugh. The meathouse had taken another beating. Its door hung from one hinge. Two screen panels had been torn off. But the black bear daylight raider had outsmarted himself. He was now blundering across the yard with his head stuck in a five-gallon can. The can was a newfangled type that had a saucer-size opening in its top. It had been half-full of cracklings.

I gathered that the bear, greedy and reckless, had jammed his head through the opening, and his ears had caught on the rim.

He was desperate. He sunfished and buckjumped. He rolled, kicking. He made a tangle-footed run and crashed into the woodpile. Then at last he got sensible. Planting both front paws on the can's top, he gave a violent shove. The can flew off his head. Saved, he now wanted revenge. He walloped the can— left, right, left—showing his teeth. Then he shook himself and loped down off the cabin bench. I followed him with the glasses. He looked promising. His quarters were chunky. His new fall coat was thick and clean. Well, I needed him. Except for the cracklings and a few pounds of last year's jerky, the meathouse had been empty. Besides, the weather signs were favorable. I figured we'd have a frost within forty-eight hours. I watched the bear until he went out of sight into the creek flat timber. He didn't reappear on the open bars.

So okay, I headed across the valley. With a little luck, I thought, I would soon sort him out of that flat.

I forded the creek. As the water was low, I didn't make much racket. There were no fresh bear tracks on the strip of sandbar. Good. Caching my packboard on the bank, I sized up the spruce-timbered flat. Seventy yards ahead there were two thickets of second-growth stuff that I couldn't see into. The wind quartered from them to me. I watched them five minutes. Nothing moved. But I had that feeling. I figured the bear was in the nearest thicket. Most likely, I thought, he was trying to work up enough nerve to finish looting the meathouse. Okay. I Injuned toward the thicket. And I felt myself grin. I do love a tricky stalk. When I had covered thirty yards, I knelt. I was now dead certain the bear was there. Maybe I had scented him, I don't know. Anyway, I reached out and deliberately snapped a pencil-thick twig. That did it. The bear busted headlong out of the thicket, grunting. I laid the Winchester's sights on him, and fired. He went down, heart shot.

"Bear bandit, I am obliged to you," I said as I prepared to hang his carcass in the meathouse he had just plundered.

Blaze . . .
My Boss Horse . . .
My Buddy

*The bull moose shook his antlers. He was an
ornery brute hunting trouble. Blaze at once
became protective. He gave a war scream and
hobble-loped to meet the bull.*

"**M**ister, we've got trouble. I can't spot our horses," young
Bill Jarvis said, his 12X glasses on the narrow spruce-timbered
gap six hundred yards below us where we had tied Blaze and
Paint. "I think that mob of caribou stampeded right over them."

"Come on," I said, and headed down the slope at a run.

This was on the remote Jones Fork of Alaska's Kuskokwim River. A bright-skied September morning. Forty minutes ago, scouting upvalley, we had sighted a nice herd of barren
ground caribou. The handsome animals had just halted on a
caribou moss bench, seven hundred yards crosswind—around
five hundred of them. We got out our glasses. The herd had
begun to feed. Several of the near-side bulls carried trophy
antlers. One was special. His main beams would average fifty
inches, and the palmation fans were ten inches wide. Bill was
enthusiastic about the head. So we rode on one-hundred yards
to good cover and dismounted to tie our horses.

My horse objected. I had expected he would. He was a
1,150-pound zebra buckskin stud, line backed with black ears,

315

named Blaze. A boss horse who plain hated to be left behind. He now grabbed my sleeve with his teeth. But I talked to him and pulled his forelock, and he let go.

It was a tricky uphill stalk. Cover was scanty and the lead cow was nervous. Maybe there were wolves in the area. Or maybe she'd once had a bad experience here. Anyway, she didn't relax. Bill's trophy bull was one of her escorts. He had found a cluster of platter-sized Boletus mushrooms, and was eating them with gourmet gusto. He drooled. He chewed with his eyes shut. The lead cow moved closer to share the mushrooms with him. But in this case she didn't rate. He bristled and swung his antlers at her. I now had a better view of his head. The middle beams would go seventeen inches. They had nine inches of palmation, with twenty-two clean points and some nubbins. A splendid head. But we still weren't in position to shoot. The range was only 150 yards, but behind the bull stood anyhow fifty caribou. We tried to isolate him by crawling to the right— and the alert lead cow saw us.

She was an operator. She reared high and snorted, the caribou danger signal. Then she took the herd hellbent down the slope, hooves thundering on the moss and shale. Bill's bull was a length behind her. The range was now two hundred yards. Bill knelt and brought up his iron-sighted .30-06 Winchester. He fired. The bull somersaulted into an alder clump, finished. The lead cow, really spooked now, swung downwind into the timbered gap where we had tied the horses. I didn't see what took place there; too many spruce tops in the way. But when Bill and I arrived on the scene, panting, both horses were on their feet. Bill's pinto was tied behind a boulder, so he was all right. But Blaze had been shoved around some. There was blood on his face and shoulders. But he had wreaked some damage too. He was spitting out bloody caribou hair. Delighted to see me, he gave a loud whicker.

"Pal, you're hard-boiled, and crazy things happen to you," I said, putting an arm around his neck. "But you're a plenty great horse."

Blaze was my friend and associate. I made a business of long, wilderness sport-and-recreation packtrain trips, and he was the best packtrain leader I ever knew. He was smart, willing, and loyal. He had everything. But, it's a fact that he was sort of drama-prone. Shucks, he was in a situation the July morning I bought him. This was out at "Black" Carlson's roadhouse in the Broad Pass. The place was then a takeoff point for travelers heading east into the upper Susitna country. I was finishing my breakfast when I heard a commotion at the corral. Agitated voices. A horse's bawl. The pound of hooves. I went to the door. A U.S. Geological Survey party had spent the night here and was packing to hit the trail. All but one of their twelve packhorses was ready. The remaining cayuse, a blaze-faced zebra buckskin stud, had decided not to cooperate.

They had got a pack on him. Now they were trying to make him accept it. One cursing packer had a grip on his halter shank. Another was taking a two-handed twist on his left ear. But the big buckskin fooled them. He faked defeat. Then all of a sudden he bounded into the air and swapped ends. He came down striking. It was too much for the packers. They dodged clear. He now began pitching, and he was good at it. Fast and strong, showing some style.

I headed for the corral. Boy, I do enjoy a competent bucking performance. I was right with him. Sitting up there loose and easy, watching his head. Moving to his rhythm. I heard myself cheering him. He now tried a couple of high rollers, and the second one did it. The sawbuck saddle slipped. The pack flopped under his belly. He kicked at it, and a heel caulk fouled on the lash rope. He fell amongst the tangle, groaning.

The packers ran to him. They untied the latigos. One of them yanked the lash rope free. The buckskin got up. He shook himself, and beat it across the corral. As he passed me I noted two things—he was single-footing, and on his side he had the white mark of a center-fire saddle's cinch. Well, mighty few horses single-foot naturally. It's taught. And today only a scattering of veteran cattlemen ride center-fire rigs. It all figured. The buckskin stud, I told myself, probably had been some old-timer's hotshot saddle mount. But something must have happened and he was sold north as a packhorse. It was a comedown and he was rebelling.

An impulse struck me. I turned to "Hurry-Up" Dick Richards, the Survey party's contract freighter, and asked him if he would take $200 for his buckskin outlaw. Hurry-Up stared. Then he grinned and held out his hand. I paid him and went over to the defiant buckskin.

"Hello, Blaze," I said. He was a top mount, for sure.

I had booked Tom Logan for a thirty-day trip westward along the north slope of the Alaska Range. There were just the two of us, with Tom doing the offside packing. We planned to end the season with a grizzly hunt. One pretty September morning we angled down to the Willow Fork, at timberline. The one-hundred-yard crossing looked mean—there had been rainfall in the peaks. But grand sport awaited us on the other side. A clearwater creek comes in there, and in autumn it is full of the world's most beautiful trout. At least that's how I rate them. They are Dolly Varden. They average twelve inches—fat and lively. And they are most gaudily colored—coral, gold, and silver. Only a few sourdoughs and Indians had fished the creek. I had told Tom about it, and he was excited. But the ford worried me. So I played it safe.

I asked Tom to hold the packtrain back. Then I rode into the stream to make a test crossing. There was a good landing spot close above the creek mouth, and I headed for it. Blaze kept snuffling the wind. I heard him pop his jaws. He had got a noseful of something he sure didn't like. Well, the gray current was swift but there were no rocks. We presently went off a bar point into swimming water.

Blaze did all right. He had a grass belly and swam high. He held his course. Two bald eagles flapped up from the willow-masked creek. One of them had a gleaming trout in his talons. Some mergansers whipped past. I saw an otter's head. The creek was a fishy place, sure enough. I began watching for drift. Some light stuff was coming down. Just forest trash. But then Tom yelled. At the same instant I spotted it—a cottonwood snag floating around the bend above us. It was a monster and was coming fast.

Blaze saw the juggernaut, and looked back at me. We were almost even with the landing bar, but had no chance to use it. The snag would soon be on top of us, so I turned Blaze into the creek mouth. He didn't like the place. He started to fight the bit. Then he flattened his ears and went in anyway. I now saw what had been bothering him. And why the eagles and ducks had taken off. We had company. Thirty yards upstream on a bar tip a baldface grizzly had appeared. He was a dark-coated four-hundred-pounder. I suppose he had been fishing. Anyway, he was soaking wet. He took a step toward us, and snarled. Blaze now got his hooves on the bottom. He bared his teeth and gave a challenge scream. Well, I heard the snag go past, its top scything brush. Then I heard Tom yell again. He was kneeling, his .375 Winchester Magnum ready. I signaled go ahead, and he fired. The grizzly spun and went down.

"Big horse, I'm proud of you," I told Blaze as we started back for the packtrain.

These long packtrain trips were my idea. I started them. They were for adventurous gents in love with the wilds. I usually had only one customer, and the best trips lasted from first good grass until snowfall. Around seventy-five days. We rode through some of the earth's finest mountain scenery. We watched game, fished, and explored. We would cover between three hundred and five hundred miles. We never met another human. There were no trails. We found our own passes and fords.

When the fall season opened, we would make a big-game hunt. I preferred an eight-horse packtrain. Each horse carried 150 pounds. I seldom worked the string more than five hours a day. They got at least three days' rest a week. Blaze was a natural in this business. He walked five miles an hour, flatfooted. He had a sense of responsibility; steady in emergencies. I trusted him.

The string also trusted him. Take the scary windup of a Dall sheep hunt I made with Jack Benton in the Yanert country. It was an overcast September noon; threatening to snow. We had been out forty days, a grand trip eastward along the game-rich north range.

A couple of days ago, when we started back to civilization ahead of winter, Jack had decided to make a sheep hunt. The best horns I had seen were in the Yanert peaks. So we turned up Wood River searching for a pass leading that way. We found one a mile above timberline. Well, we switchbacked up to the gunsight summit. I rested the horses, and started down the Yanert side—and spotted five sheep on a broken rim 150 yards above us. Two were rams.

We got down for a check with our glasses. The rams now saw us. They had been disputing right-of-way, ready to fight. They still looked hostile. One of them had three ewes with him. He was fat and slick-coated. His horns would average 14x39 inches. Neither horn was broomed or scarred. They were light amber and had eight growth rings. An elegant specimen.

The other ram was a shabby old-timer. He was sag-bellied and gaunt. His coat was mineral-stained. But he had been great. His left horn would go 16x42 inches and had twelve growth rings. But the right horn was damaged. Badly cracked and splintered, with maybe nine inches broomed off.

Jack said he wanted the younger ram. But we had a problem. I wouldn't risk shooting here. There were cliffs below us. If the packhorses spooked, we could lose him.

Disaster nearly clobbered us at that. Except for Blaze, it would have. I headed for a grassline bench. And at this point the aged ram yielded. He bounded off the rim and started across a slide area. I was watching him. I saw him dislodge the boulder. It was the size of a camp stove, and came *whumping* straight at us. I figured I was going to lose a horse or two. But then it hit a shale spire ninety feet above us and exploded.

Well, a snorty bay packhorse was struck by fragments. He bawled and stampeded forward. I had time to take my rope down. Then he slammed past the bell mare—and Blaze crowded him into a bank. I tied onto him backhand and snubbed his head against my knee. Blaze then walked him calmly sixty yards to the bench. The rest of the string had been set to take off. Thanks to Blaze they thought better of it. Jack dismounted. His .270 Winchester banged. The trophy ram toppled off the rim.

"I thank you, partner," I said to Blaze. "I owe you plenty for that."

I wasn't kidding. The string represented my total capital. Horses were scarce and expensive up here. And hard to replace. I mean they weren't expendable as in western states. When you lost one, it hurt. The nearest horse market was a couple of thousand miles distant. For example, I bought my horses on the Yakima Indian Reservation in eastern Washington. There was no handier place, and the cayuses there had Morgan blood that gave them weight. A good Yakima packhorse would cost me $300 landed at Seward. If I shopped carefully, I could outfit him with a sawbuck saddle, a blanket, sweat pad, halter, chain-linked hobbles, pack mantle, Humboldt pads, panniers, lash and sling ropes, and a set of shoes for $250. Then there was the matter of wintering the string. Ninety dollars a head was the best I could do. It all added up, and Blaze was good insurance. He watched over the horses. A formidable wrangler.

Take an episode that occurred one windy fall morning on the Dog Fork. It was Tom Logan's trip, and we had stopped here for a moose hunt. We had seen several so-so heads, but this morning we got a break. We were on a lupine ridge near camp, using our glasses. I saw movement in some brilliant birch brush two hundred yards upwind. Then out of the thickets, trotting, came a young bull moose and a heifer. The bull had been in a fight. He had bleeding gashes across his ribs, and was limping. The two passed us and went into a strip of spruces. Then here came their pursuer—a husky fourteen-hundred-pound bull. He was galloping. And when a rutting bull moose gallops, he's plumb eager. I didn't get a good look at his antlers. There wasn't time before he reached the spruces. But I thought they might go seventy inches.

We hurried after him, following the ridgetop. Five minutes later we spotted him again. He was in a yellow-flowering pea vine flat 150 yards downwind from our hobbled horses. Just standing there. Apparently he had lost track of the young pair. Anyway, they weren't in sight, and he was sore. His back hair was bristled; his ears swiveling. He now lifted his nose high, sampling the wind. A moose can't track by ground scent. His front legs are too long and his neck too short. He has to depend on the wind, and on scent clinging to brush and tall grass. I mean the low pea vine wasn't helping this bull any. He pawed the ground and grunted. I knew he was gritting his teeth. Well, the bell mare now whickered, and Blaze shouldered past her. Then the bull started toward the string.

He took maybe a dozen prancing steps. Then he buckjumped, and stomped a pea vine clump. Showing off. Blaze stood statue still, watching him. I was finally getting a fair look at the bull's head. It would go seventy inches, all right. The palms were shallow and almost square-tipped. There were thirty-two points. The brow scoops were massive. Tom said he wanted him— naturally. He rested his scope-sighted .30-06 Remington over an outcrop. The range was 350 yards.

Well, the bull now shook his antlers and trotted at the horses. He had the wind, so there was no identification error. He was simply an ornery brute hunting trouble. Blaze at once became protective. He gave a war scream and hobble-loped to meet the bull. He made a striking champion. His long mane and tail blew in the wind. The sun glanced off his satiny hide. He screamed again. Then Tom fired. The bull knelt, and fell over.

"My biggest hunting thrill," Tom said fervently.

Blaze and I fell out just once. I got rough with him, and I was wrong. A trophy grizzly was the cause of it. This was on the Dall Fork. A frost-glittering autumn morning. Sam Weston was with me. Two days earlier we had come down off a high plateau to the parky timberline river flat. I had glanced back to make sure the packs were riding okay. They were.

Then I saw something move in a willow thicket four hundred yards behind the string. I dismounted and got out my 16X glasses. A yellowtip grizzly stepped into view. A chunky 350-pounder. His new autumn coat looked good. I could see it ripple as he moved. He had just cut the horses' tracks and was busily nosing them. Maybe they were the first he had ever come across. Anyway, he was plenty interested. I pointed, and Sam reached for his glasses. The grizzly now reared, facing us. Then he loped back into the willows.

I couldn't locate him again. So we rode on a half-mile and camped in some spruces. Our medicine seemed good, for two reasons. Sam urgently wanted a yellowtip grizzly—and I had been on the lookout all afternoon for a likely horseshoeing camp. Two packhorses had thrown shoes today. When that starts, you'd best shoe up the whole string. The chore would take maybe a week, and this camp was fine. It even had a grayling stream as a bonus.

Next morning we rode out to try for the grizzly. I thought we had a good chance of spotting him. Except for a few spruces and willows, there was no cover. But we drew a blank. All we found was his tracks. He had been hanging around close downwind from the feeding horses. Now Alaska grizzlies haven't learned to kill stock—they've never had to share their ranges with stock. Just the same, I didn't like this bear's behavior.

Next morning we tried again. We rode up a blueberry ridge, and searched with our glasses. Still no grizzly. But we sighted trouble—the packhorses were in camp. Two of them had their heads stuck inside the cook tent. One look and we mounted up fast, because horses are the most destructive of all camp-raiders. When the notion strikes them, they'll totally wreck your commissary.

We took a shortcut through the spruces. Then, two hundred yards from the timber-hidden tents, Blaze surprised me. He balked. I touched him with my spurs. He refused to move; mule stubborn. So I hit him a good one. I expected him to pitch. But he just shivered and looked back at me. Sam rode alongside. Then we saw the yellowtip. He was 250 yards upwind, sneaking toward the horses. Sam slid his .300 Weatherby Magnum out of its boot. He stepped down, lined his sights, and fired. The grizzly bawled and dropped.

"I apologize, friend," I said, patting Blaze.

Back to the beginning. Blaze wasn't hurt. He had just lost patches of hide here and there. I gave him a lump of sugar. Then we went back to the downed bull caribou. I took off the head and cape, and dressed the carcass. Neither of the horses was blood-shy. So we Injun-hitched the meat onto Blaze, and the trophy onto Bill's pinto. Then, leading the horses, we headed for camp.

It was a swell morning. The sun was high now. The giant snowpeaks sheered up like mastheads of the world. The wind was full of spruce fragrance. I figured we had maybe fifteen days before snowfall in the passes. Blaze shoved me with his nose. He knew I had another lump of sugar in my shirt pocket. I gave it to him. He ate the sugar, then tilted my hat forward with his nose. The tough buckskin liked me. And I was sure fond of him.

"This is the life, hey?" Bill called.

"Amen," I replied.

Moose Are Adventure Critters

"Good to eat and fun to hunt by gosh,"
the Indian said. Whether you're after
trophy antlers or a fat carcass to live on
through the long cold winter, there is always
drama in stalking giant arrogant moose.

Friend moose, that's a dramatic war act you're putting on. I'm plenty impressed. And mystified some too, I thought as I watched the giant Susitna bull—a dun ghost-shape, wide-antlered head held high, hump hair bristled, huge ears turned rigidly forward—sneak directly crosswind through fog-shrouded clumps of orange-red-yellow-copper-scarlet creek-bank willow and aspen brush, 150 yards distant. *But I sure wish you'd sashay out into the open, hotshot. And give me a clear look at your carcass.*

I could see that he carried trophy-grade antlers, but this was my fall meat hunt. The season's big grub project.

So of course I was interested in fat quarters and ribs. Exclusively.

It would have been easy to drop the bull. Nothing to it. But I didn't want to risk getting stuck with a rut-skinny carcass. And maybe have to eat tough gristly steaks all winter, as had happened a time or two. My cherished 12X moose glasses weren't much help to me now. Layers of pearly drifting cloud-fog and the camouflage effect of massed multicolored bright leaves tricked the lenses. I didn't trust them. I needed an eyeball appraisal.

The hard-case bull apparently was making a stalk by ear, zeroing in on sounds completely inaudible to me. Suddenly he halted. He scythed those massive polished antlers back and forth. He uttered a chesty challenge grunt. Tossing his head again, he quick-stepped into some tall wolf willows where I at once lost track of him. He simply vanished. Worried now, I decided I'd better answer his war grunt. Faking moose talk isn't one of my major accomplishments, but he just might reply and give me a bearing. So I knelt. I held my hat in front of my mouth. I drew in a long breath.

Ahhhhrrrr-whuhhhh. Another bull grunted off to my left, maybe a hundred yards crosswind. Great. Wonderful.

This was taking place, folks, twenty minutes from my Erickson Creek cabin, in the western Talkeetnas. The high-country weather had turned cold overnight. We'd had a good hard frost. There was now ice on the water hole so meat would keep. I knew where several moose were hanging out—the general area, that is—and figured I could score right off. Then this doggoned ground-hugging cloud had moved in.

The first bull now sounded off again, and the one on my left answered. Then they both grunted. I couldn't spot either of them. But the hostile cusses kept swapping insults, and they were closing in. They'd meet, I calculated, in a mossy opening just ahead of me. It was a perfect bushwhack setup. Surefire, I thought. But in a moment I had that feeling that I was being watched. I glanced instinctively over my left shoulder. Naturally I'd known there was a female moose somewhere close-by. The inevitable brown siren. And there she was, forty yards distant—a plump sail-eared heifer, staring at me boggle-eyed, poised for flight.

She was the bulls' target, of course. And I was positive she'd now alert them. One alarm snort would do it. It would stampede them, ending my chances. But she surprised me, bless her.

She waggled her ears, then whirled and faded into the brush. Heading *away* from the oncoming bulls. Boy, she was something. I didn't hear even a twig crack when she took off. A seasoned cow would have wrecked my hunt. But this heifer figured, I guess, that she was strictly on her own. Let the bulls take care of themselves. Anyway, I was still in business.

I checked the iron sights of my .375 magnum and waited. Suspense built up. I was getting a terrific kick out of this, all of it—the grunting bulls, the grand blaze of leaf colors, the fog-patched creek flat, the winey smell of fermenting berries, the echoing sounds of the creek, the cushioned give of frosted moss under my pacs, the slow chill wind. I wanted to remember the whole scene. Now I saw brush shake and bend at the far side of the opening. Suddenly the warrior bulls appeared. Twenty yards apart, glaring at each other and manifestly trying to locate the heifer. The second bull was my choice. His antlers weren't much, but he had a lot of good meat on his frame. I dropped him with a neck shot. There wasn't a quiver.

I went out to the carcass and stood looking at it. I felt, as always at a moose kill, a surge of admiration for the moose race. *You long-geared brutes are tops, I thought. You are the biggest and the best, and the most rewarding. Me, I sure owe you plenty.*

We all do. Up here anyway. Visiting sportsmen are lyrical about moose hunting and resident sportsmen sure match them. But our Susitna Denna Indians are the solidest of solid moose fans. For example, consider a Denna funeral I once attended. Old "Moose Meat" Nick Stepan, of Montana Creek, had passed on. He'd been a valued friend of mine.

I had hunted moose with Nick since I was a kid. He showed me how to make moosehock moccasins and weave moose-babiche snowshoe filling. He got me started using a dried moose bladder for a tobacco pouch. He taught me that a moosehide, hair side up, is the world's best cold-weather mattress. He proved to me that the jaw muscles are the choicest meat on a moose carcass. And that a bit of its gall lends superb flavor to a moose steak.

Nick's oldest son, Mishkah, gave the eulogy. "We know there's plenty moose where you are now, Papa," Mishkah said as we stood around the plank coffin. "Big moose. Fat moose." Mishkah's voice broke, then he added, "Good to eat and fun to hunt, by gosh. You are lucky, Papa."

A mighty fine send-off, I thought.

Rutting bull moose are notional brutes. Screwball. Erratic. The tremendous sex drive that makes their necks swell grotesquely and causes them to stop eating and sleeping must also scramble their brain circuits. The noble critters are both timid and bold. Easy to hunt and all-fired tough to hunt. They ferociously attack bushes and stomp their own shadows. They grunt and answer the echoes. They are hams. And sometimes—a point to re-member, folks—they don't respect humans at all.

Take a bull I met one snow-spitting fall morning up at the forks of Erickson Creek. It was meat-harvest time again—for me the best time of the whole year. I was as eager as a lad. One reason was that this was a special hunt. I had a double project going: I wanted a first-rate carcass for the meat cache, and a big handsome wide-reaching points-studded marvel set of antlers to adorn the outside roof peak of my main cabin. The antlers display would be partly sourdough show-off. But it would also serve a more important purpose which I will presently explain.

It turned out I was plumb lucky.

But then I'd picked a fine place: the forks. Three deep-worn moose trails meet here. A beautiful spot of red rocks and wild-rose bushes, dotted with brilliantly yellow dwarf cottonwoods.

The gusty snow-threatening wind was dead wrong for me and I had to station myself on a hillside six hundred yards up-stream. But I felt confident. I'd been there maybe an hour when a cow moose came up the east-west trail. I put the glasses on her. She was a comely beast. Trim and smooth-coated. Easy moving. An A-okay bait cow if she'd be obliging and stick around.

Well, she halted at a schoolmarm snag and gave herself a vigorous massage. Rubbing her ribs and fanny against the snag's trunk. And then, doggone her, she disappointed me. She up and departed across the forks. Ah, well. I relaxed for some more waiting. Snowflakes were now riding the wind. A half-hour passed. Then I saw movement on the north trail and here came a bull. I knew before I raised the glasses that he was a winner. His antlers filled the trail. He swaggered like he owned the earth. And, praise be, he was fat.

Luck. It's wonderful.

He turned into the east-west trail and came to the schoolmarm snag. Boy, the cow must have left some fascinating scent there. He took one sniff and went daffy. He grunted. His ears swiv-eled in all directions. Then the dumbhead began charging about on the small rocky flat looking for her. He didn't try to track her. And clearly it never occurred to him that she'd crossed the forks. His brain wasn't working. He was a typical sex-goofy moose Romeo.

I knew I couldn't hit him from my position. Too much snow in the air now. So I began a stalk. I was excited, too.

I could hear him crashing around, grunting, snorting. His antlers raking the brush. I didn't try to intercept him. Instead I headed for the schoolmarm snag. And it was the right hunch, because he beat me to the spot. I rounded a red boulder and there he stood, thirty yards distant. The big sonofagun had winded me, and he was bristled. I figured at first he was bluffing. But, no. He started for me, head down. He meant it. No mistake. Okay, I stopped him—dead instantly—with a heart shot.

I now had to grin at myself. I'd been so thrilled my neck hair had lifted.

I checked the carcass. It was a great meat-trophy kill, better than I'd thought. He was a champ, a star performer.

Sure, I'm a complete moose partisan. Come autumn, moose-hunting magic really hits me hard. It's a mixture of frost glitter, harvest eagerness, the remembered drama of close stalks, the glory of winds filled with painted leaves, the banana-oil smell of my rifle, the surprises of thick-cover forest hunting, the excitement of judging a trophy head and a meat carcass, the grand arrogance of most rutting bulls, and the good blast of a rifle when you know you've held right. Potent magic, friends.

The western Talkeetna moose range is one of the newest and best. I feel sort of responsible for it. Fifty years ago moose were mighty scarce here because there wasn't enough browse for them. But a fire fixed that. I was chief smokechaser for the U.S. General Land Office when a forest fire started here in the foothills. I did my doggonedest to put it out. I battled it ten days with several large crews, but lost. Thousands of acres were burned over. I thought it was a vast tragedy. But instead it was a blessing. A fine browse crop of aspens, willows, birches, and cottonwoods soon covered the burn. And then, cheers, the moose moved in.

I keep thinking nowadays: just suppose I had licked that runaway blaze?

Moose hunters tend to label themselves: meat guys or trophy guys or meat-trophy guys. These various sporting types can be pretty clannish, but they share one urgent wish. They all hope for adventure. They usually get it.

Our unique *gigas* moose are high on the hunting adventure list. They have the color and the temperament plus a large talent for slam-bang action. They keep you on the ball, keep you busy and plotting. Often bug-eyed, too. For example, take a mid-autumn hunt I made, solo, near my upper cabin on Erickson creek. I had another double project going, the same deal—harvest my winter's meat and collect a set of antlers. Only this time the antlers didn't have to be trophy size. (In just a moment I'll tell you how come.) I'd seen fresh sign yesterday at timberline, a short two miles above the cabin. So I figured I had it made. A cinch hunt, more or less.

But things happened.

First a tricky golden leaf storm jinxed me.

I climbed a bald ridge to use my glasses. Out front was a windswept scrub aspen park with two moose in it, a Grade-A mulligan bull and a husky dark cow. They weren't together. The bull was five hundred yards distant, and almost downwind from me. He was pawing a hole in the ground, really making the dirt fly. I believe he thought he was alone in the park.

I sure wanted him. But five hundred yards is a far piece, and the air was full of blowing aspen leaves. Clouds of them. I didn't know what they'd do to a .375 slug. Deflect it? Shatter it? I simply had no idea. It was a new problem. So I stalled. Then the wind shifted freakily and the bull got my scent. He didn't exactly spook. He just shook his antlers and walked into a thicket, out of sight. I couldn't spot him again.

I did some cussing. But presently I got an unexpected break. The cow, six hundred yards crosswind, suddenly came trotting toward the thicket the bull had entered. She was lonesome, I guess, and had him pinpointed. Anyway, she now let out a loud eerie yodeling alto wail. Love-smitten.

So I could stop worrying. She'd bird-dog the cuss for me.

Okay. About those antlers. I intended them to be memorials. Reminders. Monuments. I wanted a *typical set* of mulligan bull antlers for the upper cabin's roof peak. A skimpy forty-five-inch set would suit me just fine. Savvy guys seeing them would understand. They'd know the bull had been shot for his meat, hide and sinew, and that I'd remembered him gratefully. They'd catch on and would recall with nostalgia, I figured, their own harvest hunts and the pleasant security of a full meat cache. And their indebtedness to the moose tribe. Many of us frontier roughnecks ate moose meat from fall till spring. We wore moosehide jackets, moccasins, and mittens, all sewed with moose sinew.

Aye, the narrow little non-trophy antlers would be my monument to meat bulls. The whopper set I'd taken at the forks were now spiked—spar-varnished—to the roof peak of my main cabin. They went 71¾ inches. They were beautiful. They made folks gawk. So I knew their significance was plenty clear. They stood for happy trophy-hunting adventures.

Well, the rut-struck cow was eager. She'd declared herself about as far as a cow moose ever does. But she still (a good thing for me) had a mind of her own. She halted one hundred feet from the tangled aspen thicket where my meat bull was hiding. She struck the ground with a big front hoof. She gave another high-pitched squealing wail. I saw that she was panting. But she stayed put. Obviously, she wanted the bull to come out of that doggoned brush. Well, thanks to her—she was a swell pointer—I now spotted him. A brown shadow in the weaving yellow aspens. I fired through a swirl of airborne leaves. Hoping. Hoping. And it was all right. The bull flinched and went down, finished.

Ballistics luck, maybe, but I was one happy guy. I walked down to the dead bull, sat on his shoulder, and built me a smoke.

It was a splendid meat carcass, and the head went forty-four inches.

You can't, you just can't, I told myself, beat a good moose hunt. No way.

The Way We Were

*The moral is that Mother Nature is a mean, ornery
old bat at times—but she usually makes things come
out even. If you give her a chance.*

Dedication—This one is for the dramatist, whoever he may
be, who will someday write an ace action play, with music, about
our mysterious early times mail-trail bandit, The Blue Parka Man,
and his honky-tonk gal partner, The Black Bear.

It was coming sundown. I sat at the window of the new
Matanuska schoolmarm's cabin, enjoying the flame tints and hard
purple shadows on a yonder Chugach snowpeak.

"Could you write a poem, Red-Top?"

"Maybe. I guess so—using a Squarehead saga theme I read
yesterday. Lend me a pencil and some paper, huh? Call the
verse *Ovis dalli—A Forecast*."

White Brother Of The Autumn Snows
And the wild crests of far-northern ranges,
Onyx-eyed, crafty, elusive one
With black hoofs and recurved amber horns,
I left my youth in your care.
But the paradox is that I then slew you—
Wotan-like, sacrificing myself to myself.
Today, a migrant peddler of adventure tales,
I have at last found my true mate,

Although perhaps she knows that with your death
On that high windy crag
You cheated her,
White Brother Of The Autumn Snows.

Well, she had a good poker face. I couldn't tell whether
she liked it or not. Then: "The sun has gone down. There are
no more colors on the peak. Do we want some lamplight?"

Aye, we were roughnecks and proud of it.
Elite roughnecks.
Hardfisted. Ornery. Sentimental.
With the snowshoe swagger in our legs.
And our heads full of trails, passes, fords, and distances.
Plenty good with knife and gun.
Crotch-kicking dirty fighters. Soft touches for a loan.
Squaw chasers. Whore lovers.
Practical jokers. Gamblers.
Dog-mushers. Whitewater hotshots. Far travelers.
Mountain guys.
We hated a town after the first good bender.
And we never saved a dime. Always broke or close to it.
Yeah, but the nation needed us.
We opened up a country for you, folks.
Of course it was a wonderful, wonderful life.
The greatest.
Pure adventure.
But boy, were we dumb.
We really thought it would last forever.
                                        —*Caribou Jack Hymes*

"That cheechako town up on the bench. They're gonna call
it Anchorage, I hear."
"Yeah. Instead o' Woodrow. But man, the place can't last
long. Nothin' to support it. Nothin' a-tall. By this time next
year—remember I said so—the Injuns'll be smokin' salmon in
them painted spruce-lumber shacks."
"Uh-huh. I bet you're right. An' take that crazy gover'ment
railroad. They got the rails laid past Clear Creek now, a feller
tells me, an' they're talkin' big about punchin' her plumb through
to Fairbanks. They sure must be a buncha crackpots. But anyway,

by gosh, when they get smart an' quit, we'll have us a fine dogsled trail up the Susitna Valley, huh?"

"This doggone dingbat town's been here three years now. An' about all they've done is ruin a good salmon creek. Damn it, I useta be partial to Ship Creek. Many's the time I've dried fish there for my dogs."

"Me too. It was a good creek, all right. Only, o' course, there never was any red salmon runs. Reds won't spawn in a creek that don't flow outta a lake."

"O.K., O.K., so that's *one* thing we can't hold against the cockeyed town."

"You ever eat siwash caviar, Joe?"

"Sure. It ain't bad, either. Me, I kinda go for it. Keeps ya from gettin' scurvy, too. The Injuns've got a lotta tricks like that. Stuff our white doctors ain't caught up with yet."

"Well, I don't see how ya stand the stink. *Whee-w-w-w.* Man, when they chop open one o' them frozen snowed-under pits fulla rotten salmon eggs on a winter mornin', ya can smell it a mile down the wind, I'll swear."

"Yeah, it smells. But not much worse—*haw haw-w-w*—than the young Injun gals who use urine to make their hair shine purty. An' I notice ya don't seem to mind *that* none."

Adventure I: A Quick Trip to Town

I thought the guy was just drunk. At first, that is.

He stood outside the new 4th Street restaurant I was in. Glaring through the dirty front window. A skinny, mean-looking character. Big-nosed. Sunk-in cheeks. Squinched, pale-blue eyes. Bat-eared. Sporting a red necktie with a diamond pin. Weaving a little on his feet. Lips moving as he mumbled to himself. Yeah, I thought, a town hard case. Tanked up good and on the warpath. Hunting somebody. He coughed and spit, then shuffled to the left, trying to see into the raw-plank booths behind me. And I now recognized him. He was one of the town's two barbers. Tony Spigoni, the sourdoughs called him. I didn't know his real name. But I'd heard he was a "snowbird"—a cocaine sniffer. And that he was considered dangerous. Well, the hell with him. I was hungry. I tried to catch the pretty half-breed waitress's eye, but she was busy serving three customers at the counter's far end. So I sat and waited. I could see the cook back

335

there turning hotcakes, and smell meat and onions frying, and coffee. My gut growled. I told myself I had never, holy smoke, been hungrier.

I'd hit town about an hour ago. Aboard a mixed train from Matanuska.

It was early June, I was eighteen years old, and this was my first trip to so-called civilization in eleven months.

I'd had a pack of twenty beaver pelts. Fine high-country skins, most of them blanket grade. I'd expected to get $600 for them, but the fast-talking Fur-Exchange agent offered $500. The market was shot, he said. Prices way down. It could be, he said, he'd take a loss of $500. So okay, damn him. I took the dough and headed for a restaurant. I didn't like the town. Too many people. Too many noises and smells. And the sidewalks didn't suit my moccasined feet. But I sure did like town grub. I had a typical teenage appetite. Besides, I worked hard. Tending traps. Backpacking supplies. Cutting sled trails. Building line cabins. I mean I was always hungry. I simply couldn't get enough to eat. Yeah, and I was ashamed, when I came to town, to order seconds in the restaurants. So I'd eat in one, then go to another. I once ate suppers in three joints. And was still hungry when I quit. Well, the pretty, bosomy breed waitress finally got around to me. And I ordered waffles and country sausage, with maple syrup and strawberry jam. Oh boy. I was practically drooling. It sounded so good.

Old Tony Spigoni was still glaring through the window.

Looking tougher and tougher.

Nuts. To take my mind off my complaining belly, I thought about something that had happened last week. An amazing thing, by gosh. I'd learned to hypnotize rainbow trout. An Injun kid, Billy No-Dogs, showed me. We'd hiked over to Spring Creek. Me, I had store-bought trout gear, but Billy stuck to the usual Injun outfit. A willow pole and about eight feet of linen line. No leader or lure; just a bare hook tied onto the line. But . . . the kid had inherited ten thousand years of local fishing savvy. Well, we'd brought some fresh salmon eggs. Billy baited up with a gob of them, waded into an eddy, then tossed the bait out and let it sink. The current rolled it—and *wham*, a husky fourteen-inch rainbow hit. Yeah, and it was a rambunctious fish, for sure. It jumped and jumped. Then when it'd slowed some, Billy led it in close. He eased its head out of the water. Next, taking a short hold on the line, he slowly lifted the trout straight up. And then we waded ashore with it. The fish didn't move. Nary a flop or quiver. Until he dropped it on the gravel. Then it went crazy.

Aye, a weird performance, folks, like some kind of magic. Billy said the trick was to be plumb gentle. Get the fish's nose and eyes out of the water first, then lift it easy, easy. Don't let it swing or brush against anything. All right, I tried it myself, five or six times, and it worked. Nothing to it. Naturally I couldn't explain why it worked. So, until somebody comes up with a better theory, I'd call it hypnotism.

The waitress smiled at me as she went about her chores. Nice.

And then, great day, here came old Tony Spigoni. Slamming through the front door. Teeth bared in a snarl.

Uh-huh, he'd found what he was looking for. She was in the booth right behind me, eating ham and eggs. A classy blonde sporting gal known as The Peroxide Kid. I'd seen her before and heard talk about her. Compliments mostly. Well, Tony sure didn't fool around. He yelled that she'd lifted his wallet last night. Then he grabbed a handful of her hair and yanked her across the table. She let out a scream, and slapped him. Good for her, I thought. Well, the three guys down the counter now came hurrying to watch the fun. Applauding. Tony belted the gal one as they arrived, and cut her mouth. Blood ran. Produce his wallet, he yelled. And then, oh man, he flashed a razor. None of the three watchers moved to take it away from him. Shucks, they were still grinning. The no-good S.O.Bs. Okay, I spotted an open case of Carnation Brand canned milk behind the counter. Armored cow, we called it. And I figured a can or two would get the job done the easiest way. So I vaulted the counter. Old Tony, yelling again, now had his razor at The Peroxide Kid's throat. I made a careful pitch.

And scored good.

The can of milk smashed Tony's big nose. Knocked out some teeth, too. I saw them land on the table, in a spray of bloody spit, as he fell backward over a chair. His razor skidded out of view across the floor. Well, the three customer heroes spun to face me. Looking real hard-boiled. And The Peroxide Kid, no dope, tried to dodge past them to the front door. But she wasn't fast enough. One of them grabbed her arm and twisted it into a hammerlock. So have fun sucker, I thought, and I let go another can of milk. It clobbered him, *splat*, on his left ear. And down *he* went. The Peroxide Kid headed for the street again, and this time made it. Well, the other two customer jackasses should have laid off me. But I guess they were friends of old Tony. Anyhow, they started over the counter. My, my. I dropped them both. One can of milk apiece. Took maybe five seconds. Then, gents, I got the heck outa there. Via the back door. I knew I was a cinch to make jail, and the fine—yeah—would be exactly $500. My beaver money. So I sprinted down to the depot, where a northbound freight train had stopped for orders.

Five minutes later I was in an empty boxcar, bound for Matanuska.

Hungrier'n a wolf pup in January. But laughing.

It sure had been the quickest trip, by gosh, I'd ever made to town.

Notes and Stuff

A tip for snowshoe hare hunters. And for guys who use talcum powder to prevent cold weather aftershave facial chap. The hind paw of a snowshoe hare taken in winter makes a great— hell, the greatest—powder applicator. Women like 'em, too. They're prime dressing-table novelties.

The penis bone of a bear is useful as a penholder. It's hard as ivory, and takes a swell polish. And it's shape is A-okay for comfortable writing. Yeah, a practical trophy. Ornamental, too. But most hunters—and I guess you can't blame 'em— don't even know it exists.

Things I wonder about:

How come we're told that "Denali" is the Injun name for Mt. McKinley? Every Injun I know in the area calls the mountain "Delaykah," which means, simply, "That big peak over there."

And what's the scoop regarding roast moose nose? Hunting-adventure novelists used to praise it extravagantly. Pierre, the faithful Canuck guide, always prepared it, by gar, after a moose kill. It was, they claimed, marvelous grub. By me, gents, I unfortunately find a moose's nose plumb inedible—roasted, boiled, broiled, fried, or whatever. And this mystifies me. Did the early day camp cooks have a secret recipe? If so, I sure wish I possessed it.

Aye . . . and how on earth did the Tin Fiddler, a well-known sporting gal up here some forty-five years ago, get her curious nickname? What did it signify? Man, I lie awake nights trying to figure that out. And cuss myself for not having questioned her about it.

The Arctic loon "flies" underwater. That is, it uses its wings as paddles, chasing fish. Startles you when you first see one, because the sonofagun is really fast. An underwater speed merchant. Swift enough, by gosh, to catch trout or grayling.

To settle an ancient argument, I hope, I can report that the lynx *does* scream. I once saw one screaming, on a Cannonball Creek (northern Kenai) gravel bar. The sound was shrill, with a whistle-like carrying quality. I got the impression the cat was plenty sore about something.

"What was the most spectacular thing you ever saw happen, Red-Top? In nature, I mean."

"Well, that's easy. It was two bald eagles mating. The big tough birds might've been grotesque doing it on the ground. But listen, this pair was three thousand feet above Chinitna Bay. Right after daybreak. A calm sparking morning. With a smoke-blue half moon behind them. Shucks, I thought they were fighting, and put my 12X glasses on them. They tumbled, one clasping the other with feet and wings. Falling end-over-end. Spinning. Spiraling. Diving. Twice they separated and came together again, with the same eagle in the clasping position. Then I realized I was watching the world's most thrilling sex drama. They parted two hundred feet above the water, and coasted out of sight amongst some gray sea cliffs. I tried to imagine what it must have been like. And concluded it was something only bald eagles could know. Only overeager don't-give-a-doggone, air-daffy bald eagles trying for the most."

She sighed.

"Oh-h, I wish I'd seen that. I think I envy her."

Adventure II: The Belt Knife

"You speak Injun, Joe. What does 'Matanuska' mean?"

"It means 'The Island People.' An' the word has quite a history. Used to be, five or six Goat-Eater Denna Injun families lived on a river island about where Esai Slough comes in now.

They was plenty scared o' the Knik Injuns, I hear, an' felt safer out on that island. Then the army stationed some soldiers opposite 'em on the river's north bank. An' the GIs, not knowin' any better, called their camp Matanuska, too. Well, then a coupla sportin' gals come up from Kodiak, an' worked first in a tent, then in a cabin they hired some guys to build. An' then that fall a Boston cheechako put together a wash-boiler still an' starts peddlin' moonshine hooch. Yep. An' shortly thereafter the Ragtime Kid blew in from Nome an' opens a dugout gamblin' joint. O' course, ol' Tex Cobb was there from the beginnin', huntin' meat fer the town an' gamblin'. But man, the place was honky-tonk. A good spot to get Mickey Finned in an' lose your poke. Well, then the railroad came, an' ever'body moved up here, to be near the rails. An', sure, they brought their Matanuska (Island People) town name with 'em. That name sure sticks, huh?"

"Yeah. But the important thing is, we still got ol' Tex Cobb."

"Uh-huh. Him and the mountains."

This Injun kid was something. He'd been sitting on the plank sidewalk outside Phil Allen's Matanuska roadhouse for three hours now, intently studying a dead silver marmot. Turning the carcass this way and that on his lap, in sunlight and in shadow. Staring narrow-eyed, his brow concentration wrinkled. I guessed he was maybe fourteen. A typical long-haired brush Injun kid. Aye, you could smell the urine-tanned moosehide moccasins and leggings he wore. Phil winked at me when I came in to buy some matches. The kid was sorta batty, he said. But, man, he sure could carve purty things outta wood an' bone. Animals, birds an' fishes, mostly. Plumb lifelike, too. You wouldn't believe it, by gosh, less'n you saw 'em. His name was Kashka, Phil added, and he lived with his father in an old-time soda *bara-bara* hut down by the rivermouth. Uh-huh, a full blooded Matanuska. One o' the few left around.

"Hey, Kashka. Whatcha doin' with that *hai-hai* marmot, huh?" Phil hollered through the doorway.

The kid turned. His concentration look suddenly gone. White teeth flashed in a smile.

"Well, I want—I try—hard—hard," he replied, "to see what it looks like."

I thought, impressed: *I'm gonna ask that kid to carve me a sheephorn knife handle. Covered with all the magic good-luck hunting and war signs that he knows.*

It was a pretty spring day. Robins yelping. Geese and cranes overhead. A spruce-scented slow wind blew along Matanuska's short, grassy, main drag. I had dropped in at the schoolmarm's cabin for a visit, and found her painting her nails. This was a project I'd never before witnessed. And it fascinated me. Maybe because it was so feminine and she seemed so artistically absorbed in it.

"Tell me a story Red-Top," she said presently. "Another story about bald eagles, please."

"Okay. . . . Sure. . . . Uh, I've got one with a moral. A plenty tough moral. It happened last spring in the Big Susitna country. I'm rustling some breakfast-fire squaw wood one morning when a hen bald eagle flies over camp. She's low, heading for the river flats, and she's carrying a load of wild hay in her beak and talons. Which means, of course, that she's got a nest thataway. Probably close. Well, two or three days later I find it. It's a tall, skinny Balm o' Gilead cottonwood on the bank of a river slough. Just a clumsy-looking platform of sticks, dead grass, and moss. Yeah, and it's occupied. Several fuzzy eaglets have their heads stuck over the nest's rim, watching me. The hen eagle, I figure, is out hunting. Killing grub for her nestlings. She's obviously a hard worker, too, because the ground is plumb littered with eagle garbage—feathers and small bones that the youngsters have discarded. Lucky brats, I think. They're really eating first class. Okay, I start to move on—and then, holy cow, I spot something that makes me plenty mad.

"It's the skull of a kit beaver. And some scraps of fur.

"Well, I get the picture. A pair of bank beavers has moved into the slough. The female's had a litter of kits, and the eagles had started picking them off. (They'll harvest 'em all, too. That's a certain-sure copper-riveted cinch.) Okay, I'm sore. And I know what I oughta do. I oughta blast a half-dozen .30-06 slugs through the bottom of that nest. Because, my gosh, beavers are valuable critters. A colony of 'em is like money in the bank. But shucks. . . . I do hate to kill young stuff. So I head back for camp, thinking it over. The male parent eagle shows up now, and screams at me. I tell him to haul fanny or I'll feed him a

220-grain softnose. . . . Y'know, Miss, doggone it, I'm now confused. I argue with myself the rest of the day. And I finally decide there's a soft streak in me. And that I'd better get rid of it, fast. I mean I'd better beat it back down there, come morning, and knock off that whole family of beaver-eating eagles. Yeah, wipe 'em out like any sensible trapper and hunter would. Otherwise I'll never be a success on this frontier.

"So next morning, at first shooting light, I start down to the river. Hating the chore ahead of me. Cussing my medicine. Feeling all-fired sorry for those baby eagles. Shucks, I hadn't enjoyed my breakfast. But—yep—I'm a determined assassin. At least I think I am. . . . And then I come to the slough. Both parent eagles are circling the place, screaming. But, great day, I don't see the nest tree. It's disappeared. Just not there anymore. I guess my mouth musta hung open. I break into a run, to check on what's happened. Well, the answer's plumb simple, it turns out. The beavers won without anybody's help. Last night the chisel-toothed cusses felled the doggoned nest tree. It crashed into the slough. And the eaglets—I can see 'em—are lying dead in their big, ugly nest. Either drowned or killed by the fall. . . ."

She'd finished painting her nails. And she now gave me a long look. A new kind of look from her, I thought. Like she was making up her mind about something. "But the moral, Red-Top. You said there was a moral."

"Uh-huh. I did. The moral, Miss, is that Mother Nature is a mean, ornery, murderous old bat at times—but, by gosh, she usually makes things come out even. If you give her a chance."

It was showdown.

Between the stranger and me. With $150 in the pot.

And I wished the hell, folks, that I'd never gotten into this game. I wished I was back at the cabin yarnin' with my partner, Tex Cobb. Or maybe reading one of the Jack London books that had arrived by mail today. Anything but this. Not, holy smoke, that I was worried about losing. Shucks, I figured the pot was mine for sure. In fact, I was sorry the stranger had called. I would have upped it some. Bet the ten bucks still in front of me. No, my worry wasn't dough—it was superstition and a sense of trouble. (We were all superstitious up here. It was part of being a roughneck frontiersman. Although, natch, nobody ever admitted it.) Right now a chill was jittering up my spine, and I felt my neck hairs tingle. Prime warning signals. We were playing in the lobby of Phil Allen's roadhouse, five of us. With a half-dozen spectators. The stranger, a husky, hard-eyed gent, now turned his cards over. Two pairs—jacks and sixes. And they weren't good enough. And I guess he suspected they weren't. Anyway, I saw him bite down on the Optimo cigar he was smoking.

So. . . . I showed my hand. A full house. Three eights and two black aces.

The dead man's hand.

It was suddenly quiet in the room. Then somebody muttered, "Sonofabitch."

Aye, I'd drawn Wild Bill Hickock's last hand. The one he'd held when a gun-sneak shot him in the back of his head. Eights, aces, and death. I'd heard the superstition all my life. You'd win the hand, sure, but you'd never spend the money. Not a chance, man. Something would happen. Well, by heck, I'd never let on that I believed this. Nor would anybody else present. They all began kidding me, laughing, when I raked in the pot. Shucks, I even heard myself chuckle. Sounded all right, too. But the game now broke up. The stranger allowed that he was due back at his camp. He nodded and went out the door. Walking Injun easy. I'd noted that he was a pro woodsman. It showed in various ways. In his clothes. In a snow-squint he'd acquired. In the fact that, like the rest of us, he had no hair on his hands. (You burn it off stoking campfires.) And in his knife. It had a Kobuk-carved fossil-ivory handle, and he carried it in a sinew-sewed rawhide sheath, snugged behind his right hip bone. With two inches of the handle sticking up. Yeah, he was a pro. But from other parts.

I stuck around a few minutes.

Joked about the cards. Bought a can of pipe tobacco for Tex.

Then I left—and, yeah, felt my neck hairs tingle again.

Me, I trusted my instincts. And they sure were telling me to watch it. Danger ahead. I stood on the sidewalk, letting my eyes get used to the night. I could smell cigar smoke eddying in off the trail Tex and I used. Well, no surprise. I *had* drawn Wild Bill's death hand. And guys had been way-laid for a heap less than the $160 now in my poke. Okay, I touched my knife and got going. A thin fall moon had risen, speared on a Chugach peak. But the trail was brush-bordered, banked with inky shadows. Well, so what? Hell, I liked darkness. Always had. It suited me. Gave me confidence. Tex said I was one of the night born. I drifted along, my moccasins making no sound on the hard-packed trail. I honestly hoped, folks, to avoid trouble. But if some larcenous S.O.B. out there wanted to play games, why, swell. I'd sure cooperate. Actually I was beginning to enjoy this. Then, fifty yards ahead in a patch of moonlight, I saw movement. It was a man—the stranger, I believed. Anyway, he'd spotted me, and quickly stepped aside into some shadows. I felt myself grin. All right, mister, I thought. So we'll play games.

I halted in the gloom of a willow clump.

The only weapon I had with me was my knife.

It was all that I needed. The Eskimos, the Finns, and the Alaska pro woodsmen are said to be the world's top knife experts, and old Tex, yeah, he was a master. And he had paintakingly taught me everything he knew. We used our knives constantly. For everything from pelting furbearers and butchering game to trimming our hair and paring our toenails. We ate with them. If sudden danger threatened, my knife was the first weapon I thought of. Old Tex had a grim joke. There were only two really showy ways to demolish an opponent with your knife, he declared. One was to stick the knife in his belly and then quickstep around him while hanging onto the handle. The other was to drive the knife plumb through him, hang your hat on its point, and walk away whistling. Me, I had a rapport with my knife. I seldom consciously drew it. When I needed it, it just appeared in my hand. It had an eight-inch blade of handworked Swedish steel. And the Injun kid, Kashka, had carved a sheephorn handle for it—a beautiful job, covered with magic masks and signs. Aye, a good knife. Like I said, I didn't need any other weapon tonight.

I knelt. And faked a nervous cough. I wanted the guy to think I was really scared.

Ready to wet my pants.

It might make him careless. Well, a couple of minutes passed. And I couldn't pick up a sound or spot a movement. But that cigar smoke was still in the wind. Okay I was in no hurry. I had all night. To keep myself in the mood, I remembered an episode on the Metal Creek trail last month. Tex and I were headed up there, with five pack dogs, to bear-proof a cabin. One of our dogs was new. A powerful ninety-pound King Island husky that Tex had bought from the Malamute Kid. Like many of the island dogs, he was brindle-colored and short-tailed. Also unfriendly. We'd named him Togo. Well, one morning I went out to cinch the panniers on him, and the cuss growled at me. I now saw that he was sick. Foaming at the mouth. Panting. His eyes wide and crazy. *Uh-oh*, I thought—rabies. Before I could step back, he jumped at me. What happened next was pure reflex on my part. Togo was in the air, jaws open to grab my face. Then the knife was in my hand. Got there by itself, it seemed. I remember a gush of blood. Then Togo was on the ground, dying, his head cut half-off. A sad, bad, hair-raising business.

Well, some nice suspense had built up by now.

It was now time to surprise the guy.

He'd vanished into the shadow of some aspens across the trail. And I didn't think he'd moved. I'd have heard him. There was a lot of brittle dead stuff over there. Noisy. So okay, I catfooted through fifty yards of easy thickets, and came out opposite to aspens. Right at the edge of the trail. I could no longer smell the cigar, so apparently I was upwind from it. But I could sense the guy's presence. He was there, all right. And he was plenty good. Even the cigar smoke had been an okay nerve-jangling trick. You could respect such a man, by gosh. Well, enough games. I stepped into the trail. "Come on out here, Mister," I said. "You and I have a chore. We are gonna finish a super-stition. Prove that Wild Bill's famous hand is just eights, aces and baloney. O' course, it may take some doing. So let's get at it, huh?" There was no reply. But. . . . I now heard foot-steps farther up the trail. Then, with the moonlight on him, here came—Tex. Aye, no mistake. I'd have known that wide-shouldered silhouette and that loose-hipped snowshoe-swagger walk any-where, anytime. He'd seen me, and now raised a hand in greeting.

"Evenin', Redhead," he said. "I run outta tobaccy. Gotta go buy some. Uh, if'n it's any o' my business, who was you talkin' to in there?" He gestured toward the aspens.

"Two guys. A poker-playin' stranger—and Wild Bill Hickock's ghost," I said and handed Tex the can of tobacco I'd bought. "Here. I saved you a walk to town."

"Be doggone. Thanks." Tex smiled at the aspen clump. "Quiet sort, ain't they," he said, then turned and we headed for the cabin.

I'll never be sure. But I thought I heard a low laugh behind us.

A Short Bibliographical Essay
on Russell Annabel's Books

Since launching the five-volume series of Russell Annabel books, we at Safari Press have received a fair number of inquiries as to all the books published by Russell Annabel. A short bibliographical essay based on the research we did follows.

Annabel's first book is *Tales of a Big Game Guide* (Derrydale Press, 1938, New York, 198 pages). It consists of magazine articles from *Outdoor Life, National Sportsman,* as well as apparently original material. The book was limited to 950 numbered copies. It is now very rare and commands hundreds of dollars in the rare-book market. It is noted for having a fair number of pictures of Russell Annabel in the Alaskan game fields, which in itself is rare since pictures of Annabel in any of his books is rare. Essentially this book is a compilation of short stories on Alaskan big-game hunting: Dall sheep, moose, grizzly, black bear, and caribou.

The next book Annabel wrote is entitled *Hunting and Fishing in Alaska* (Alfred A. Knopf, 1948, New York, 341 pages). This book is substantially larger than his first book. Many of the chapters of this book were also previously published in *Outdoor Life, Field & Stream, Sports Afield,* and the *Saturday Evening Post.* However, a substantial part of this book does appear to be original material. Again, this is a book of short stories for the most part, although some chapters seem to follow each other with a common thread running through them. As the title indicates, this book also has fishing stories.

The third book written by Annabel is possibly the most obscure of all his titles. It is entitled *Alaskan Tales* (A.S. Barnes, 1953, New York, 137 pages). It is substantially smaller than his other books. Research shows that some of the chapters were previously published in *Field & Stream.* In this book, Annabel recalls his first meeting with Tex Cobb and his Indian mentor Oolinka.

Next comes *Alaskan Days, Mexican Nights,* which was published by Amwell Press in 1987. It features 455 pages and has a total of 42 chapters. It contains eleven chapters from *Tales of a Big Game Guide* and *Hunting and Fishing in Alaska.* It also contains some chapters from *Alaskan Tales.* The remaining thirty-odd chapters are articles from *Sports Afield* and other magazines. Again, this is a book of short stories with only very few chapters making a transition from one story to the next. Most of the stories are on hunting in Alaska, but some contain fishing tales, and others are about Mexican big game.

The last set of books by Annabel is from Safari Press. This is a five-volume series of books, and they are entitled *Alaskan Adventures* (Volume I, 1995, 351 pages), *Adventure Is My Business* (Volume II, 1997, 341 pages), *Adventure Is in My Blood* (Volume III, 1997, 384 pages), *The High Road to Adventure* (Volume IV, 1997, 375 pages), and *The Way We Were* (Volume V, 1998, 350 pages). All have a frontis photo of Annabel and line drawings by either Michael Coleman or Louise Lopina. All were issued in a limited edition of 1,000, numbered, signed, and slipcased copies. All five volumes are signed by Mrs. Dell Annabel Lamey (Russell Annabel's widow) and their son David Russell Annabel.

BIBLIOGRAPHY

"Blue Blizzard in Sonora," .... *Sports Afield*, June 1970

"Epitaph for Killer Grizzlies," .... *Sports Afield*, July 1970

"Pronto Was a Lion Killer," .... *Sports Afield*, August 1970

"Wolf Trouble," .... *Sports Afield*, November 1970

"Fifty Years in a Grizzly Pasture," .... *Sports Afield*, Annual 1971

"Berserk Brownies I'll Never Forget," .... *Sports Afield*, January 1971

"The Demon Bull of Denna Lake," .... *Sports Afield*, February 1971

"Die-Hard Dueler of the Crags," .... *Sports Afield*, May 1971

"Beach Bears Can Be Fatal," ....*Sports Afield*, June 1971

"Champ Dalls Come Tough," .... *Sports Afield*, November 1971

"Deadly Hunter of the High Country," ....*Sports Afield*, December 1971

"You Can't Beat Luck," ....*Sports Afield*, February 1972

"Those Killer Tramp *Tigres*," .... *Sports Afield*, March 1972

"Saga of a Hunting Cayuse," .... *Sports Afield*, April 1972

"High-Up, Way-Out Adventures with Goats," .... *Sports Afield*, May 1972

"Believe It . . . Black Bears Attack," .... *Sports Afield*, October 1972

"1,000 Pounds of Trouble," .... *Sports Afield*, December 1972

"Grizzlies with Short Fuses," .... *True's Hunting*, Yearbook 1973

"Adventures with Rut-Crazy Moose," .... *Sports Afield*, March 1973

"Grizzly Fever," .... *Sports Afield*, April 1973

"Adventures with Dall Sheep," .... *Sports Afield*, December 1973

"Grand Stalks for Smart Billies," .... *Sports Afield*, Annual 1974

"Don't Turn Your Back on a Black Bear," .... *Sports Afield*, May 1974

"Jake and the Willow Ptarmigan," .... *Sports Afield*, July 1974

"The Grizzly Is One Big Surprise," .... *Sports Afield*, September 1974

"Grand Stalks for Giant Moose," .... *Sports Afield*, Annual 1975

"Stalks of the Alaska Rangers," .... *Sports Afield*, November 1975

"Adventures with Giant Moose," ....*Sports Afield*, May 1976

"How Tex Cobb Came Up an Alaska Legend,"*Sports Afield*, December 1976

"The Greatest Grouse Dog," .... *Sports Afield*, Annual 1977

"Grand Stalk for Great Dalls," .... *Sports Afield*, Annual 1977

"Goats of the Skyline Rim," .... *Sports Afield*, Annual 1977

"Black Bears Were My Neighbors," .... *Sports Afield*, Annual 1977

"Blaze . . . My Boss Horse . . . My Buddy," .. *Sports Afield*, Annual 1978

"Moose Are Adventure Critters," .... *Sports Afield*, May 1978

"The Way We Were," ....*Sports Afield*, December 1979